WHY AQUINAS MATTERS NOW

WHY AQUINAS MATTERS NOW

OLIVER KEENAN

BLOOMSBURY CONTINUUM
LONDON • OXFORD • NEW YORK • NEW DELHI • SYDNEY

BLOOMSBURY CONTINUUM
Bloomsbury Publishing Plc
50 Bedford Square, London, WC1B 3DP, UK
29 Earlsfort Terrace, Dublin 2, Ireland

BLOOMSBURY, BLOOMSBURY CONTINUUM and the Diana logo are trademarks of
Bloomsbury Publishing Plc

First published in Great Britain 2024

Copyright © Oliver Keenan, 2024

Oliver Keenan has asserted his right under the Copyright, Designs and Patents Act, 1988, to be identified
as Author of this work

For legal purposes the Acknowledgements on pp. 218–219 constitute an extension of this copyright page

All rights reserved. No part of this publication may be reproduced or transmitted in any form or by
any means, electronic or mechanical, including photocopying, recording, or any information storage or
retrieval system, without prior permission in writing from the publishers

Bloomsbury Publishing Plc does not have any control over, or responsibility for, any third-party websites
referred to or in this book. All internet addresses given in this book were correct at the time of going to
press. The author and publisher regret any inconvenience caused if addresses have changed or sites have
ceased to exist, but can accept no responsibility for any such changes

A catalogue record for this book is available from the British Library

Library of Congress Cataloguing-in-Publication data has been applied for

ISBN: HB: 978-1-3994-0418-1; eBook: 978-1-3994-0417-4; ePDF: 978-1-3994-0416-7

2 4 6 8 10 9 7 5 3 1

Typeset by Deanta Global Publishing Services, Chennai, India
Printed and bound in Great Britain by CPI Group (UK) Ltd, Croydon CR0 4YY

To find out more about our authors and books visit www.bloomsbury.com
and sign up for our newsletters

For Rachel

Contents

Introduction   1

1. Conversing   13
2. Reality   32
3. World   56
4. Symphony   81
5. Frontier   97
6. Belonging   126
7. Consummation   160
8. Postlude   198

Notes   203
Acknowledgements   218
Bibliography   220
Index   227

Introduction

St Thomas Aquinas was a reluctant revolutionary. His work unleashed an epoch-shaping explosion of theological creativity and philosophical controversy in the thirteenth century, the shockwaves of which continue to reverberate in the contemporary university. This fact alone is enough to establish that Aquinas should be read, but it does not say anything about why Aquinas matters now. In fact, Aquinas deserves much more than just a reading. His work addresses and interrogates the present moment with relevance and urgency. But why should we listen?

Someone deserves to be read because they have something interesting to say. What they have to say might very well be interestingly wrong, out-of-date or of distant historical significance. Someone *matters* when they have something interesting and relevant to *show*, when what they have to offer exceeds the sum total of what they can say. They might gesture towards a new way of living, a new horizon for human inquiry or a fresh perspective on what it means to be human, but they show us more than they can tell; their thought expands the world of our thought. Someone matters *now* when what they show us resonates with the historical moment to the extent that we cannot afford to overlook their contribution. Significance of this kind captures something urgent that is of pressing concern, perhaps something that we might otherwise be struggling to even articulate or see clearly. Aquinas matters now, not because he was right about everything he said (or even about most things on which he had his say) but because he can teach us a way of looking at the world that we ignore at our peril.

Arguing that Aquinas matters to today's reader implies some sense of where we are and how we got here. This is potentially perilous, especially in a short book: it sometimes feels as if there are as many analyses of the contemporary historical moment as there are philosophers. It would be arrogant to paint with too broad a brush, but pointless to make vague lamentation of things not quite being what they used to be. Every era has thought itself to be modern and been forced to grapple with continuity, decay and disruption. There are times when the pace of change is more rapid than others, but no crisis is as unprecedented as it feels.

Nonetheless, Aquinas speaks directly to a widespread feeling of alienation that haunts our world. To be alienated is to be disconnected from the rhythms of the natural world, to feel rootless in society, homeless and lonely, and disenfranchised from politics. To live in alienating times is to be more aware of the fragmentation of humanity than we are of our commonality, to witness the political consequences of fear and anxiety, to sense that despite the enormous technological advances and expansion of knowledge, something – perhaps the most important thing – is missing. Alienated bodies are restless, stressed and burned out. Alienated minds are easily prey to a cheap and easy cynicism.

Things may not always feel quite so bleak, but if even an iota of this portrait corresponds recognizably to the world of today, then Aquinas matters now. At a time when war, injustice, poverty and conflict threaten to alienate us from one another, Thomas offers a robust account of community, of justice, friendship and peace. As we face the threat of alienation from our natural habitat by the climate emergency, Aquinas offers a vision of humanity flourishing in responsible co-existence with the non-human world. As widespread technologization and consumerism threaten to alienate us from ourselves – even from our own bodies – Thomas shows us how to live in friendship with our bodiliness, to value and enjoy sensuality and passion. As we continue to reckon with the devastating psychological and social impact of Coronatide, Thomas is a reliable guide to the interior caverns of our hearts and minds. Thomas's vision is urgently needed because it is profoundly non-violent, refusing nothing that is authentically true and beautiful. In a world that is so often dehumanizing and inhumane, his political vision begins with each one of us becoming human, and so living humane and humanizing lives.

INTRODUCTION

COMMUNICATION

Aquinas matters in divided times because he can show us how to communicate. Communication, for Thomas, is not simply a matter of exchanging information. Communication is the opposite of alienation. As Thomas understands it, communication involves communing: the sharing of life, giving and receiving of gifts; learning to live, move and act in harmony with others. This rich sense of communication is not fundamentally a matter of embodying our thoughts in words, whether written or spoken. It is instead the rather more demanding task of fully embodying ourselves well within the communities that make up our world. Communication is the whole tapestry of human practices that make our lives live within the story of the world, the praxes by which we become whole humans by belonging to the human whole.

To be fully alive is to live a life of deep and profound communication. Deprived of communication, we are doomed to misery and frustration. The journey into freedom that Thomas shows us cannot be achieved by withdrawing into ourselves, seeking an escape from all the things that move our hearts and distract us, whether by attraction or repulsion. Thomas recognizes that we must take the risk of entanglement with the world (and especially with other people), even if this means we are at risk of failure, frustration and vulnerability. We must even allow ourselves the greatest risk and infinite adventure of becoming entangled within God. Such a journey of human becoming, into which Thomas's work beckons us, is as personally demanding as it is intellectually challenging, precisely because it is totalizing. But the alternative is even more terrifying: a life that opts out, which rejects this invitation, whether intellectually, emotionally or spiritually, is a life that is not actually being lived.

Language is not the only tool for communication that we have, but it is the most pervasive and powerful. Language so shapes human existence that Thomas thinks it sheds light on the communicative shape of reality. Aquinas matters now because he can show us that to be is to belong to a world that speaks. To exist at all is to share community with the whole of reality, to belong to a conversation that embraces all other creatures. To be human is to be empowered to bring those relations to conscious expression, to live responsively and responsibly as co-workers with God in bringing the world's story to a harmonious and integrated conclusion. The gift and the obligation of being human is to dwell in the world of the present moment and yet to live beyond it, moving from simply belonging to the world as given into an active shaping of the world as a home. To be human is to live that story into existence.

Thomas's universe is structured like a conversation. It has the same kind of unity that an old-fashioned conversation between friends has. Made up of distinct parts, its meaning is more than the sum of its parts. Like a conversation, the universe unfolds as the interaction between different centres of freedom and meaning; it is possessed of a narrative flow or arc with a beginning, middle and ending, albeit one that developed on an almost infinite number of parallel stages and that contains an endless array of subplots and individual stories. Without prejudicing the autonomy and integrity of each element, Aquinas intuits their manner of belonging to the whole conversation.

Like a conversation, the universe can be fulfilling and enjoyable. When there is miscommunication, manipulation or deception, it can become heated and even devastating. At such junctures, it can seem like the only way forward that avoids violence is to terminate the conversation early, to refuse to cooperate any further. But to live a *human* life is, as Aquinas sees it, to perform a role in the conversation of the universe. To opt out (whether by refusing to listen or refusing to speak) is, then, not only to give up on some element of being human, but also to communicate definitively and violently (and therefore to enact the very thing that was to be avoided). So, knowing how to go on with the conversation is of the utmost importance. It is for this reason that Aquinas matters profoundly at a time when many feel their voices do not matter, and where the loudest and most sanctimonious voices threaten to dominate the conversation.

AQUINAS IN THE CANON

Arguing that Aquinas matters is subtly different from arguing that Aquinas deserves to be read. In fact, it is hard to deny that Aquinas has earned a place in the normative canon of philosophers and theologians. Beyond the importance of his teaching, Aquinas is a truly impressive exemplar of academic rigour and integrity. He was a synthetic genius with an almost terrifying capacity for analytic clarity, bringing vastly divergent systems of thought together into a uniquely fruitful conjunction. An unsurpassed exposition of Roman Catholic theology, his thought – in both its content and its style – has shaped and formed the intellectual culture of Western Europe in ways that are hard to overstate.

As a theologian, Aquinas remains the indispensable guide to understanding the sociological significance of global Catholicism and its cultural legacy. A poet, a wordsmith and an innovative pedagogue, Aquinas, by the force of his intellect, shaped the language and literature of his day, forging a new communicative register by crafting a genre of reflection aimed not only at the effective transfer of knowledge from teacher to student, but also at the cultivation of academic rigour and the formation of a certain kind of scholarly subjectivity. His experimental pedagogy shaped the university in its emerging and formative decades, bequeathing to the contemporary academy both a model of seriousness and some of the essential structures and categories through which we now innately understand our shared pursuit of the truth. The range, extent and breadth of Aquinas's intellectual itinerary – and the domains in which his thought continues to exert its influence – are astonishing, ranging from political and legal theory (not least his account of the common good and distinctive expression of just war theory) to human psychology (offering the most detailed analysis of human emotional life available for several centuries). Some of his explorations, while superseded by more contemporary science, are staggeringly brilliant for their time. He developed an elaborate theory of perception, speculated on open questions in human biology, tried to account for the mystery of sleep, offered a rudimentary treatment for depression and wondered whether angels could talk to each other.

In short, Aquinas was what Foucault would later term a 'producer of discursivity': his work not only made decisive contributions to a number of existing conversations, but it was also generative of an entirely new discourse and horizon for human inquiry. For all this creativity and diversity, Aquinas's work is united by a single overarching concern with *how* we are to live well, of *how* humanity can truly flourish. In a time of seemingly unprecedented social upheaval, this alone seems to justify Aquinas's relevance. Only by knowing where we have come from can we know how to proceed. Knowledge of ancient answers concerning the *how* of life can and should aid our own discernment of how to endure and live fruitfully amid the trauma and tragedy of fractured times.

INTELLECTUAL DWELLING

As I have already said, none of these contributions, extraordinary though they undoubtedly are, not even the sum total of them, adequately captures why Aquinas matters now. Such approaches to Aquinas frame the significance of his work in *archaeological* terms, undertaking the task of locating Thomas's significance as *past-tensed*, concealed within a distant – perhaps lost – history, upon which we certainly depend but from which we are inalienably remote and excluded. The value of Aquinas is, then, at best foundational or genealogical. It is a foundation upon which we walk; we might certainly benefit from a greater awareness of it, but it is still basically an artefact or monument of an intellectual tradition. On this account, the dominant mode by which Aquinas's value can be accessed is one of excavation and uncovering.

As someone who matters now, who has something urgent to show us, Aquinas holds for today's thinker a value best understood in *architectural* rather than *archaeological* terms. Aquinas's vision of the world that speaks cannot be recovered simply through argumentative excavation, but through an invitation to indwelling. Throughout his career, Aquinas was preoccupied with the question of communication, writing in such a way as to induct his readers into deeper conversation with reality. In particular, the uniquely refined style and structure of Thomas's *Summa Theologiae* offers an intellectual abode from within which we can hear the world that speaks and to renew our engagement with the world-conversation in morally and politically responsible, as well as intellectually rigorous, ways. The occupant of this intellectual home does not need to accept the correctness of Aquinas's conclusions in every detail. Rather, they need only accredit the basic soundness of its architecture, to acknowledge that the strength of its walls, arches and foundations is weight-bearing, and that the beauty and intellectual power of the vista it offers are worth the arduous labour involved in entering its confines.

PLAUSIBILITY

The breadth of Aquinas's thought raises the question of how plausibly and directly his thought can address today's reader. His thought world is both historically remote and irreducibly – indeed, dogmatically – shaped by Christian convictions. For all that this diversity of scholarly interest is bewildering to today's academic specialist, it was, for Aquinas, unified within the task of Christian preaching. It was as a preacher – and for the sake of preaching – that Thomas studied anything and everything. In the rich intelligibility and surpassing beauty of the created order, Aquinas saw a glimpse of the infinite beauty and goodness of the God whom he was ordained to preach. No sector of reality could be overlooked, since only the endless array of truths that God has buried within the world can begin to capture and communicate the inexhaustible richness of God. So the Christian thinker had, Thomas thought, an intellectual duty to think about everything from the vantage point of faith.

Aquinas was certainly no pluralist. He believed that knowledge (and acceptance) of Christian truth is necessary to human flourishing. Like his contemporaries, he believed in the existence of an eternal hell and developed an unusually sophisticated account of its justice. So at first glance it seems wildly implausible to contend that his teaching might resonate with our own pluralist age, in which we rightly celebrate diversity. Yet Aquinas was also no fundamentalist, and granted the theologian no intellectual hegemony over the non-believer. In fact, a closer look at the way in which Aquinas held to his Christian convictions reveals a rather complex picture, from which contemporary pluralism can learn much. Although committed to the exclusive, unalterable and universally binding character of Christianity's truth-claims, Thomas did not believe that these beliefs were immune from intellectual scrutiny or rational critique, even by non-believers. Nor did Aquinas believe that the gift of faith bestowed a privileged starting point on the believer, from which they could gain an automatically clearer perspective over the world.

Holding firm to deep convictions, even religious ones that are taken to be accredited by God, is, for Aquinas, no obstacle to openness to insights from other traditions. The ends of dialogue are not best pursued by watering down our deepest convictions. In fact, the stronger the conviction, the broader the degree of openness to others can be. Even in his most explicitly religious moments, Thomas exhibits great confidence in the universality and power of human reason as the basis upon which humanity can communicate in the shared task of getting to the truth of things. The free exercise of reason plays a crucial role in overcoming our alienation from one another, and even if the task of translating from one cultural or linguistic context to another seems endlessly labour-intensive, it is not ultimately impossible. Indeed, faith does not demand that we step back from reason, but rather that we ask reason to do more, to work more intensively and extensively. Aquinas thinks that authentic faith strengthens rather than diminishes the power of reason.

Although in today's secular university philosophy and theology are quite distinct (and sometimes opposed) faculties, Aquinas would not recognize such a sharp disjunction. He is both a theologian and a philosopher, and often both at the same time. Conventionally, the boundary lines between these two disciplines have been drawn in terms of revelation: philosophy concerns matters accessible to the natural powers of unaided human reason, while theology begins with principles beyond our natural grasp, given by God's freely-willed disclosure of them (pre-eminently in the Bible). There is truth in this account, but readers of Aquinas ought not draw the boundary lines too firmly or too quickly. Certainly, Aquinas does not subscribe to the deceptively attractive idea that philosophy is the science of unanswerable questions, whereas theology is the cashing out of God's definitive answers. For Thomas, the boundary between theology and philosophy is much more porous, not least because theology uses the tools crafted by philosophy, and because theological progress is often achieved by joining a revealed truth with a philosophical insight.

Together, theology and philosophy exhibit the deep human desire to fashion a home within the world by making sense of the meaning of our existence. Both disciplines concern the highest reaches of human potential. Humanity alone needs philosophy and theology, since we alone among the animals are confronted with our existence as a question, a puzzle or a project rather than a brute fact. Theology and philosophy are necessary bedfellows, then, in that they both begin with a sense of wonder, and share a common attunement to the mystery of existence, albeit from quite different angles. Philosophy and theology alike push at the limits of human capacity, striving both to widen the horizons of human understanding and come to terms with the systematically elusive character of reality, the fact that we cannot bring everything under our control, that the world in which we live is always beyond our mastery. Philosophy pushes at the boundaries of human possibility from within, stretching reason as far as it can go. Theology pushes at the same boundaries from without, enlarging our minds in

INTRODUCTION

the awareness of the infinite world of meaning and possibility that confronts us from without.

THE DESERT

I will have more to say about Aquinas's historical remoteness in the next chapter. I will not, however, attempt to explain the strangeness of his world view away. I drafted an outline of this book while trekking through the Mojave Desert, where I had gone hoping that its remote, unfamiliar and intrinsically challenging landscape might yield a fresh perspective. This serves as an apt metaphor for how I see the journey into Thomas's thought. No matter what preparatory work is done, there is nothing that can really prepare you for the first encounter with the magnificent desolation of the Mojave. Along the way, you will inevitably meet people and discover that there are as many reasons for undertaking the journey as there are pilgrims. Some are escaping from the buzz of the modern world, others seek a sense of perspective on the world's challenges, some are trying to exorcise personal demons, others are indulging a desire for the extremes, some want to find a place of encounter with God. Some people probably just want to say that they have been, and others cannot explain why they love it. But whatever reason people have for venturing into the desert, the difficulty of getting there is intrinsic to its value.

There is something of the desert about Thomas Aquinas and his *Summa Theologiae*. It is magnificent and kind, full of surprising pockets of life, but it is also relentless and unforgiving to those who come ill-prepared. Pilgrims are attracted to the *Summa* for a range of reasons (some good, some bad), and the first-time visitor is wont to be overwhelmed by the strange and startling terrain they encounter. For anyone who enters into conversation with Thomas's work for any length of time, the difficulty in entering the world of Aquinas is part of his value. Aquinas's strangeness is our opportunity. It is my hope that this book will help prepare those who have not yet encountered Aquinas directly to undertake that journey of their own, and all of us to persevere in allowing Aquinas's strangeness to remain strange.

Nonetheless, the task that I have set myself is not to offer an exposition of Aquinas's thought, but to show that Thomas's thought matters now. While this obviously entails some degree of exposition, it also allows me to take certain liberties and to engage in a certain amount of provocation. I cannot, of course, hope to be exhaustive, and among many themes that could have been given more extensive treatment the account of creation (omnipresent in Aquinas's thought) is ranked in first place. My hope is simply to show those who feel more at home in the world of Foucault, Peterson, Lacan, Žižek or Badiou that Aquinas is worth engaging with; that, for all of his strangeness, he has something to say and something to show us; and that many of his central convictions are both rigorously thought through and deeply intuitive.

THE JOURNEY

Each of the chapters that follows examines an indispensable element of Thomas's conversational universe. A special place within that world is reserved, of course, for the human person. Uniquely, we find ourselves by bringing the world into speech. The consequences for overlooking the 'conversational' character of the universe prove quite paralysing, both to the intellectual life and to human existence more generally. A conversation is always a mysterious thing. It can never be simply a matter of exchanging information. A conversation is always complex and multi-faceted, operating on a number of levels and communicating across a range of registers, some of which are immediately obvious and others deeply concealed (and, as Sigmund Freud and St Paul both taught us, hidden from the view of the interlocutors). To miss one of the dimensions of a conversation is to misjudge how to participate within it and consequently to limit the range of authentic responses that are open to us. The results of such communicative misfires range from crossed wires through severe embarrassment to unwittingly inciting violence. Similarly, treating the non-human world as merely a repository of information to be mined and described (something that seems to be a perennial temptation of post-Enlightenment thought) severely hampers our efforts to belong within the world.

An examination of the consequences of such a 'flattening' of the world into a single register of meaning will recur in what follows. Nonetheless, there is one overarching consequence of seeing the universe as being structured like an ongoing conversation that is worth emphasizing at the outset. We are often intuitively primed with a

INTRODUCTION

pragmatic account of truth: the value of knowledge lies in what we can achieve with it, whether that be by developing technology or by achieving freedom for ourselves and others. Paradoxically, we can adopt a similar attitude towards freedom as important for what we do in it: we desire freedom so as to declare our truth, to live the truth of ourselves without restriction. By pulling truth and freedom apart in this way, we can inadvertently weaponize them. We can appeal to freedom to justify our irresponsible behaviour towards others. We can appeal to truth-telling to justify causing offence and hurt.

In the Thomistic universe, 'truth' and 'freedom' (or, if you prefer, 'love') are neither in competition (and could never be) nor separable. We cannot use the truth as a weapon to imprison, nor can the imperatives of freedom excuse us from the obligation to fidelity. Knowledge of the truth is precisely the freedom to respond well, and the freedom to move in the conversation of life is inevitably the road to truth. Since our freedom is always a matter of participating within the conversation of reality (along with all other beings that make up our world), so the pursuit of truth requires no further legitimation in terms of artificially constructed frameworks of relevance or impact. Intellectual inquiry always has social and political ramifications stitched into its very fabric (whether for good or for ill), not least in the type of citizen that intellectual inquiry forms.

Thomas Aquinas matters not only because he recognized these truths and developed their implications with an unsurpassed consistency, but also because his thought maps out a way of living that equips today's readers to negotiate the demands of reality in ways that are humane and humanizing. In times of unprecedented fragmentation, the seemingly remote wisdom embodied within the rigours of Aquinas's thought can help us to find wholeness, by listening to what the world is telling us and intuiting within it an integrity crying out for our co-creative completion.

OUTLINE OF THE BOOK

The theme of conversation unites each of the chapters. The first chapter sketches a portrait of Thomas Aquinas as a participant in the world-conversation and the tradition of theological reflection, and suggests that Aquinas intentionally crafted his writings so as to stimulate conversation – not so much with himself (or our peers), but with reality itself. Chapter 2 outlines Thomas's account of the fundamental building blocks of reality as dynamic and communicative centres of 'speech'. These individual voices participate in different ways within the single world-conversation, because all communicative life takes place within an infinite and eternal horizon (which Thomas calls God); this is the theme of Chapter 3. The fourth chapter moves into more explicitly theological territory, showing how Thomas understands God's own life in communicative terms, as a symphony of bliss. The unique mode of human participation within the world-conversation is the subject of Chapter 5, which draws attention to Thomas's account of the forms of 'interior conversation' that are uniquely human. Chapter 6 explores how human beings belong to the world-conversation by shaping their lives in projects of meaning. Chapter 7 examines this facet of human life and the tools that enable us to negotiate the task of becoming human in a world of change. The final chapter considers the ways in which God speaks directly within the world, and raises human beings into the conversation of friendship with Godself.

I

Conversing

THE LIFE AND WORK OF ST THOMAS AQUINAS

Martin Heidegger offered an infamously terse biography of Aristotle, seemingly stressing the dominance of arguments by downplaying the importance of the historical figure that produced them: 'He was born. He worked. He died.'[1] A similar reverence for Thomas's textual legacy and its arguments over the accidents of biography is tempting in the case of Aquinas. His life was essentially a long story of fidelity to the task of teaching, and he seems to have intentionally produced texts that are detachable from the sites of their production, inviting very little reflection on the author's state of mind or private intention. Consequently, today's reader can find Aquinas's work bloodless and dispassionate, even bewilderingly abstract, as if the medieval 'Thomas' holds himself at a comfortable distance from 'Aquinas' the academic *persona* we encounter in his writings.

Nonetheless, Aquinas consecrated himself to the task of becoming a conversationalist: somebody deeply engaged in the business of listening to the world-conversation and contributing to it in the best way that he could. The bulk of his working life was spent engaged in the hard business of helping others to embark on the same adventure. It was no bloodless undertaking. The astonishing breadth and extent of Aquinas's work can only be explained by a passion that Thomas generally – perhaps intentionally – concealed from public view. It could be that Aquinas presupposed a common passion, shared with his students, which he sought to sharpen and direct through the hard discipline of intellectual graft. After all, Aquinas self-evidently understood himself to be a preacher before anything else: it was not his job to artificially make the subject matter interesting or relevant; he could presuppose that his students already knew this to be a matter of life and death, worth staking their life on. The defining characteristic of Thomas's life is that he was a member of the Order of Friar Preachers, a then novel, creative and highly contested form of religious life. It was to the defence of this new way of life that Aquinas devoted some of his most intense bursts of intellectual energy. This defence of the way of life to which he was committed produces some of the most trenchant and passionate work of his early career, including some of the rare moments when Aquinas seems to have been angered by his opponents.[2]

Given the apparent remoteness of Aquinas's way of seeing the world from our own, some attunement to the creative foment in which he lived reveals some surprising commonalities. The details of Aquinas's life are well-established, particularly in intellectual biographies by the Dominican scholars James Weisheipl and Jean-Pierre Torrell,[3] and the scholarly work of Simon Tugwell.[4] Thomas was born to a noble family in Roccasecca, became a Dominican friar, and lived for about 50 years. He died in 1274 after an accident, having shortly before experienced some kind of mystical or neurological event that – for reasons that are shrouded in mystery – put an end to his scholarly career.

CONFLICT AND CONTINUITY

Thomas's 30 years of life as a friar preacher were marked by study (Naples, Paris and Cologne), and above all by teaching (twice in Paris, in Orvieto, Rome and – probably also twice – at Naples). If our image of Aquinas is that of the gentleman scholar with vast quantities of uninterrupted time to roam around the world of ideas, we are utterly mistaken. In a way with which many of today's academics can empathize, Thomas's scholarly work – supported though it was by a range of devoted assistants – was interrupted by administration, various extremely tedious meetings (some of which were important), the demands of travel and several forays (generally though not entirely reluctantly) into ecclesiastical and secular politics. He also involved himself in what we would now call the ecumenical movement and preached popular sermons. Much of his preaching, in stark contrast to his academic writing, seems rather boring and unremarkable, certainly comparable with his contemporaries. With the notable exception of his double stint in Paris and his remarkably prodigious output (roughly eight sides of A4 for each day of his working life), the rudiments of his relatively short life do not immediately suggest the extraordinary intellectual itinerary that is disclosed by his writings.

In three respects, Aquinas's life resonates with our own times: his experience of conflict; an intense awareness of marginality; and the feeling of rapid, perhaps uncontrolled, social and intellectual change. Although it is not immediately apparent from his mellow style of writing and from the generally irenic character of his philosophical method, Aquinas was deeply familiar with conflict and the instability it brought to social and political life. He inhabited an era in which philosophical and religious ideas easily mixed with contestations of political sovereignty, as witnessed by the Crusades to the Holy Land and the fight against the Cathars.[5] The incursion of Islam into Christendom, particularly in the Spanish Kingdom of Granada, pinched Christian self-understanding and aspiration, frustrating the desire to extend its religious culture and social order across the entirety of known human geography and civilization.

Closer to home, Frederick II was challenging – both on the level of ideas and in the bloody reality of warfare – the extent of the Pope's 'secular' (more bluntly, military) power and authority. The Treaty of San Germano,[6] enacted when Aquinas was about six years old, marked an end to the tumultuous War of the Keys, but the relief was temporary, and the politics of the region that comprises modern-day Italy would remain dominated by the conflicting interests of Papacy and empire for decades to come. The Aquinas family seem to have been periodically implicated in the conflict and to have intermittently nurtured pro-emperor sympathies. The new University of Naples was founded by the emperor with the intention of providing for the bureaucratic needs of the empire's enormous administrative superstructure, but with the implicit goal of forming a cultural and intellectual counterpoint to the papal foundations at Bologna and Paris.

As a result of all this, Aquinas, like many of his contemporaries, would have been more immediately aware than previous generations of the location of his cultural and religious life at the frontiers, adjacent to a whole world of contradiction and confrontation. The

Abbey of Monte Cassino, where the young Thomas was taken for education from 1230 until 1239 (seemingly on account of his family's aspirations for him to rise to lofty ecclesiastical office there), sat directly on the frontier between the Kingdom of Sicily and the Papal States. Aquinas's fundamental intellectual formation was, then, located at the fault line of an unstable religious and political synthesis. More significantly still, the University of Naples – to which Aquinas would be displaced by conflict at Monte Cassino – represented an *intellectual* frontier, functioning as a gateway through which startling new ideas could flow from the immense civilization of the Islamic world that lay just across the Mediterranean. This flow of ideas included a fresh mediation of Aristotle's thought, an influx of an exciting new world of thought and inquiry that would decisively shape Aquinas's own theological and philosophical projects. In short, from his most formative years onwards, Aquinas would have been acutely aware of a cultural and intellectual 'Other', a tradition of thought that could, in sophistication and richness, compete with his own. This functioned for Thomas not merely as an antidote to cultural hegemony, but also as intellectual stimulation, providing a rich battery of conceptual tools and new sources of philosophical insight. The times not only promoted innovation; they also required it.

Framed by this attunement to otherness and a felt sense of liminality, Aquinas's intellectual project – and indeed his entire life – can be read as a patient and intelligent negotiation of stability and change: the continuity of fidelity to an inherited tradition and the discontinuities of its confrontation by the creative novelty of the 'cutting-edge' deliverances of philosophy and the natural sciences. The potency of the emerging intellectual world seemed to be both an opportunity, opening new horizons of human understanding, and an intimidating threat to the stability of Christian wisdom. In all of this, there was for Aquinas no question of a straightforward 'defeat', whether of the old by the new or *vice versa*. At their point of encounter in Thomas's mind, neither world view remained unchanged or unenriched, but nor were they simply fused into a 'third thing' as if an entirely new synthesis was formed by the merger of these two world views. Rather, without underestimating the real discontinuities, each world view seemed to open out and unfold itself within the other, with each retaining its basic integrity in the process. (Though, of course, in accordance with his vocation as a preacher, the Christian tradition always held priority and wielded the power to correct).

The task of reconciling Aristotle and Christian philosophical theology seems to have been facilitated by the particular character of Thomas's genius as a 'conversationalist'. Alongside the prowess of an intensely sharpened analytical mind, Aquinas enjoyed a rare capacity for synthesis, an ability to penetrate to the conceptual heart of a text or a set of ideas, and so be able to inhabit for himself the living dynamism that held a particular world view together. By seeing apparently contradictory systems of thought 'from within', Aquinas was able to detect the hidden commonalities and convergences, as each opened out onto some aspect of reality in its unsubduable richness and complexity. Above all, it was a profound confidence in the power of reality – the world-conversation that transcends all of the necessarily fragmentary attempts to capture its meaning – that funded Thomas's confident pursuit of a synthesis that could only have been vaguely intuited in advance. Along with this strategy of slow, penetrative and synthetic 'reading-for-wisdom', it is the unshakeable confidence in the power of reality to truly disclose itself that Aquinas exemplifies to today's historical moment.

FEROCIOUS IRENICISM

Each of these three strands of Aquinas's life experience – conflict, attunement to the other, and the negotiation of change – converge and were intensified in the university, the setting for Aquinas's life's work and intellectual development. Thomas was a highly skilled practitioner of professional university life. As Marie-Dominique Chenu has observed, Thomas's philosophical work is inconceivable apart from the relatively newly inaugurated intellectual atmosphere of the universities, which provided the context, impetus and scholarly frame for Thomas's thought.[7] The universities had become intellectual hotbeds, not only in terms of numbers but also vitality. The early universities succeeded in attracting a radically new kind of student than had the monastic schools with which earlier generations of theologians (like St Anselm) would have been familiar. This new breed of student was to be educated in a domain of intentional encounter between cultures and ideas, and this demanded fresh reflection on pedagogy.[8] Throughout his work, Thomas self-consciously reflects on the best and most effective ways to communicate complex ideas to his students and (perhaps more importantly) to form within them the discipline of conversational engagement with the world that speaks, through the cultivation of virtuous intellectual practices and dispositions.

As the locus of the Church's intellectual life shifted more resolutely from the monastery to the university, Aquinas could sense enormous intellectual opportunity amid the obvious threat to conceptual stability. The universities were themselves sites of entrenched conflict (along both intellectual and political lines). Thomas's openness to Aristotelianism was fiercely resisted by traditionalist Augustinians, who feared the new philosophy would imperil theology's supremacy and eliminate the mystical. Careers were marked and marred by long and intractable disputes between secular professors and those drawn from religious orders; and there were infamously rancorous disputes between members of the Franciscan and Dominican orders themselves (sometimes involving theft, threats of violence, slander, mass brawls, allegations of poisoning and occasional displays of Christian reconciliation). The university within which Thomas thrived was but a microcosm of the complex and changing times in which he lived.

The ability to thrive in this complex and contested world is reflected in various paradoxes of Thomas's personality that can be reconstructed both from his writing and from historical witnesses.[9] Aquinas could be characterized as something of a living contradiction: ferociously irenic. On the one hand, his intellectual temper is characteristically peaceable, with the capacity to remove the heat from a debate and proceed calmly, rationally and with remarkable justice to conflicting authorities. On the other hand, when necessary, Aquinas shows no aversion to conflict, and no trepidation in entering into the most robust refutation of his opponents.[10] In these moments, Aquinas has no compunction in exposing the weakness of his interlocutors and their arguments.

In fact, a similar paradox is evident in descriptions of Aquinas's very physicality. He was notoriously large and robust – nicknamed 'the Ox' as a student – and yet unusually sensitive to physical pain and to the movement of the emotions. Often found to be lost in the contemplation of complex theoretical problems, he was known to be frequently abstracted or absent-minded, yet he was fearsomely perceptive and extremely insightful when it came to political and personal matters. Both his biography and his theoretical work suggest this lover of silence and solitude (even with a certain contempt for frivolous conversation) had a sustained capacity for deep and meaningful friendships.[11] As a younger professor he was known as a friendly, witty and amusing interlocutor. Evidently skilled in the deployment of logical argument with a clinical precision, he was also an accomplished poet and a wordsmith. Some evidence suggests a degree of musical training and proficiency.[12]

The profound complexity of Aquinas's thought is the fruit of a strikingly complex man coming to terms with an enormously complex social world. Yet Aquinas's religiosity is disarmingly simple. His vernacular preaching was (insofar as we can tell) simple, direct and unostentatious. It was so unremarkable, it seems, that relatively few of his sermons – especially his university sermons – have been preserved. Surprisingly, Aquinas does not seem to have been particularly devoted to the Virgin Mary, but always carried with him a relic of St Agnes, with which he reportedly effected a miraculous cure of his friend and secretary Reginald (in commemoration of which he held an annual party for his students). Deeply devoted to the presence of Christ in the Holy Eucharist and to the contemplation of the events of Christ's earthly life, Aquinas was fond of praying in front of a crucifix, but he never proposed any particular spiritual technique or method of meditation: prayer is simply a matter of asking God for things that we need.[13]

Aquinas's theology and spirituality seem to have helped him to come to terms with episodes of trauma in his life: a sister killed by lightning as he slept in the same room left him with a lifelong fear of storms; the trenchant – even violent – opposition of his family to his vocation (involving the temporary deprivation of his liberty); and a non-consensual encounter with a woman (possibly a prostitute) that was apparently intended by some family members to upset his equilibrium and dissuade him from pursuing his dreams.[14] Echoes of these darker memories can be heard periodically in Thomas's work, not least in his lengthy investigation of the emotions (and of sexual passion) and his account of divine Providence in the *Summa Contra Gentiles*, written (it seems) at the same time as the *Commentary on Job*, a book Thomas takes to be 'the demonstration by probable reasons that human affairs are ruled by divine providence'.[15]

CHRISTIAN VISIONARY

Aquinas died on 7 March 1274, while travelling – at Pope Gregory X's request – to participate in the Council of Lyons, which was intended to heal the wounds of a dogmatically divided Christendom. A month or so earlier, absent-minded as ever, Thomas had tripped over and struck his head against a branch; evidence suggests he never fully recovered and, indeed, progressively weakened. In early December of 1273 – around the feast of St Nicholas, and while Thomas was celebrating Mass in the Saint's chapel – Thomas experienced something unusual, registered by his companions as 'an astonishing transformation'.[16] Without notice, Thomas suddenly stopped work and, with an uncharacteristically dramatic flourish, destroyed his writing equipment. He initially said simply that he could not go on. When pushed, he declared that, compared to what he had seen, everything he had written was straw.

Explanations of this event vary widely, and tend to reveal more about the interpreters than they do about Aquinas. Hagiographers diagnose an intensely relativizing mystical encounter. Those inclined to a more natural account propose a physical explanation in terms of a stroke or other neurological event, but there is evidence that Thomas retained the capacity for theological reflection and continued working in a limited way, albeit only when asked. Perhaps the most likely explanation lies somewhere between these two extremes: after many years of intense labour, it is easy to sense Thomas's growing fatigue and exhaustion. It seems likely that the physical and emotional toll taken by his extraordinary workload could have contributed to a cataclysmic breakdown as Thomas grew older. Of course, this is by no means incompatible with a mystical encounter. The spiritual tradition attests that such moments of disruption are often powerful occasions of grace; painful encounters with our own finitude can often be the site of unusual spiritual and theological insight.

One thing about this strange incident can certainly be excluded: the reference to his writings as 'straw' should not be taken as synonymous with 'trash'. Aquinas is not here disavowing or discarding his written work. The terms he uses are familiar enough to the lexicon of medieval logicians, serving to distinguish the reality aimed at ('the grain') from the conceptual framework ('the straw') that leads to and supports it.

Thomas is not devaluing his theological work but rather re-valuing it in the light not so much of its failure as of its *success* in leading him to a point where he could now *see*. The practice of intellectual reflection had taken him, by grace, to a place beyond conflict, marginality and endless change, where ultimate reality could disclose itself to him and, for the first time, he could see something that had hitherto been concealed. This is the point of Aquinas's teaching and the possibility that his intellectual abode offers today's reader: to deliver us to a new place, a new standpoint, where we can finally see for ourselves.

Aquinas's death brought to a conclusion a life that was extraordinarily fruitful and yet profoundly ordinary in its fidelity to the mundane realities of daily academic and religious life. Taking a synoptic view of Thomas's life has proved a challenge to biographers over the centuries. The complexities of his work and the times in which he lived problematize efforts to locate his thought in ways that correspond to the categories of the present day. Aquinas was certainly a preacher and a professor, a philosopher and a theologian. He also made important contributions to psychology, speculative biology and political theory; he is a notable poet and liturgist and, on some accounts, deserves to be seen as a mystic. He was a medieval 'man of letters', a passionate communicator whose primary tool was language and who fashioned a style of writing and an associated scholarly vocabulary that coupled power with clarity, balancing precision and flexibility. His work pushed existing genres to their limits, reshaping the disciplinary field around the importance of new fields of questioning. Rather than renewing already established conclusions, Aquinas's work gives first place to questioning, with questions having a priority even if they could be answered decisively from existing authorities. Without questions, the human mind would grow static and thus miss the true significance and redolence of the answers that are already within our grasp.

To the modern academic, it is the scope of Aquinas's questioning that is perhaps the most remarkable feature of his work. The extent of his work is determined by the twofold object of the theological science as he understood it: God in God's own intrinsic perfection, and all other things as they relate to God and receive a finite share in God's infinite perfection. The theologian of Aquinas's day was not relegated to a small corner of the humanities faculty with the tacit agreement that they will be left alone on the condition that they avoid embarrassing the university by speaking up. The theologian could (and, indeed, *should*) interrogate everything and anything, since it is the task of theology to provide the wisdom by which anything and everything fits together in a comprehensive whole.

Cornelius Ernst suggested that Aquinas might best be portrayed as a 'Christian thinker',[17] one who was concerned not so much with knowledge production as with the task of thinking rigorously about every facet of human experience from within a basically committed orientation towards reality. That Thomas's life was fruitful precisely in terms of knowledge production indicates the urgent necessity of thinking in this richer sense of free intelligent exploration of reality in all of its richness. This type of thinking cannot, however, be indulged simply as an end in itself. It is seeing, rather than thinking, that was the end point of Aquinas's working life, the grain towards which the straw of his voluminous writings and herculean labours were orientated. In thinking, Aquinas was concerned to open up a new way of seeing reality, to excavate – for himself and for his students – a mode of intellectual belonging, lived in the presence of ultimate reality, in which reality could be seen for itself. The ambiguity with which the figure of Aquinas sits within today's university ought, perhaps, to raise the question of whether such thinking and seeing – and, indeed, such belonging – can flourish within the universities of today. And if not there, then where?

HEDGEHOG OR FOX?

Isaiah Berlin famously proposed categorizing writers as either foxes or hedgehogs. As the ancient saying has it, foxes know many things, but hedgehogs know one big thing. An intellectual fox's interests are diffuse and widespread, drawing from many sources and experiences, and their many ideas refuse reduction to any fundamental principles. By contrast, the intellectual hedgehog's thought is unified by a central concept or insight, repeated or implemented across many iterations. For the hedgehog, there is a key that unlocks the unity of the world, but for the fox the rich complexity of reality can only be adequately reflected by refusing any single synthetic viewpoint. Vaguely amusing as an academic icebreaker, the distinction cannot be applied too simplistically or rigidly. Every thinker has a balance of instincts that resemble both fox and hedgehog. Nonetheless, postmodernity has tended to celebrate the fox's victory: the postmodern is trained to sniff out and reject even the merest hint of a unifying meta-narrative. To the postmodern, Aquinas is an irredeemable hedgehog.

Aquinas was certainly a hedgehog, but a hedgehog in fox's clothing. Without a doubt, Aquinas's thought world is unified by a relentless and singular focus on the infinite mystery of God. Insofar as everything else exists by depending upon God as creator and – more acutely put – sharing in some finite way in the gift of God's existence, Aquinas would hold that the most rigorous of hedgehogs must necessarily be the most expansive foxes. Only the fox's breadth of inquiry can support and sustain the hedgehog's unitary vision.

Reflecting these two aspects of his thought, the community of Aquinas's readers must always exist in a balance or tension between foxes and hedgehogs. There are those who focus on the particular detail of Thomas's individual teaching: Antonia Fitzpatrick on Thomas's account of bodily identity,[18] Paul Rogers on his account of prophecy,[19] and Nicholas Lombardo on Thomas's theory of emotion.[20] For all their necessity and brilliance, such studies are complemented by those who attempt to capture something of the broader Thomistic landscape: Herbert McCabe's *On Aquinas*,[21] Eleonore Stump's *Aquinas*[22] and Marie-Dominique Chenu's *Toward an Understanding of Saint Thomas*.[23] Without the detailed focus on the particular, these visionary accounts could risk slipping the bonds of Thomas's actual work. On the other hand, without periodically stepping back to survey the broader vision, the precision of the particular study risks getting lost in the detail, much of which is deeply historically conditioned.

The balance between fox and hedgehog is held together in Thomas's thought by his understanding of creation as the relationship of all things to the infinity of God. Creation occupies such a prominent place within Thomas's thought that G. K. Chesterton famously remarked that, following the Carmelite custom of attaching a fitting epithet to a saint's name, Aquinas might be known as 'Thomas of the Creator'.[24] Quite apart from the explicit attention given to creation in Thomas's writing, Josef Pieper suggested that the doctrine of creation is also a hidden, structuring, element of Thomas's thought.[25] Attentiveness to creation meant, in Aquinas's day, keeping abreast of the latest developments in scientific inquiry. Aquinas lived and worked at the zenith of what has been termed the medieval '(re)discovery of nature'.[26] If nature had once appeared to be a secretive, obscure and elusive force – as if pulling the strings behind the world that is accessible to the senses – nature was now personified as a teacher, not merely transparent to human investigation, but actively giving herself to be known and loved by the attentive observer.

The rediscovery of nature left Aquinas, along with his contemporaries, with the challenge of achieving a harmonious synthesis of two potentially conflicting accounts of nature. The first, taken from the natural philosophy of antiquity, interpreted nature as an internal principle of movement that worked within things to guide their movement towards their fulfilment. The second, overtly theological, account was inherited from the theologians of the early Church and stressed the natural world's status as the theatre of divine self-communication. On this theological rendering, nature is fulfilled in the expression of something beyond itself: held in existence by the creative power of God, nature is the instrument of God's providence.

The unique power of Thomas's account of creation lies in his recognition that these accounts of nature – more like aspects of a single reality than competing theories – stand or fall together. The integrity of nature's internal, causal structure is secured by the affirmation of its transcendent origin and fulfilment; the possibility of the natural world communicating anything of the supernatural depends upon the integrity of its internal constitution. Theology, philosophy and natural science are ultimately non-competitive: whatever the doctrine of creation affirms, its fundamental concerns are not ones that can be proven or disproven by the scientific study of the world.

The doctrine of creation is, for Thomas, not primarily an account of how God got the world-conversation started. Rather, it is an account of a form of communication that is taking place in every instance of time, the way in which God continually provides the silence that hears us into speech, a silence that is filled with the world that speaks.[27] More personally, it is an account of God's constant invitation to participate in the world-conversation, a silent and gentle questioning that provokes us into life. Profound spiritual experiences are simply moments when we become aware in a transient way of something that is 'going on' all of the time. The doctrine of creation is not really about getting our facts about the world's origins right but, more importantly, the cultivation of a mood of attunement to the giftedness of existence.

Consequently, Aquinas's understanding of creation can only be fully articulated as a contemplative posture – a moral and spiritual attitude towards the giftedness of existence – albeit one that is inevitably accompanied by a set of intellectual practices. The heart of this contemplative attitude is an intense and systematically developed awareness of the utter gratuity of creation. Creation is in no sense necessary.[28] Our existence, individually and collectively, is not the outcome of logical necessity. Creation is freely and lovingly willed into existence in an outpouring of the divine life that has neither preconditions nor determination outside of God's sovereign and free desire to share the gift of being with creatures. From this quasi-mystical intuition of creaturely fragility, Thomas, as we will see, extrapolates a way of living marked by gratitude that unfolds into a social programme, a politics of friendship and solidarity.

Although Thomas has very strong hedgehog-like instincts towards the development of a unitary world view, he is not a systematic thinker in the way a modern philosopher such as Hegel could be said to be. In this sense, systems aspire to completeness and to closure, to the achievement of a definitive 'picture' that can account for everything. Thomas does not aspire to such a determinative account of reality. In fact, by unifying his philosophy and theology around the infinity of God, Aquinas forecloses the possibility of precisely this kind of system. As infinite, God is uniquely without boundaries or limits, and could never be accommodated within a system of understanding. Thomas recognizes that, no matter how sophisticated our understanding, there is always more that could be said, and the reality of this excess is a necessary condition for the possibility of saying anything at all. Thomas's version of systematic thought is not ordered towards the production of a system, but to systematically tracing the relationships that exist between the truths that make up our thought world. Thomas looks systematic because he sees everything to belong in relationship to everything else, but this relationality is more like the organic dynamism of a living body (or the vibrancy of a conversation) than the processes of a machine.

WAYS OF APPROACH

As I noted in the introduction, a major impediment to the 'indwelling' of Aquinas's thought is the perceived inaccessibility of his world view, often framed in terms of its historical remoteness. The question of how to negotiate the (at least partial) inaccessibility of Aquinas's thought has dominated scholarly approaches to Aquinas for more than a century. Roughly speaking, two basic approaches can be observed. 'Speculative' readers (exemplified by neo-Thomism)[29] generally emphasize the transcultural accessibility of Thomas's *arguments*. Although the style, idiom and content of his work may very well be utterly alien to the contemporary reader's perspective, the hard labour of reasoning can extract logical arguments from his textual corpus and – perhaps aided by the commentatorial tradition – follow Aquinas's pathway so as to reach his conclusions. This approach exhibits a certain kind of confidence in the universal power of human reason: reason is not so alienated from itself – or its earlier historical forms – that Aquinas cannot be read intelligibly.

Historical readings of Aquinas adopt quite a different approach, stressing the culturally embedded character of his work. Without some attunement to the thought world of the thirteenth century (and its profound difference from our own) the truly explosive character of Thomistic thought will be lost.[30] Historical readers likewise exhibit confidence in human reason, but stress its role in the laborious task of historical reconstruction as providing a set of tools that offer points of connection with the medieval mindset. For many readers who adopt this approach, the extraction of logical arguments from Aquinas's corpus perpetrates an interpretative violence against the texts themselves. Part of the revolutionary genius of Aquinas's approach lies in the way his arguments operate within a much broader, more composite and complex, body of literature, with considerations ranging from the order in which questions are presented, the systematic use of liturgical allusion, dense scriptural intertextuality and the evocation of the much broader landscape of sense and reference that Aquinas would have shared with his first students. In other words, Aquinas can only truly be read if his texts are situated within the cultural nexus in which they naturally and organically live.

For speculative readers, Aquinas matters because of what he says: the solidity, rigour and robustness of his argument. For historical readers,

Aquinas matters because of what he did with what he said: the ways in which he crafted an intellectually robust response to the needs and challenges of his day. It must be acknowledged that the fruits of both approaches (which, except in extreme cases, are more like tendencies held in creative tension) are clear to see. The speculative approach can find considerable support within the texts of Aquinas himself (as well as in Aquinas's own methods in appropriating the thought of others). Quite clearly, Aquinas systematically cultivated (especially in the *Summa Theologiae*) a highly disciplined style of writing that prioritized economy of expression and clarity of argument. The texts directly invite the reader to engage in conversation with them, presenting themselves as works of rigorous argumentation and debate. To refuse this invitation would ultimately amount to a violent refusal of the literal sense.

Nonetheless, historical readings also rightly point out the vast panoply of literary genres and registers of meaning within which Aquinas operates. Alongside the highly argumentative and conceptually dense works like the *Summa Theologiae* and *Summa Contra Gentiles* (as well as the disputed questions) lie the more literary and discursive works such as the biblical commentaries and shorter treatises, as well as heartfelt prayers and beautiful poetry. By attending to these more literary texts as philosophically instructive in their own right – and therefore as illuminative with respect to the adjacent argumentative texts – historical readings have helped scholarship to recognize the same poetic registers as operating within the *Summae*. From the perspective of an historical approach, speculative readings err not by engaging argumentatively or by affirming the transcultural portability of Aquinas's arguments, but in the employment of the reductive strategy of extraction, implicitly or explicitly positing that Aquinas *only* matters because of arguments that can be extracted and captured in the bloodless language of crisp, analytic logic. The greater holism offered by historical modes of reading has allowed Aquinas to come into view as both philosopher-theologian and mystic. In this broader perspective, Aquinas is a master not only of the Sacred Page, but also of the ways of the human heart.

REMOTENESS AS OPPORTUNITY

A first encounter with Aquinas's writing is often jarring and bewildering. Thomists probably feel something similar when they approach Lacan:

the sense that the acceptance of a few axioms would unlock a thought world of intricate complexity, the undeniable presence of a formidable intellect, and the intuition of something of profound significance, but ultimately a sense of exclusion, whether by jargon, cultural distance or straightforward lack of initiation. It is tempting for Thomists – who often pride themselves on being the 'straight talkers' and common sense merchants of the theological world – to deny this. The truth is that Lacan's disciples have no monopoly on what Roger Scruton called the 'nonsense machine'.[31] Aquinas's contemporary relevance cannot be found by attempting to port his thought across the centuries of historical displacement, or by an antiquarian interest in re-creating the culture of a bygone era. No advocate of Thomas's contemporary value could dissolve the sense of his historical remoteness, nor should they want to. Aquinas's historical remoteness, occasional obscurity and psychological distance – together with the intellectual investment that this writing demands from his readers – contributes positively to why he matters today.

In the first place, remoteness serves as an enabling condition for the kind of architectural indwelling that makes Aquinas so valuable today. Since so little of Aquinas's biography intrudes into his texts, the texts can be engaged as texts in their own right, without an excess of the unhelpful interposition of the vagaries of human personality. In short, we can read Aquinas without hearing his voice. This helps to explain the extraordinary valency of Aquinas's thought, as even the most cursory survey of contemporary 'Thomisms' indicates. There are ways of indwelling Aquinas's thought that disagree quite radically concerning the internal logic of Thomas's system and that dispute the correct reading of some of his most central and foundational axioms. While Thomists frequently disagree about the plausibility of these competing articulations of their master's thought, these disputes are themselves textually mediated through an engagement with Aquinas's texts. This confirms, rather than undermines, their valency: the texts are able to provide a framework and a common grammar – a set of philosophical tools and categories – that facilitates a fruitful and well-specified kind of constructive disagreement.

Secondly, the remoteness of Aquinas's thought (and, in particular, the periodic strangeness of his assumptions and sometimes bizarre questions that he adjudges to hold great significance) manifests an historical contingency that confronts and exposes the provisionality of our own intellectual worlds. Grappling with a theory that is so manifestly intelligent and insightful, and yet also so patently marked by ancient prejudice and presupposition, ought to raise rather acutely the question of what limitations mark our own basic assumptions about the world. In other words, reading Aquinas necessarily also involves allowing Aquinas to read and interrogate us.

Related to this is a third value that can be identified in Aquinas's remoteness. On account of its strangeness, indwelling Aquinas's thought involves a certain kind of intellectual humility, even an asceticism of mind. Entering the conceptual abode of Thomas Aquinas does not come naturally or even easily to a mind raised within the intellectual milieu of later modernity. It requires – demands – a great investment of time, energy and, above all, very intense thought. This kind of thinking is (Aquinas argues) a form of human excellence in itself, a life-giving and fulfilling activity that brings integrity to our intellectual lives and manifests one of humanity's highest and most distinctive capacities. More than one philosopher has observed that simple disavowal of falsehood does little to displace the constellating power that such known falsehoods can exercise over our thinking and acting. To displace such engrained and habituated frames of reference requires lengthy practices – bodily if possible – that perform a cognitive reorientation and reconfiguration. The alterity provided by Thomas's remoteness, with its refusal of any straightforward assimilation, posits the necessary conditions for the possibility of precisely such a deeply liberative mode of intellectual grappling.

The best kind of historical approach to Aquinas has two aims. First, that of enabling a more richly speculative engagement with Aquinas's arguments and concepts in their holistic totality. Secondly, and simultaneously, the aim of *intensifying* the sense of our own distance from Aquinas, so as to avoid depriving Aquinas of the power to interrogate and confront.

RHYTHM, RESONANCE, MOVEMENT

Movement – and the question of how to move well through life – plays a decisive role in structuring Aquinas's thought. As he indicates in his *prologue* to the monumental *Summa Theologiae*, Aquinas encounters his student as somebody on the move, engaged in the journey of self-determination and growth. The role of the teacher is to lead the student by the hand (*manuductio*) through an intellectual itinerary that the teacher has already navigated for themselves.[32] In so doing, the professor necessarily constitutes herself in a position of intellectual vulnerability, since (in an approach Aquinas himself frequently exemplifies) they cannot simply present their conclusions with an *ex cathedra* authority but must show the route that has been taken to reach these conclusions. In exposing the reasons that support their beliefs, good teachers open themselves up to critique, to the possibility of being outsmarted, and of discovering that they are mistaken in some fundamental belief about the world.

A similar pedagogy of movement is reflected in the microstructure of the *Summa Theologiae*. Each of the basic units that make up the *Summa* (the 2,669 articles that are distributed across its 512 questions) embodies a dynamic movement, an oscillation between objection and counterargument. This relentless, and almost antiphonal, rhythm of the *Summa* is fashioned and cultivated in order to evoke and provoke the student's full personal engagement with the question under consideration. This not only fosters a fresh engagement with familiar – perhaps even presumed – truths, but also summons the student to leave behind the premature stasis of fragile conclusion, inviting them into an intense intellectual movement.

This movement is generated by carefully crafted and strategically deployed questioning. In a world of premature exclamation marks, Aquinas matters because he can remind us of the importance of questioning and of formulating our questions well. The particle *utrum* ('whether') appears with monotonous regularity in the *Summa:* Aquinas crafts his text not primarily around the defence of theses, but in pursuit of answers to questions, often using those questions to state his thesis more precisely and to allow its significance to be unfolded. Learning to dwell with questions – not to eliminate them with immediate answers, but to experience the value of puzzlement – is, for Aquinas, a matter of intellectual and spiritual maturity. Indeed, Thomas himself clearly found intellectual pleasure and conceptual fecundity in the experience of being interrogated. Quodlibetal disputations – in which the professor would accept questions on any point, without prior notice – were a key feature of his academic practice, at which he seems to have excelled. The preserved records of these disputations show both a mind-in-motion and an intellect that flourished under the intense pressure of dialogical scrutiny.[33]

The structural significance of movement is not, however, confined to the level of the distinctive microstructure of each particular question and sub-question, but informs the overall macrostructure of the *Summa*. As Marie-Dominique Chenu demonstrated early in the last century, the plan of *Summa* tracks the movement of all creatures as they emerge from God by creation ('*exitus*') and return to God in Christ ('*reditus*').[34] Rather than being determined by abstract methodological principles, the shape of Thomas's teaching is moulded around the structure of reality. Theological and philosophical inquiry is not simply a human *response* to the world that speaks but, insofar as it maps onto the communicative movement that is 'built into' the structure of reality itself, a participation within that conversation. Indeed, Aquinas understands human reasoning to play a uniquely indispensable role within this dynamic movement of reality. Through characteristic motions of knowledge and love, human creatures contribute to the fulfilment of creation in its speaking back (*reditus*) to God. Knowing and loving are lodged within the resonant frequency of reality's rhythms, directing or misdirecting some small part of the world-conversation to flourishing or to failure.

MOVING IN INTELLECTUAL DANCE

To know, then, is to catch wind of the conversation of reality and be caught up in its movement back to God. Knowing contributes in a small, dependent and derivative way to God's governance of the world. For all that the world is often a cacophonous din of clashing forces and ideas, the question that faces us is not *whether* or not to involve ourselves in the conversation of reality, but *how* to make the next communicative move in a world to which we already unavoidably belong. Moving well primarily involves an attentiveness to discovering a mode of life lived in basic attunement to the rhythm of the world-conversation, but it always involves more than this. Discerning the form that our reality-attunement ought to take in a contested global sphere involves both knowledge and love, cohering as wisdom: it draws upon both knowing *that* and knowing *how*. As the philosopher Ludwig Wittgenstein observed, understanding and knowing how to go on – that is, what the next move is and how to make it – are fundamentally inseparable.

2

Reality

ENCOUNTERING THE WORLD THAT SPEAKS

The Mesquite Dunes in Death Valley are a forceful display of natural vitality. The name 'Death Valley' suggests a lifeless, echoey chamber in which a retreat into solitude – an escape from the technologized hustle and bustle of life – might open up a space in which the call of the transcendent can be heard. But it is hard to believe that anyone truly finds solitude in the desert. Far from being a barren place of inertia, the landscape pulses and throbs, never ceasing from a relentless push and pull, give and take. The senses are bombarded with movement. The burning heat rises in waves through the soles of our shoes. The air tastes and smells of salt. The inescapable howl of the wind traces both movement and resistance, punctuated by the sound of cracking salt plains. There is simply too much movement for the eyes to take in here, even when it is shrouded in the darkness of night. Standing at Mesquite shatters the illusion that humanity is the only locus of life in the cosmos. The desert unfolds itself before us, not as a blank canvas or a vacuum, but as a place of such vital intensity that it has performed a work of liberation upon us, breaking through our self-induced anaesthesia so that we might see the life that has been concealed before our eyes.

These experiences of natural extremity and the questions they provoke offer a route into understanding St Thomas's philosophical account of reality. Like the surprising vitality of the desert, Aquinas finds reality teeming with life and movement. Aquinas's philosophy of reality works as an anti-anaesthetic, a therapy to awaken us to the living dynamism of reality that is hiding in plain sight. Aquinas offers us a chance to change the way we look at reality, a philosophical therapeutic through which all that once seemed to be dead and inert can impress itself upon us as inescapably vibrant and alive: the power of a world that speaks.

Changing how we look at the world is, of course, easier said than done. The work of philosophical therapy it demands challenges us to consider the way in which some of our most intuitive assumptions about reality might turn out to be radically misleading. Aquinas's philosophical account of a world that speaks can feel as remote from our inherited assumptions as Death Valley is from the urban sprawl of Manhattan. Nonetheless, the journey into Aquinas's reality is worthwhile and rewarding; learning to see the world in a new way has never been more important.

We are – quite rightly – acutely and painfully aware of the political, social and ecological problems that face us, but we are less well attuned to their emergence from the tapestry of a world that speaks. Our instinctive response to the crises of our day is problem-solving: to diagnose and prescribe as quickly and effectively as possible. Aquinas offers a complementary approach that might be termed 'contemplative'. Rather than framing the present situation in terms of problems and solutions, Aquinas invites us to reflect on the broader question of what reality is trying to say to us, in all its rich complexity. Aquinas wants his student to incline their ear to hear as clearly as possible the groans of a creation that seeks liberation. This is not to deny that we must act urgently and responsibly, but to acknowledge that an authentic moral response can only emerge within the context of deep listening.

REALITY AS SPEECH

Listening is an appropriate metaphor for this kind of contemplation because, for Thomas, realities are things that show themselves, things that speak into the world-conversation. Speaking and communicating are so deeply embedded within human experience that we can easily overlook the mysterious complexity of speech. Consider the types of language use that characterize our daily existence: an exchange of pleasantries, the telling of jokes, asking for directions or transacting business. To bring any of these social tasks into speech we need first to be able to use our bodies to shape sounds into phonemes, then our minds to select meaningful words from a battery of vocabulary, and then our creativity to relate them in a flow of intonation and coherence as a sentence. Once that has been achieved, we are only scratching the surface of complexity: we are inevitably always using our speech to shape narratives, to cultivate a certain style that patterns our identity, and as a persuasive rhetorical tool to convince others to join us in projects of becoming. Each added level of complexity depends upon the more basic levels, and ultimately on our inherited biological skills. To say that reality speaks, then, is to say that everything that exists is also a nested collection of complex processes and skills. Aquinas's analysis of the most fundamental building blocks of reality (his metaphysics) functions to describe every instance of reality as operating on three equally primordial levels of 'speech': reality communicates something meaningful, achieves something practical and belongs within a narrative.

Something is real insofar as it has the power to reveal itself in the self-communicative action of existing. The real 'speaks' – perhaps better, 'presences' itself – simply by existing. 'Reality' as a whole is the totality of that which has the power to disclose itself in an indeterminate number of future manifestations: a place of surprise, wonder and mystery. The journey into reality is the great adventure of our lives: reality in this total sense is the ultimate horizon of all of our projects of love and learning, the theatre in which the drama of our lives can unfold.

The 'really real' (the things that are really 'out there' in the world, quite apart from our minds) can be distinguished from the merely mentally real (the things that exist only in our minds) by the fact that they do things to us as they speak. The 'really real' invades our minds via the senses, bumping into us and making an impact on our lives and on other entities in the world: failure to acknowledge the difference between the 'really real' and the 'mentally real' is a dangerous business.[1] This element of risk that the really real poses to us is, however, not a matter of the world harbouring a violence towards us. Rather, it is a symptom of the innate generosity of reality. Insofar as they are real, realities 'give themselves': they move out from beyond their own individuality, speaking themselves into manifestness and thereby forming the relational and interactive 'community' that is reality taken as a whole.

This moving, communicative character of the really real has two fundamental dimensions, one positive and one negative. Negatively, individual realities are marked by a certain incompleteness: they are not in themselves utterly self-sufficient, cannot be taken to 'possess' the whole of reality, and therefore tend towards their fulfilment and completion in relation to other existents that they share the community of reality with. Positively, however, precisely as 'really real', these particular realities possess an innate (but limited) perfection and tend to realize this perfection diffusively (by communicating themselves to others).

REALITY RE(VE)ALS

Reality, as Aquinas understands it, would be better captured with a verb than with a noun. Reality is not reducible to 'stuff' and cannot be portrayed principally as a state of affairs, whether as a very large collection of objects, or anything that could be entirely captured in the form of information. Reality is an event, a happening, a communicative motion in the slipstream of which human beings are uniquely entangled. Encountering the world as a movement of self-communication might have been second nature for much of the history of humanity, but it has proved deeply counterintuitive to many modern philosophers. Thanks to the legacy of mind-centred philosophers like Descartes and Kant, the ambient intellectual culture of our day habituates us into thinking of the world beyond our minds as something that we gaze out upon from behind our eyes: 'stuff' that we apprehend and bring new life to as we fashion them into more complex, beautiful and functional artefacts.

In such a world view, a deeper understanding of reality can be achieved through fragmentation: by breaking complex objects down into smaller and smaller parts so as to analyse the most foundational elements in the most microscopic detail. To understand a car, we look inside: opening the bonnet, assessing the movement of the engine's components, analysing chemical reactions, modelling the kinetic interplay of forces, and so forth. Aquinas's instincts are almost exactly the opposite of this fragmentation. As we will see, true understanding is not to be found through fragmentation, but by prioritizing the integrity of wholes (particularly *living* wholes), and seeing how they make themselves available for meaningful interaction with the other wholes that populate our world. Without denying the importance of an analysis of components, the highest level of understanding lies not concealed within, to be discovered through a destructive analysis, but on the surface, in the way a particular whole gives itself up to its relationship with others. The highest meaning of a car is, then, to be found in its utility, the way in which it is used to transform life and empower its occupants.

Although the idea of a world that speaks might sound like an abstract or even mystical matter, Aquinas brings it down to earth. Our experience of reality's speech is primarily an encounter with the causality that is embedded within the world. The way in which reality speaks is as the dynamic process by which the potential in one thing is brought into actuality, whether that take places through an encounter with something else (as when water is made hot by the heat of a flame) or through a natural unfolding, the realization of a potential that is intrinsic to the thing itself (as when a baby grows into a mature woman). Negotiating the change of causality is so fundamental to our experience that it is only under certain rather artificial conditions that we ordinarily catch a glimpse of the causal processes themselves: as I see the page before my eyes, I do not immediately imagine that the potential of my eyes is being activated by the coloured marks on the page. I simply read the text and am struck by its meaning. Similarly, for most of our daily lives we 'read' the text of reality and are struck by its significance. Nonetheless, the causal relations that give rise to such meaningful encounters are, for Aquinas, not secondary additions to reality but integral aspects of the world, built into the structure of existence itself. Reality as we encounter it *is* the great interplay of causal flux. Reality speaks because everything that exists is involved in the world of causing and being caused.

BEING AND BECOMING

At first glance, this suggests an identity of being and becoming: that to exist is to emerge in a process of growth and change. A student of philosophy will immediately recognize an ancient debate concerning whether stasis or flux is the most basic feature of reality (Heraclitus v Parmenides).[2] Is the flow of change all there really is (with the static appearing to us only as a means of creating some point of stability for ourselves within this endless movement), or is change only an illusion of the senses, with ultimate reality being unchanging?

With Aquinas, the starkness of this opposition appears less a rigid decision than two complementary perspectives on the same reality. Thomas's emphasis on the dynamism of change as the hallmark of reality as we encounter it ought not be taken to imply that his understanding of reality is so thoroughly dynamic as to construe being solely in terms of becoming, as if any point of stability in the ocean of change is a mere illusion. In fact, Aquinas seeks to avoid both extremes. The basic elements of reality are neither absolutely static (building blocks, lumps of stuff that await propulsion into motion) nor absolutely dynamic (pure flux, endless change, swallowing everything up into movement). At each level of his analysis of reality, Aquinas understands the speech of reality to emerge through an interaction between a dynamic principle of life and a static principle that captures this movement in a concrete instance, bringing limitation and specification of the particular. As we will see, this has a profoundly important consequence: everything that exists is utterly unique, possessed of its own inalienable wholeness and integrity, but is nonetheless always already transcendent of its own individuality, connected by the fact of its existences to the totality of reality. Consequently, the stability provided by determinate individuality and the dynamic of belonging are not competitive features of life, but mutually reinforcing and complementary.

Aquinas sees this connection and interplay of dynamism and particularity playing out in three interlocking layers of complexity. The first concerns the most basic question that can be considered of anything at all: the fact of its existence (its 'that-ness'). The second concerns the identity of something that exists: the 'what-ness' in which something that exists is determined to be a particular that belongs to a certain type of reality. The third concerns the way in which a reality manifests itself in the very concrete particulars of its existence: the 'how-ness' of something's emergence within the world, the contours of its growth and change, and its development over time and in relation to other realities in the world. To point to my newly acquired Maine Coon Sigmund is to point to each of these three aspects of the speech that is his reality. In the technical terms of Aquinas's metaphysics these are (1) the specification of existence by essence; (2) the determination of matter by form; and (3) the qualification of substance by accidents. Each of these levels corresponds to one dimension of the world's speech: the meaningful, purposeful and emplotted character of reality.

EXISTENCE

Like all good cats, Sigmund spends as much of his life as possible doing absolutely nothing. But even in doing nothing, Sigmund still does something good, something I expect him to do: he exists. In fact, the kind of nothing that Sigmund does is a very particular feline kind of doing nothing, and if he stopped doing this kind of nothing a trip to the vets would be in order. We could say that in doing nothing Sigmund 'cats': he exhibits the existence that is proper to cats. Along similar lines, Aquinas holds that it follows from something's being real that it is active in a certain sense, even if it is a stone or a grain of sand under a microscope. All individual existents are beings-in-act,[3] whether or not they seem to be doing something or nothing at all.

Thomas's technical term for the primordial act by which something is real is '*esse*'. *Esse* is usually translated as 'existence', but it is in fact not a noun but the infinitive form of the verb 'to be'. Translators have attempted to mark the strangeness of this word *esse* with the deployment of a neologism like is-ness, izy-ness, or to-Be, but this too misses the point: for Aquinas it is important that an entirely ordinary word can be charged with a special meaning that opens it out into an enormous conceptual plasticity, without any loss of connection with its mundane use. However it is translated (and it might well be better to leave it in the Latin), *esse* articulates the act of existence, the 'to-be' by which a particular reality speaks itself into the world-conversation. *Esse* consequently answers one of two basic questions about any particular thing: the question of whether or not something exists (*an sit*), leaving open the other major question, the specification of what exactly that thing is (*quid sit*). In the careful differentiation of these two basic questions about a reality we can find a route into apprehending Thomas's most basic metaphysical axiom: the 'real distinction' between essence and existence.

Esse is a dynamic energy, impulse or movement, unlimited in itself, that is specified by the static principle of essence that captures the act of existence by, as it were, focusing it into the mode of existence that is proper to a particular type of thing.[4] In this sense, essence 'limits' existence: Sigmund's essence of cat-ness means that he 'cats' rather than 'dogs'. We can see that essence and existence must be distinct by reflecting on the non-necessity of everything that we encounter in the world. All the phenomena that make up the world might cease to exist or might never have existed at all: there is nothing about Sigmund's cat-ness that means there had to be a cat called Sigmund, or indeed any cats whatsoever. We need two different questions and answers to get at the fact that Sigmund is a cat and that he exists. Since there is nothing intrinsic to any particular thing that makes its coming into existence absolutely inevitable and irreversible, everything must receive its existence from elsewhere, from something that does not define *what* it is to be that type of thing but merely specifies *that* it exists at all. Aquinas holds that all realities (apart from God, as we will see) are marked by this real distinction of essence and existence, which consequently forms the most basic and fundamental type of composition we encounter in the world.[5]

Importantly, the *esse* of any given reality – whether really real or only mentally real – is neither a thing nor an idea in itself, but rather that by which every given thing exists. A glance at the rather strange sentence 'the singer sings' can help to illuminate the point. The singer exists as a singer (rather than as a swimmer) in-and-by the act of singing. Unless there is singing, there is no singer. But while the singer exists as a real reality, 'singing' itself does not: it is the act by which the singer is constituted in her identity as a singer. In the case of a singer, of course, there is something (indeed, someone) that exists prior to the act of singing (which consequently modifies their identity), who could – at another moment – be a swimmer. In the case of the act of *esse*, however, absolutely nothing exists prior to the act of *esse* that could receive the qualification or be modified by it. Just as the question 'whether singing sings?' is frankly incoherent, so the question of whether *esse* exists is also – though perhaps less obviously – incoherent. The act of existence is neither an abstract thing nor a simple concept, but an act, the distinctive act by which all realities are themselves real, the driving force of a world that speaks.[6]

In calling the distinction between essence and existence 'real', Thomas does not mean that we can go around carving the world up into essences and existences. This distinction can be arrived at by philosophical abstraction only, not by empirical investigation. We do not find essences lying around the world waiting to be activated by existence. Nor do we find the pure power of existence lurking in the shadows, seeking out an essence to activate. We encounter *esse* only as it manifests itself in realities, as the act that brings things into speech. Consequently, essence and existence are better seen as two different moments or aspects of the speaking of a particular reality into the world-conversation. *Esse* is the dynamic moment of activating generosity; essence is the static moment of stable self-identity and essential integrity. Essence is *what* is said; *esse* is the act of speaking.

In construing the relationship of essence and existence in this way, Aquinas seems to invite us to think the unthinkable, to posit a limiting substance that is really distinct from that which it limits, without in any way existing apart from the act that it supposedly restricts. Without denying that there are paradoxical features of Aquinas's formulation, it is important to understand the sense in which he takes 'essence' to be limiting with respect to *esse*. The contribution made by essence is never simply negative. Human experience shows that the acceptance of certain kinds of limitation or restriction can make possible the reception of otherwise unobtainable goods (as, for instance, when somebody undergoes the tightly specified and rigidly limited relationship with a therapist so as to make possible the otherwise unachievable goods of a therapeutic relationship). We can only use the water of an ocean by putting it into a smaller container. Similarly, essence limits existence only as a limited mode of reception, so that the power of existence can be 'harnessed' in particular realities.

Two important consequences can be unfolded from this. First, the fundamental distinction of essence and existence gives philosophical voice to the existential paradox of contingency: the absolute non-necessity of any particular existent actually existing. The speech of reality is simultaneously mighty and vulnerable, powerful and precarious, enduring and yet permanently liable to destruction. To exist only through the reception of existence from beyond one's own essence is simultaneously to enjoy a finite share in the powerful generosity of *esse* itself, but only to the extent that this is always haunted by a radical and absolute dependence on the other, which is manifest in the incapacity of existents to endlessly sustain their own existence. To embrace the medieval idiom of reality as composed by the 'real distinction' is to face up to the experience of angst that has fascinated many contemporary philosophers: the intuition of the unavoidable possibility of one's own de-composition.

Second, an implication of this picture of the limitation of existence by essence is that existence is not a binary, a digital 'on or off', 'yes or no', in which something either exists or does not. Rather existence is an analogue scale that runs along a spectrum of possibilities. Not everything has existence in the same way or degree of self-possession. Some realities have a higher share in the dynamism of existence, and so a greater degree of reality to them. An analogy of this is found in the way in which we use the concept of 'life': in a fairly intuitive sense, a cat is more alive than a cactus – it moves more freely and lives more dynamically – but a human being is more alive than any other reality we encounter within the world. The more something exists, the more closely it approximates and images the self-subsistent perfection that is ultimate reality (which, as we will see in the next chapter, Aquinas calls 'God').

FORM

Esse synthesizes: it make a particular essence into a whole, bestowing upon it a togetherness that accounts for how realities real-ize themselves within the world. Some questions, however, remain, particularly those that relate to the *what-ness* of realities, and how particular individuals are the type of things that they are. Sigmund is inalienably particular and yet obviously just one of a certain type of creature. Answering these questions requires attentiveness to a second level of metaphysical composition, that of form and matter. When it comes to Thomas's use of these technical terms, there is good news and bad news. On the one hand, whereas the translation of *esse* arouses considerable controversy, the terms form (*forma*) and matter (*materia*) are universally accepted. On the other hand, they are extremely misleading translations, as Thomas's originals assume a technical significance that is quite remote from their sense in everyday English.

Form is the configuring 'idea' that gives shape and purpose to a particular reality. It is the meaning of the reality that speaks itself into the world-conversation. Distilled to its most basic meaning, form is the name that Thomas (following Aristotle) gives to the principle that determines a particular reality to be the kind of reality that it is, rather than any other kind of reality.[7] Form is often – but unhelpfully – illustrated by reference to inanimate objects like furniture (the form of a table being its design as a moderately weight-bearing assemblage of a particular shape), but Aquinas takes his starting point in the realm of living things. In the world of life, form designates not so much a shape or an idea as a 'skill':[8] form is a kind of performance, through which a particular form of life 'presences' itself within the world. Form is a mode of survival, of flourishing, through which an entity sustains itself in a sometimes hostile world. It is true that an organized configuration (a 'shape') is a part of that skilful presencing, but it is not the whole story. Attentiveness to the realm of life draws attention not only to the dynamic character of form, but also to its intimate connection with function. The form of a table is ultimately understood in relation to its function as a load-bearing platform of a certain type. Form determines the way in which a particular thing is rendered accessible to the world and present to that which lies beyond it.

It is the fact that furnishings are artificial that makes them such impoverished exemplars of form's meaning. Artificial objects do not configure themselves, but have a shape imposed upon them from without. By contrast, living things have a certain intrinsic self-identity and capacity to move themselves: 'form' is more like the way in which living things organize themselves within the world as distinctive entities. Form is not an idea lurking behind or beyond an animal's body, but rather the dynamic process and praxis through which an animal's body realizes itself as the animal's body. The form, then, specifies the way in which some reality is present within the world and functions with respect to the whole of reality. Form determines both what a thing is and the ways in which it makes itself available to other realities within the world. Form is simultaneously self-determining and relational.

The dynamic principle of form is conjoined with the specifying principle of matter. The language of matter is, unfortunately, immediately suggestive of dust and atoms, playdough and plasticine, and other 'stuff' that could be shaped into more meaningful configurations. This is emphatically not its meaning for Aquinas. Rather, matter is nothing that could ever be seen or observed, no matter how powerful our microscopes and telescopes become. Matter is pure potentiality, pure receptivity. Just as an essence receives existence without pre-existing it, so matter receives the perfection of form without existing in any way prior to the form that activates it. So why should we bother with it? Is it not just another mythical construct that can serve no justifiable scientific purpose, better cut away as an embarrassing residue of medieval mythology?

A better approach is to reconstruct the idea of matter by considering its function within Aquinas's thought. The genius of Aquinas's account of matter lies in its capacity to simultaneously answer two apparently distinct questions. First, how can there be multiple instances of the same type of thing (various iterations of the same form)? Second, how can there be some kind of real continuity when one entity changes or develops from one kind of thing to another kind of thing (which would apparently be the replacement of one form by another)? In both cases, matter functions as the principle of individuation, the provider of the unity of singularity. In the first case, matter is the provider of particularity for the uniqueness of each given instance of a form; in the second case, matter is the principle of continuity, securing a particular kind of identity in the face of obvious formal change. In some sense, the 'matter' contributes the moment of specific 'this-ness': the indexing of a particular for a here-and-now, a concrete history of change within a particular situation. If form is the meaning of the word that is spoken, matter is something like the particular voice that speaks it.

The explanatory value of form–matter analysis, which had great value for the natural scientist of Aquinas's day, is unlikely to convince today's sceptic (though some Thomists have been quick to point out surprising points of connection with contemporary science, not least in the way Aquinas allows wholes to relate causally to the parts that compose them).[9] Nonetheless, a view of reality governed by immanent form – as imprinted with meaning – is, even if it is adopted merely as a heuristic, deeply revolutionary. Form–matter analysis gives a primacy not only to life but also to the *surfaces* that living wholes present to us. A surface analysis is by no means a superficial analysis. Indeed, because form is the process or praxis by which a reality speaks itself within the world-conversation, reality is itself identical with a certain type of purposeful activity. Just as human speech simultaneously communicates and performs, so the speaking of reality not only *says* something, it also *does* something.

MEANING AND PURPOSE

This intrinsic meaningfulness and purposiveness is not a secondary feature of reality, subsequently added on top of existence, but neither is it some kind of intellectual blueprint embedded within reality. Rather, purposeful movement is an inalienable dimension of every existent's distinctive act of self-realization: form (as the meaning of its existence) specifies the 'aim' towards which an entity's act of being naturally moves, unless it is otherwise impeded. All of reality, precisely because it speaks meaningfully, is intrinsically goal-directed. Aquinas follows Aristotle in giving an important place to an analysis of the natural purposes that things serve – 'ends' or 'final causes' towards which they move by nature – in his explanation of reality.[10]

Much contemporary science reacts with unnecessary violence against the idea of including 'final causes' within an explanation of natural realities, for two broad reasons. First, since the end (*telos*) of a thing is future-orientated, using it to explain a causal relationship seems to posit backwards causality, in which the future exercises a determination over the present and pulls the present into the future and out of the past. Secondly, final causality seems principally to concern the provision of means–ends reasons and thus ought to be restricted to the practical work of intelligent life, characterizing the domain of rationality and deliberative moral agency. Both of these concerns, however, can be answered through a clarification of the character and logical 'location' of the final causes themselves.

Final causes are necessarily distinct from, but related to, what Thomas (following Aristotle) calls 'efficient' causes. Efficient causes are 'movers': things that contribute to an effect by the fact of their acting. Bluntly, efficient causes are like engines of change: they concern the provision of impetus, energy and propulsion. By its nature, movement is necessarily directed: it goes somewhere, and it has to if it is to be movement. It is awareness of this directedness of reality's movement that final causality adds to scientific explanation. Final causes are, therefore, not distinct or subsequent movements (like 'pulls' coming into the present from the future), but simply contribute to the causal pathway by focusing – directing or configuring – the movement of an efficient cause. Final causality might better be seen as the focusing aspect of efficient causality; final causes do not exist outside the movement of efficient causality, but are a necessary component embedded within it. This qualifies the extent to which rationality is a necessary presupposition of goal-directedness. While intellect is certainly necessary for the identification and articulation of final causes, the final cause itself is merely an explanatory feature of a particular movement: it amounts to saying that a movement is going somewhere, not to the claim that the movement knows where it is headed. To the same extent as the movement of efficient causality is present to the senses, so too is the final cause (albeit in a more implicit manner). Knowing the efficient cause to be the efficient cause requires the same level of ratiocination as the apprehension of final causality; not all final causes are produced through a process of deliberative reasoning.

There is an important difference between final causality as it operates in human action (and perhaps in divine and angelic action, as we will see) and as it operates in the realm of nature. This difference concerns not so much the 'location' of the final cause (which is always nested inside the movement of efficient causality), but rather the relationship between the efficient cause and the effect that it brings about. In the case of the production of an artificial reality (whether it be a sculpture or a machine), the final and efficient causes combine to act upon the effect from outside it (they are 'extrinsic' to the object, shaping it from without). A simple example of a sculpture makes this clear: human intelligence and skill act upon the lump of marble to fashion it into an object of beauty and edification. In this case it is possible to see a number of levels of final causality operating. There is a simple and unmodified form of final causality in the production of the sculpture as the end towards which the artist's action moves (*finis operis*). There are also more complex aims and intentions embedded in this production, ranging through the social, aesthetic and economic outcomes she intends to achieve, which are often a prime motivating force. These higher and broader elements of final causality rarely terminate in the *finis operis*, and indeed may not necessarily coincide with it at all. In the case of natural realities, however, they are, by definition, characterized by the capacity for *self*-movement. The kind of finality under consideration in these cases is not a directedness added by an extrinsic cause, but rather the innate focus of the intrinsic cause of self-movement, the 'existential target' or shape that form takes as the process and praxis of skilful self-presentation and self-realization. The purposiveness of a natural reality is ultimately an aspect of the manner in which its formal self-realization within history is directed.

AUTOMOBILES: SELF-MOVING SOULS

The chief characteristic of a living thing, in Aquinas's understanding, is the capacity for self-movement. As Herbert McCabe famously observed, living things are auto-mobiles (self-movers), quite unlike cars.[11] Living things are not simply moved about by other things (in the way that stones and footballs are) but exist by moving themselves (in however limited a way). For Aquinas, to be alive – to be a limited self-mover – is to have a soul (an *anima*), a term he reserved not simply for human beings (who uniquely among the animals have *immortal* and *intellectual* souls), but extended to plants and to non-human animals (each having their own unique type of soul).[12] Importantly, in Aquinas's world, to have a soul is not the same as having consciousness or the capacity for elaborate intellectual acts like thought, prayer and anxiety. These capacities are proper to humans, as human beings are the type of self-movers that move themselves around in free and intelligent ways, and thus can deliberate about the things they want to do and the projects to which they intend to commit their lives. Non-human animals and plants have more limited souls, in that they can move themselves in more limited and less expansive ways. They do not encounter reality as a theatre of existential possibility.

Notwithstanding Thomas's emphasis on the unique capacities of human beings, he affirms the real continuity between human beings and other living things.[13] An important consequence of the way that Thomas parses the difference between the living and the non-living relates to how he understands parts to relate to wholes. In the case of a living being like a dog, its self-movement depends upon the good functioning and relatedness of its parts (the legs, eyes, lungs and heart all play their essential part in the dog's chasing of the postal worker). Similarly, the movement of a car depends upon the smooth functioning and operation of its engine and wheels, as well as the moving instruments that communicate between the two. While there might be a sense in which we give some limited kind of non-moral blame to the dog (some types of dogs are banned for good reason), there is no sense in which the car is blamed for speeding round the M25 (even if it's a Formula 1 car, it would always be the fault of whoever took it there).

A crucial difference turns out to be that while the parts of the car exist prior to the car, the parts of the dog do not. In fact, the relationship between parts and whole is inverted. The dog's heart exists *only* as an organ of the dog, whereas the car *only* exists by the coming together of its parts. To have a soul means *not* to be an assemblage: the parts of living things acquire their identity and their meaning from their status as organs of the whole, rather than *vice versa*. There is a residue of this emphasis on the living whole over the parts in the way in which we talk about the parts of the human body as performing functions of the whole (as when the eyes are said to see something). To understand a living thing is to give an account of the whole and to see the parts within the light shed by that whole.

This relatively simple distinction has tremendous importance for scientific inquiry. Whenever a living reality is studied as if it were a non-living reality (by supposing it to be determined by its parts, rather than parts shaped by the whole), the explanations that are delivered will necessarily be as fragmented as the method that is adopted. If scientific explanations are to penetrate to the understanding of life, due priority must be given to comprehensive wholes as the determinative units of our experience.

LANDSCAPES OF REALITY

The two basic forms of metaphysical composition that have already been examined – essence and existence; form and matter – map out the coordinates of a multi-dimensional landscape of reality. This can be seen by noting how a form–matter analysis interacts with the essence–existence distinction to secure the basis for an account of reality's diversity in such a way that natural difference is affirmed without either being swallowed up by the whole or becoming disconnected from the broader reality of the world. As noted above, the essence–existence distinction serves this diversity in the vertical dimension of ascending degrees of existential perfection. The form–matter distinction operates on the horizontal axis, providing for natural diversity within and across the same level of participation in the hierarchy of reality.

An additional dimension is added to this landscape through the third level of metaphysical composition, that of substance and accidents. The distinction between substance and accidents explains two curious features of our experience that contemporary philosophers might instinctively handle as quite unrelated problems: first, that some realities undergo astonishing and dramatic kinds of change – such that they might be entirely unrecognizable in different phases of their history – without ceasing to be the same reality (as in the case of human maturation from infancy to adulthood); secondly, that there are some realities that exercise a quite determinative influence over our lives but which we can never conceive of catching in themselves (like the number three, or the colour red).

Aquinas addresses both these challenges by distinguishing the principle of a reality's enduring continuity (its 'substance') from the things that befall it in the changing phases of its existence (its 'accidents'). Strictly speaking, accidents are those things that do not exist in themselves but only through another: thus, we never clap eyes on the colour red, but we know redness to be a reality as it is the visible feature of various objects. Accidents are perceived by their presence to the senses, but it is the intellect that penetrates to the knowledge of the substance in which the accidents inhere, and which is not perceptible aside from the accidents that manifest it. As that which underlies the accidents in their manifestation to the senses, the 'naked' substance does not (and cannot) present itself to direct observation, but is known through intellectual judgement, as the mind reflects upon the myriad data of the senses. The relationship between substance and accidents is, however, by no means loose and arbitrary but intimate and necessary: certain substances have certain kinds of accidents necessarily, in accordance with the substantial form that constitutes their meaning (hammers are, by definition, hard).

Like the language of 'essence' and 'matter', the word 'substance' evokes for most English readers the impression of stuff (substance in the sense of a resistant material out of which something is made – metal, wood or plastic). Although much more dynamic in Thomas's understanding, the words function in the medieval's lexicon in a somewhat more minimal and even deflationary way. From *substare* ('to stand under'), a substance is essentially a hook in the relational web of reality's dynamism: a centre of action or being acted upon. As the principle of continuity for a reality's self-identity, substance is implicitly a relational term: the unfolding of form's process and praxis of self-realization necessarily involves interaction – exchange and communication – with other realities within the world. The boundaries of a substantial identity are, therefore, like a cell's semi-permeable membrane, simultaneously securing the integrity of individual distinctiveness while serving as the point of interface with the other. The self-identity that is secured by substance is, then, not one that is intrinsically opposed to change (like the eternal and perfect immutability of God), but rather one that enables change, and, in so doing, requires it.

SUBSTANCE, SPEECH AND STORY

There is, then, a third dimension to the speech of realities into the world-conversation. The speech of the world is not only meaningful and performative, but also – because it takes place across time – 'emplotted', that is, it manifests itself as a story. 'Substance' picks out the element of a reality that is amenable to having a story told about it (whether or not the substance is capable of articulation). Accidents are the unfolding of this story, features that qualify the substance's reality at particular moments: by the accidental features of its narrative, a substance exists in this particular way, at this particular moment, in this specific place. Consequently, although substance is a profoundly dynamic reality, its role within the substance–accident coupling corresponds not to the dynamic moment (like existence and form) but to the concretizing moment, alongside essence and matter. It is the accidents that have the task of dynamically unfolding a substance into narrative, as the vehicle through which the potentialities of a particular subject are actually realized.

The significance of placing the *accidents* in the dynamic position of unfolding a substance's life across time should not be overlooked. Thomas does not show contempt for the physical and contingent world that is manifested to the senses by relentlessly opting for the stability of the invisible world of the intellect. Even though accidental, the appearances are a *reliable* manifestation of reality and a rich unfolding of its perfection. Indeed, like the co-constitution of matter and form, in the normal run of material creatures, substances and accidents do not exist independently or in isolation from one another (though Aquinas famously makes an exemption from this principle in the case of the eucharist). In this way, the dynamic function of substance is synthetic: it holds a particular reality together. As a dynamism, the character of substance is of a perpetual holding together, the internal centripetal force by which a reality refuses to give itself up to dissipation. According to this model of reality, accidents are like the correlated centrifugal force that projects a substance outward into the world of space and time. The synthetic force of substantiality therefore simultaneously operates in two distinct dimensions. First, the substance integrates a reality in the here-and-now of the present moment: the accidents perceived by the senses at a particular instant of time are held together in a meaningful unity by their existence through inherence within the particular integrating substance. Second, as already noted, it is the dynamism of substance that unifies the life story of a particular reality across time, precisely by enabling its temporal growth and development.

Some contemporary thinkers will question the merits of substance-language (not least because substances as Aquinas understands them systematically elude any attempts to perceive them directly). Nonetheless, it is precisely this resistance to direct observation that bestows vital importance to substance-language in Aquinas's metaphysics. Alongside the explanatory value of substance as a synthesizing principle, it is substance that uniquely has the capacity to safeguard the interiority of particular things. Without in any way relativizing or diminishing the central importance of the relations of exteriority that a form's surface makes possible, the notion of substance prevents reality being collapsed into those relationships. Consequently, it is the dynamic character of substance, as Aquinas understands it, that secures reality's basic freedom from total extrinsic determination, which ensures that there is a reality that speaks, and not just reality's speech floating on the winds of change.

THE DENSITY OF REALITY

This dynamic account of reality as that which realizes itself and presents or shows itself within the world of our experience culminates in one of the central features of Aquinas's metaphysics, the so-called doctrine of the transcendentals.[14] The 'transcendentals' are a set of properties that are co-extensive with reality: they are found wherever reality is found and reflect different aspects of what it means to say that something is real. The transcendentals are so called because they transcend (or 'jump over') all the divisions by which we might try to categorize or carve up the world of reality. In the technical sense, they are convertible: rather than adding something new to reality as a secondary property, they cash out distinct aspects of what it means to call something an instance of reality. Like reality itself, the transcendentals are possessed in different degrees of intensity or perfection. The more real a particular given existent is, the more intensely it will exhibit each one of the transcendental properties.

In his *Disputed Questions on Truth*, Thomas presents a fairly standard list of such transcendental properties: being (*ens*), thing-hood (*res*), unity (*unum*), distinctness or identity (*aliquid*), truth (*verum*) and goodness (*bonum*).¹⁵ To these we can helpfully add beauty (*pulchrum*).¹⁶ The speech of reality always possesses these characteristics adverbially, in the degree to which something is real: most immediately, the world speaks lovably, truthfully and beautifully, as a unity-amid-diversity. With the exception of beauty, which plays in the interstitial space between two other transcendentals, these properties can be paired up to form a dynamic coupling in which one pole maps the interiority of reality and another the exteriority of reality as it gives itself away in communication: *res-ens; unum-aliquid; verum-bonum*. The world speaks not in a monotone, but as a symphony of goodness, truth, beauty and life.

Among this set, the term '*res*' (from which our word-concept 'reality' is derived) is the hardest to fully articulate in English, being a distinctive concept of Latin-language philosophy and simultaneously wielding considerable conceptual power, covering an enormous semantic range. *Res* refers in some sense to the deepest ground or rooting point of an entity: whereas *ens* functions as a participle, so as to point to the entity's unique act of being, *res* captures the idea of the centre of individuality, the subject that possesses the act of being.¹⁷

The interaction of *unum* and *aliquid* has already been touched upon in the account of the hierarchy of being as determined by wholeness. Unity (*unum*) captures the sense in which each and every natural reality is an intrinsic unity, 'sustained inasmuch as it is not divided into parts'.¹⁸ Distinctiveness (*aliquid*) captures the correlated idea of each self-realizing unity as set apart from all other things. As the intensity of a reality's unicity increases, so it distinguishes itself more intensively and perfectly from all the other entities that make up the domain of reality. The principle of *aliquid* is, however, not simply about dividing entities up, but rather relating them to one another. As noted above, formal delimitation always implies relatedness to the other. To posit distinctiveness as a transcendental property consequently makes the rather powerful assertion that where there is reality, there is also a kind of relatedness. We are used to thinking of relationships as being accidents that are acquired by already existing centres of agency, but the form of relatedness implied by *aliquid* is quite different. It is not added to or subtracted from a particular subject, but is rather inscribed in its basic reality.

The dynamic and relational understanding of reality helps to clarify the ways in which 'goodness' and 'truth' function as transcendentals.

To be real is to be desirable by the will (which is to be good) and to be knowable by the mind (which is to be true).[19] For an entity to be real is, then, for that entity to realize itself in a particular orientation to the knowing mind: that which is spoken can by definition be heard; that which is real is by definition knowable. In some ways, this is not a startling claim. It amounts to saying that there is no reality that can be apprehended as real without at the same time being known to be true. More difficult, however, is the correlated principle that the realm of reality does not extend beyond the realm of that which is orientated to the knowing mind. In essence, however, this claim amounts to little more than the idea that reality is endlessly surprising, that it will continue to indefinitely present itself to us in ways that exceed our grasp and thereby require an endless revision of our theories, as the excess of reality repeatedly confronts our intellect and surpasses all of our desiring.

TRUTH SPEAKS

Nonetheless, in a way quite alien to most contemporary philosophers, Thomas takes truth to be a dimension of reality.[20] All extra-mental realities have something within them on account of which they can be said to be true, and this is identical with their essential reality itself. In this way, there are in fact two dimensions of truth:[21] the dimension that resides within the things themselves, and the dimension of the perceiving intellect. In its richest sense, truth is not a property of sentences that happen to correctly articulate states of affairs, but a perfection of reality as it discloses itself to our minds. Truth is more than the right information or a collection of facts; as a transcendental, it shares the living, dynamic vibrancy of reality itself.

This account of truth is funded, for Aquinas, by a theological distinction between God's knowledge (which is creative) and our caused knowledge (which is basically receptive).[22] As we will see in more detail in the chapter on creation, Aquinas holds that to be real is to be known (and loved) into reality by God (and thus to be orientated to mind as the production of the divine mind). Created realities are in this sense intellectually suspended between two minds: the first, creative, mind of God; the second, created, mind of God's creatures. Nonetheless, elements of this picture are broadly detachable from Thomas's theological presuppositions. Aquinas distinguishes two measures of knowability. The first is determined by the character of the object that is known, and the other by the character of the subject that does the knowing. The standard analogy to unpack the meaning of this distinction is drawn from the world of visual perception, where visibility is determined by how much light is present. In one sense, the sun is the most visible thing in the solar system, since it is maximally bright (the source of all light) and so all our seeing depends upon its illumination. On another level, however, the intrinsic brightness of the sun makes it impossible to perceive it directly: its brightness simply overwhelms the eye. In this analogy, reality is to the mind as light is to the eye.[23] Reality is the medium upon which intellect depends, but which the intellect cannot perceive directly in its totality. Just as the sun is in a sense too visible to be seen with the naked eye, so there are realities – particularly the realities of God's own life – that are so intrinsically intelligible that they can never be truly apprehended by the finite human mind (on account of the latter's imperfection, rather than on account of any lack of intrinsic intelligibility).[24]

Many contemporary theologians have stressed that beauty also belongs among the transcendentals. Readers of Aquinas have debated whether or not he regarded beauty in the same way. On the one hand, the list of transcendentals Aquinas offers in *de Veritate* does not include beauty, but on the other hand, elsewhere Thomas clearly speaks as if it were a transcendental, as if the beauty of reality were a participation in the infinite beauty of God.[25] Indeed, beauty is in some ways particularly apt to function as a transcendental, as it captures something of the self-disclosive and diffusive character of being. For Thomas, beauty emerges in a kind of dance between goodness and truth. Beauty adds to the desirability of the good a particular kind of orientation to the intellect. While it is the goodness of reality that ultimately satisfies the desires of our appetites, the apprehension of beauty unleashes a kind of pleasure within the mind. Interestingly, beauty thereby plays an integrating role, drawing intellect and will together in the contemplation and enjoyment of reality. The well-ordered enjoyment of beauty is by no means to be thought of as exciting dangerous passions, but as a way in which the soul can be re-integrated and healed.

Indeed, attentiveness to the beauty of truth plays an important role within Aquinas's theological method. He frequently has recourse to arguments from fittingness, which, rather than handling questions of logical necessity or counterfactual possibility, serve to show and unpack the well-ordered beauty of God's dealings with humanity.[26] Fittingness arguments serve not to determine what the facts are, but to unpack how those facts belong together to form a beautiful and well-ordered pattern or economy, governed by the supreme wisdom of God. The philosopher (like the theologian), as a servant of reality, is required to show not only the skills of logical and argumentative rigour, but also the capacity for narrative insight, the crafting of metaphors and the speculative reconstruction of a plan and purpose that shapes reality (and our belonging to it). The beautiful aspects of God's wise ordering of reality are resistant to simple description and sit adjacent to the task of simple causal explanation. In an era marked by the temptation of mechanization (even within the human sciences), the power of fittingness arguments points to the ever-excessive density of reality.

This 'excessive' character of reality is particularly captured by the transcendental 'goodness', which evokes the human will's innate drive or desire. The good, for Aquinas as for Aristotle, is 'that for which all things seek'. While the goodness of reality does not depend upon its valuation by humanity, its innate goodness – and thus its aptitude for such valuation – manifests something of reality's intrinsic relationality. For Thomas, the goodness of reality follows from its actuality: goodness is the presence of some perfection that renders an entity apt to be valued and desired, which is thereby perfect in the entity itself and (at least potentially) perfecting in relation to others. Importantly, this type of goodness is neither identical with (nor totally unrelated to) the moral valuation of particular acts and omissions. As a transcendental, goodness belongs not to the 'ought' of how things are to be used and valued as means and ends, but to the 'is' of each entity in its own intrinsic value as particular instances of reality's 'generous' self-presentation. The aspect of goodness underlines the 'admirable' character of reality.

The transcendentals goodness and truth are perhaps the most counterintuitive for a modern reader to grasp. Instinctively, we locate goodness and truth within the realm of the decisive contribution made by human intelligence (and, by analogy, the products of human agency, like social and political structures). They are, however, central to Thomas's account of the way in which reality is the natural habitat of the human being and, derivatively, of the account he gives of the unique survival skills with which human beings are equipped to negotiate that environment. Indeed, so intense is the relationship between reality and the human person – the latter being in some sense a microcosm of the former – that an understanding of these transcendentals requires some anticipation of Thomas's understanding of the human person.

Taken together with *verum*, the transcendental *bonum* indicates a rhythm that is inscribed into the very structure of reality itself.[27] This can be seen by analysing the distinction between the relationship of truth and goodness to the human intellect, in the form of knowledge and love. As we will see in Chapter 5, Thomas has a profoundly intimate understanding of knowledge as the unfolding of reality *within* the mind. The truth of reality, then, indicates its aptitude for being drawn into the mind, a movement towards unification with the knower in a most intense form of communion. Love, however, moves in the opposite direction, stretching the soul outwards towards that which it desires. The goodness of reality, then, articulates the power that reality has to provoke and evoke us into action, to draw us out from where we are, towards a deeper and more profound encounter with the world. The truth of reality indicates an introverted movement, a centripetal force that corresponds to the centrifugal motion of love. The rhythm of these two 'moments' constitutes a resonant frequency that catches the human being up in the flow of reality. But before offering a more complete account of this 'catching' of humanity up into reality, we will first require an account of what it is that makes reality a world.

3

World

GOD THE UNKNOWABLE HORIZON

The Mojave Desert gives itself to the visitor as an experience, a place and a project. As an experience, the desert can be overwhelming and bewildering. The visitor is exposed to the forceful extremes of nature and the antagonism of an inhospitable environment, but the sheer expanse of the desert is hard to articulate or comprehend. It must ultimately be encountered. As its vast expanses unfold ahead of us, the desert presents the visitor – and everyone *is* a visitor, because nobody can quite subdue it into a home – with a radical experience of containment: there are no easy escape routes, few places to hide and no quick route to traversing its enormity. As we enter the Mojave, we are quickly disengaged from the normal texture of time and the habitual way in which we move through space. The desert slows us down; resistance to its modification of our pace is simply futile. In short, we do not take an adventure into the desert, the desert takes us into itself, and so to visit the desert is to give oneself over to an experience that can neither be pre-determined nor absolutely controlled.

Even if it alludes our mastery, the desert is also a project. It engages us in the task of survival, of finding ourselves within the beauty of its expanse. The containment that the desert offers is inevitably an experience of relativization, which brings with it the task of re-orientating our lives. Faced with the natural expanse, it is hard not to feel small and profoundly situated. The cares of the moment are relativized along with us, and questions of ultimate importance present themselves easily. Yet the reference points of the desert are so huge and the vast expanses so apparently limitless that it quickly becomes impossible to orientate oneself in terms of location and speed. With no other marker, the point of reference is the limit: the horizon, which simultaneously marks the point beyond which one cannot see and insinuates that the desert itself can be contained, that it is not a limitless chaos but a comprehensible whole that can itself be surveyed from afar. Without the promise and possibility offered by the horizon, the desert would simply be undergone; only by knowing the horizon do we know the desert as a place of possibility and discovery.

THE INFINITE HORIZON OF REALITY

Like the Mojave, reality is a place, an experience and a project, but this place we call life. For Thomas, the human person is so deeply inserted into the fabric of reality that they belong to it with the same complex intimacy with which an eye belongs to the visual field. Reality never comes to us except as something that contains us, as a place to which we belong. Our unique forms of human attunement to reality are a relativizing containment of the kind that we become aware of when we undergo the experience of the desert. Another way of putting this is that reality is always for us a world: not simply a chaotic expanse without form or function, but a coherent whole. As a world, reality is an unfolding expanse of possibility and significance; it can be known only in encounter. But reality is also a project, giving itself to us as the theatre of possibility in which we discover and define ourselves. In doing so, we recognize that although we are defined by our belonging to the world, we are not limited by it.

Like the desert, it is the horizon that makes reality a place of possibility and discovery. Maintaining a basic sense of orientation in life requires a horizon that marks out the world from a 'beyond', which constitutes the world as the coherent entity that it is. Knowledge of this horizon promises a breadth and depth of vision, but the horizon is also the ever-present backdrop against which the world and everything that is contained within it can appear. By looking towards the horizon, beyond the immediate things that seem to demand our attention, we can avoid getting so caught up in things that we cannot see them clearly. Seeing things for what they are requires distance, and that is provided by the horizon. St Thomas's word for this horizon of possibility and discovery is 'God'.

Paradoxically, Aquinas's most sustained efforts to come to terms with the world-character of reality are condensed into his so-called 'Five Ways', which have generally been taken by interpreters as arguments for the existence of a God-beyond-the-world rather than as a treatment of the character of reality itself.[1] On the face of it, the Five Ways seek to demonstrate the existence of God by tracing causal pathways that we can identify in the world back to a primordial first cause. By interrogating the finite causal structure of the world, Aquinas seeks to expose the infinite causality of God residing within and behind it. This cause, Aquinas argues, is that which 'all people call God.' Whether they begin with creaturely experiences of (1) movement; (2) causality; (3) the existence of possibility; (4) the graded hierarchical ordering of the world; or (5) the evident motion of the world towards an end, the ways ultimately converge on the same primordial reality that is *called* God.

The subsequent interpretative tradition has given a much greater prominence to the Five Ways than Thomas himself afforded them.[2] Nonetheless, there can be no doubt that Aquinas judged the arguments contained in the Five Ways to be sound and valid, delivering truthful conclusions from true propositions via legitimate intellectual procedures. What has perplexed readers of Aquinas, however, is the task of specifying more closely the role that the arguments play within the thought world of the *Summa Theologiae*. Certainly, the arguments might be taken to equip a believer with a set of basically apologetic tools, but they are not intended as an answer to the objections by anything like the world view of a contemporary atheist. Likewise, the arguments do not function to get God-talk started or to justify the intellectual legitimacy of theological reasoning:[3] the question on the existence of God follows the question concerning the scientific character of theology, which presupposes God's reality and affirms the necessity of God's self-disclosure for the work being undertaken.[4] The arguments are not, then, presented as a prolegomenon to theology – what today might be called 'philosophy of religion' – but are already embraced by and interwoven with Thomas's *theological* project.[5]

Tellingly, the Five Ways each treat reality as a world: the arguments take the world as a coherent whole, as something like an 'object' or 'artefact' about which a particular set of questions can be asked fruitfully and meaningfully.[6] In other words, they raise questions not just about the individual things that make up the world, but about the whole of reality, precisely as it is a whole. Each of the Ways is a sustained reflection on one particular aspect of the totality that comprises the world. This changes in a crucial way the type of arguments that the Five Ways constitute. Aquinas works with a distinction between two kinds of demonstration. The first type, known as a *propter quid* demonstration ('on account of which'), starts with a definition and moves towards its effects.[7] If we know that oil is less dense than water, we know that oil will float on water. The second type of demonstration, known as *quia* ('that'), moves in the opposite direction: observing oil floating on water, we know that it must be less dense than water, even if we do not know what oil is (and even if such a demonstration could never yield a definitional knowledge of oil). If we are seeking an explanation of one particular entity within the world, the answer we move towards could – if we had all the relevant facts – be offered in terms of a *propter quid* demonstration, identifying a causal pathway that moved from something that is known to its effects. The Five Ways, however, operate in the direction of a *quia* demonstration: we do not know the 'definition' of God, but we can proceed towards some limited knowledge of God from an observation of God's effects.[8]

AN EXPERIMENT IN INTERROGATION

Individually and collectively, the Five Ways are an extended experiment in the investigation of the world-character of reality.[9] They constitute an experiment in interrogation, by which Thomas pushes a certain line of questioning to its limits and simultaneously confronts the reader with the legitimacy of the question and the unknowability of that which answers it. Throughout the question, Thomas treats reality as a world: a maximally expansive, utterly encompassing whole, the character of which is disclosed by the fact that it is sensible to ask certain types of questions concerning its character. Taken together, the force of the Five Ways establishes nothing if it does not establish the validity of interrogating the world's contingency. Since the Ways demonstrate the intellectual legitimacy of interrogating the contingency of the world in this way, they also demonstrate that there is an answer to the questions that they raise, otherwise the questions would be nonsense. And that answer is what is *called* God. God simply is whatever answers these most basic questions about the world's existence.

The experiment in interrogation works by systematically exposing a distinctive and ultimately radical form of contingency. This can be seen by probing the meaning of inquiring about the 'why' of a particular thing's existence. To ask why something within the world exists is to (albeit indirectly) indicate the possibility of its non-existence. Interrogating the causal pathway that led to my birth in the world involves a whole array of interactions and facts that could easily have been otherwise (my parents might never have met, they might themselves not have been born, and so on). My existence or non-existence, however, does not touch upon the reality character of the world: the fact of my (non-)existence does not make the world any more or less real. The fact of my existence is not the filling of an Oliver Keenan-shaped hole in the fabric of reality, not actualizing a potential within the world for the presence of Oliver Keenan. To say that Oliver Keenan might not have existed is, in the end, just to say that the world might have been otherwise than it actually is. This, however, is only one way of answering the 'why' question, and the type of contingency that it exposes is not the most radical form of contingency. The type of causal 'explanation' that the Five Ways seek to expose can only be reached by weaning ourselves off questions that can be answered by another version of the world. These questions demand attentiveness to the more radical possibility that the world need not be a reality at all, of why there is something rather than nothing at all.

There are good reasons why we generally confine ourselves to the first type of 'why' question. It obviously yields useful and usable information in a way that the second type of 'why' question does not. Pushing our questioning towards the more radical form of contingency evokes a certain kind of existential dread. For Thomas, however, the more radical 'why' question is far more important than the more superficial 'why' question. Attunement to the deepest forms of contingency indicates radical political and moral implications, the full extent of which can be seen by a consideration of the type of demonstration that this extended experiment in interrogation amounts to. The 'answer' to the form of interrogation indulged by the Five Ways cannot be sourced from any entity that is entirely contained within the world and thus which could have the first type of contingency (that could have been otherwise).

Consequently, the extended experiment in interrogation ultimately delivers two conclusions: first, that presupposing the world-character of reality is a legitimate and meaningful undertaking, corresponding to definite characteristics of the world as it gives itself to be known. Second, that the world does not contain within itself the resources to account for its own world-character. Something beyond the world is necessary if the world is to be presupposed in the way that has been shown (by questioning) to be legitimate, and it is this that all people call God.

Read in this way, the Five Ways are primarily a refusal: a refusal to limit the realm of human questioning to simply that which can terminate within the first form of intra-worldly explanation in terms of a world that might have been otherwise. Put theologically, this is a refusal of idolatry. The Five Ways are not so much concerned with the intellectual atheism that explodes in a post-enlightenment culture, as with a practical form of atheism that allows the finite to practically displace the infinite.[10] Seen another way, the Five Ways mark a turning of the question back upon the questioner: since reality is sensibly – and quite naturally – taken as the world, what forms the central explanatory principle for this coherence? Who or what fulfils this role? Who or what are you worshipping? The perennial temptation – from which theologians are far from immune – is to lay hold of something *within* the world as the principal source of meaning and value (capital or productivity, for instance). The Five Ways serve to expose these false ultimates as merely provisional, allowing one who follows their path to be gradually led away from these premature terminations of intellectual inquiry over the course of a lifetime of struggle. In this, then, we find the roots of a Thomistic politics: the perpetual recognition of radical contingency should culminate in a systematic refusal to locate absolute power of authority within any person, community, structure or other thing that can be contained within the world.

THE UNKNOWN

Although the Five Ways have often been taken to embody a limited optimism concerning the power of the human intellect to prove God's existence, a careful reading suggests something quite different. The Ways are preceded by an argument that God's existence is not immediately self-evident,[11] but nonetheless demonstrable through the sustained effort of human reasoning.¹² Indeed, the Ways point to the inaccessibility of God, who is known by reason only as a definite other that stands beyond the horizon of knowledge that is constituted by the world. This unknowability of God is determined both objectively (according to the character of God) and subjectively (according to the limitations of human knowing). Nonetheless, even as the Ways proceed by demonstrating the radical dependence of the world upon God, they also show the world to be possessed of a certain kind of autonomy.

Subjectively, the necessity (and the possibility) of argumentative demonstration underscores the fact that God's existence is by no means immediately and intuitively apparent in the way that the deliverances of the senses are. It is not possible to directly read God off our encounter with the world; denying the existence of God (foolish, in Aquinas's mind) is not possessed of the same kind of irrationality as suggesting that the earth is flat (which involves the direct denial or repudiation of the senses). Objectively, the Five Ways deliver us to the threshold of an Unknown. For the idolater, a faithful application of the Way will move from the domains of the knowable to that of an unknowable beyond, an Ultimate Mystery. In the case of a genuine agnostic, the movement is from an indeterminate unknownness (an indetermination within their own mind) to a determinate unknownness (an objective acceptance of the definite existence of that which is most properly Unknown).

Not every reader of Aquinas will be convinced that this presentation corresponds to Thomas's intentions; others will be unconvinced by the validity of Aquinas's arguments. Some would rather abandon the intuitive sense of reality's world-character (and suggest the questions indulged by the Ways are therefore invalid) than concede the theistic implications embedded within it. In one important respect, however, the contemporary philosopher – whether atheist or not – ought to concede an important principle. The Ways point to what might be called the 'immanent failure of description': however comprehensively and rigorously description is performed, the practice of description cannot itself deliver a completely satisfying description of reality. Indeed, just as the world cannot account for its own world-character, so fidelity to the task of description will ultimately demand more than description alone can offer. This 'excess' of the world beyond description was complete (and consummated) for Aquinas in theology, but others might have recourse to poetry or visionary ethics. Whatever route is charted beyond simple description, it will necessarily have to come to terms with elements of radical unknowability and a reality that surpasses our conceptual and technological mastery.

GOD THE UNSAYABLE

The extended experiment in interrogation constituted by the Five Ways delivers the wayfarer to the affirmation of a definite Unknown: the unknowable ultimate reality of God beyond the world and beyond all thing-hood. The decision to begin his theological argument with a studied meditation on the world-character of reality is motivated neither by a simple refusal to despise the deliverances of the senses – an Aristotelian reverence for the empirical – nor by apologetic expediency, but by theological convictions concerning the reality of God. The Five Ways underline the reality that God surpasses everything that can be known or said. Consequently, the task of the theologian necessarily begins with the world, because – quite unlike God – we can grasp hold of it.[13] The beginning of any authentic account of ultimate reality is the attempted articulation of the radical difference between the Unknown God and any of the naturally knowable realities that populate the world. Consequently, a special place is given to the work of 'unsaying', the task of systematically reminding ourselves that the ways in which we speak about ultimate reality inevitably fall short of the reality of God's infinite perfection. So, the theologian necessarily begins with the world, because she has nowhere else to start than with the reality that our intellects can grasp. But the first move she must make is one of negation: the things we know of intra-worldly realities must be negated of God.[14]

This is particularly the case when it comes to what scholastic philosophers called 'quidditative knowledge'.[15] This is the type of knowledge that penetrates to the essence of a thing, identifying its particular nature or kind. Within the horizon of the world, as Aquinas sees it, we can obtain knowledge about the what-ness of a thing (its essence) through an analysis of its distinctiveness and defining features. In this, Aquinas broadly follows Aristotle's mapping out of reality according to the specific difference that particularized a species within a genus. In the laconic, but useful, definition of a human being as a 'rational animal', the essence of humanity is located within a group (animals) and according to its unique features (having rationality).

Extended across the whole range of the world, reality is seen to be made up of continuities and discontinuities, with groups of similar types of things with shared characteristics and the discontinuities that make each species the unique type of thing that it is. To know what any particular thing is, is to be able to locate it within this landscape of continuity and discontinuity.

The landscape of continuity and discontinuity marked out by specific difference is, however, an analysis of the composition of the world. Since God is beyond the world and enters into philosophical discourse as an explanation of the world-character of reality, God cannot be located within its frameworks.[16] To put this negation in a more positive form, the unsurpassable and incomparable uniqueness of God is such that God cannot be 'contained' by anything greater than Godself. There is no point of natural comparison between the way that God exists and the way that other realities exist. As the source and origin of all difference and similarity, God is both beyond all comparison and resistant to any categorization. Since God cannot be 'contained' by a genus, God cannot be localized through the identification of any specific difference.[17]

The basic function of a genus is 'catching' things up into groupings. From this alone it is clear that the uncatchable God could never belong to a genus. But could God *be* a genus? There are two basic reasons why God cannot be said to be a genus. First, a species can be said to activate a possibility that is latent within a genus. The octopus realizes the possibility of an animal having eight limbs (hydrostats, tentacles, arms, or whatever they are). Human beings actualize the possibility of an animal being rational. As there is no potentiality within God, there is no sense in which God could be taken to be a genus. Secondly, the specific difference that defines each species (rationality or 8-hydrostatedness) is extrinsic to the definition of a genus, insofar as each distinct species must introduce something new and different into the hierarchy to which it belongs. There can, however, be nothing that exists that is extrinsic to being, and so God cannot be a genus from this perspective either. Moreover, the language of *specific* difference is entirely inappropriate to God, because the difference between God and any other reality is infinite (and thus unspecifiable, emphatically not *specific*). In fact, the word 'difference' – which depends upon comparison – entirely fails to capture God's radical incomparability. Any attempt at divine-creaturely comparison is simply nonsensical. That we continue to talk in ways that seem to presuppose such comparisons might just indicate that not all nonsense is equal:[18] some of it is useful in pointing towards otherwise inarticulable truths.

IN PRAISE OF IGNORANCE

The account of God's reality that Aquinas develops is, then, in continuity with the intellectual procedure of the Five Ways. Its primary concern is to systematically resist any premature, idolatrous identification of ultimacy with something that we can lay hold of. The emphasis on the way of negation is not supposed to establish that we can have no *true* knowledge of God, but rather that we can have no simple *positive* knowledge of God.[19] Anything that we can truly say about God is necessarily subjected to a degree of negation and qualification, accompanied by an ever-greater unsaying that resists the premature foreclosure of idolatry. Attention to the grammar of God-talk can wean us off the idea that true knowledge is always necessarily expressible (if not actually expressed) in terms of the assertion of facts.

Even for those who do not share his theological convictions, Aquinas's studied intellectual humility when it comes to ultimate reality offers an important lesson. The acknowledgement of ignorance indicates the value of conceptual restraint and the importance of specifying known areas of ignorance within the intellectual life. When it comes to his theology, what Aquinas does *not* say – indeed, what he *refuses* to say – is more important than anything that he does say. The attunement to the necessity of silence focuses attention on the unsayable 'background' upon which all of our speech depends, including an intuitive grasp of reality that precedes and accompanies everything that we know and say. As the scientist-turned-philosopher Michael Polanyi would put it some centuries after Aquinas, we inevitably know more than we can tell.[20] An honest and intellectually rigorous acceptance of the limitations of our articulate capacities can liberate us to find value in our areas of ignorance. Ignorance, of a certain kind, is, after all, a necessary pre-requisite for the joy of discovery and the thrill of investigation that makes our minds truly live. The challenge is to value the right kinds of ignorance.

Aquinas shows that not all ignorance is equal, and that ignorance is not simply a blank space within our mental frames, but a multi-dimensional phenomenon with hidden depths and expanses. There are forms of absolute ignorance in which the unknown is unacknowledged, shrouded by noise or, worst of all, unknown even as a question: moments when we are not even aware of the possibility of thinking or of calling into question some aspect of reality. Aquinas shows the intellectual validity and importance of moving from absolute to relative ignorance, in which the areas of ignorance and unknowability are respectfully acknowledged. While contemporary intellectual practices give precedence to the statement and argumentative defence of theses, and affords a central place to expert opinion, Aquinas rightly sees the value of clearly stating what we do not know and investigating realities of which we could never anticipate achieving comprehension. This procedure allows Aquinas to locate our knowledge within a particular evaluative framework. A probiotic drink contains five billion live bacteria, and it would theoretically be possible for a team of scientists to begin the task of identifying the location and movement of each and every one. Clearly, this process would yield true and verifiable knowledge, but it would utterly lack value. Given that we know in general terms how the bacteria behave, some things about the probiotic are best left unspecified if we want to get anything done. Such silences afford us the opportunity to determine what questions are valuable and worthy of exploration, and the silences Thomas places around his doctrine of God allow him to focus his questions onto areas of the most profound existential significance.

At times, this first step in unfolding the Five Ways into a more complete doctrine of God appears not to be a direct affirmation of anything about the divine transcendence or about God's infinite perfection, but rather the sketching out of the limits of language, stabilizing a conceptual grammar that recognizes what later theologians called the 'infinite qualitative distinction' between God and the world. It is seemingly by tracing out the ways in which God always transcends the powerful dynamism of our knowing that we can begin to intuit the height and breadth of divine otherness (albeit indirectly). Whether or not this is entirely fair to Aquinas's intentions is a matter of some disagreement among Thomists. Leaving such debates to one side, it is clear that Thomas is not concerned simply to acquaint his student with the incapacities of human language. Paradoxically, attunement to the failure of God-talk underlines the power and plasticity of language, including its power to simultaneously assert and negate.

SILENCE AND SILENCING

However we parse the intricacies of Aquinas's account of the way of negation, it is clear that an important role is played by silence.[21] Thomas attends to the silences that fall between human words, silences that are by no means empty but saturated with meaning. It is these silences – to which Thomas listens with great intensity – that provide the necessary conditions for the meaningfulness of words. There is, however, a difference between restraint and constraint: between the respecting of an already existing silence – a refusal to 'break' a silence with inappropriate speech – and an act of silencing, by which a space of silence is opened within a domain of noise.

Thomas's negative way harmonizes both strategies. On the one hand, Thomas effectively places a silence around everything that we can say about ultimate reality, so that there is an inevitable haunting of theological wordiness by the power of silencing. On the other hand, the world, if seen correctly, is always already surrounded by a 'halo' of silence; there are spaces of silence that are built into the framework of our experience, silences that ought to be respected and heard. This is negative thought in the mode of restraint: as the philosopher Ludwig Wittgenstein would later put it, 'whereof one cannot speak, thereof one must remain silent.'

The mode of constraint is not so immediately obvious from the surface level of Aquinas's text. To find it, the questions on the existence and nature of God must be undergone as a form of spiritual exercise. Here Aquinas subtly exposes within us the seemingly natural temptation to speak about God in certain ways that feel obvious and intuitive. Aquinas seeks not to invalidate these ways of talking, but rather to show that they must not be taken as ultimate or definitive. They must pass through the purifying fire of a form of 'silencing' that allows us to speak their truth more forcefully. Thomas's negative way 'silences' the elements of untruth within God-talk, which, even as they must necessarily be spoken if we are to avoid absolute silence, must simultaneously be silenced if we are to avoid blasphemy. The student who seeks some firm 'hold' over the mystery of God – a stable point upon which to fasten all of their habitual claims about the divine nature – is supposed to come away from this experience frustrated and yet enlivened by the experience of grappling with ultimate reality in the dance of saying and unsaying.

Obviously enough, given the vast corpus of the *Summa Theologiae* that extends well beyond the doctrine of God, Aquinas does not intend the constraining and restraining action of the negation to reduce us to an absolute mystical silence. We do not need to find a philosophical argument or theological endorsement that secures permission to bypass a prohibition on speech. There is no sense for Aquinas that the inevitable failure of language ought to deprive it of all value; quite the contrary. Rather, Aquinas is affirming that (in this life) any intellectual inquiry into ultimate reality will be unavoidably, entirely and perpetually conducted in the mode of discovery. The reality of God's own life is never that of something definitively discovered, as if God's self-revelation constituted God as an uncovered datum or historical fact.

The qualification ('in this life') is an essential one, touching upon two structural axioms of Thomas's account of ultimate reality, one concerning human nature and the other concerning God. First, the human person's capacity for knowing and loving has a sort of in-built orientation towards ultimate reality.[22] God is the final horizon of our knowing and loving; anything less that God will always be unsatisfying and penultimate. Secondly, as the ever-greater, God cannot be adequately mediated by being brought 'under' any concept, image, category, or sign.[23] The knowledge of God that fulfils the human quest for the ultimate can only be an intuitive and unmediated form of knowledge, in which God is known in no other way than by God alone. This is the direct vision of God's essence (the *visio beatifica*) that comprises the infinite happiness of heaven, a place and a state, in Aquinas's account, of absolute natural and supernatural satisfaction.[24] Even then, when God gives Godself to be 'possessed' in the form of direct and unmediated encounter, the divine essence remains infinitely other and inexhaustible and is, in a sense, always and eternally discovered.[25] Even in the state of heavenly repose, God remains sovereign over God's self-bestowal and un-determined by God's gift of self, which – while then definitively given – has not thereby become something over which the recipient can lay claim. In this future consummation, the Saint has true and (in a sense) positive knowledge of God, but it remains the knowledge of gratuitous encounter rather than the production of linguistic reasoning or abstraction. This knowledge escapes negation only because it is not fitted to the status of a wayfarer, utterly surpassing the intelligible frameworks by which we negotiate the world.

NEGATION AND PLENITUDE

Thomas's emphasis on negation ultimately serves the positive reality of divine plenitude. Theological attentiveness to the incapacities of our knowledge and language is only a means to the end of a deeper intuition of the glory of God's ultimate reality. Indeed, the element of negation is introduced only within a prior affirmation – established by the Five Ways – of the world's dependence upon ('that which all people call') God. The power of negation is not absolute, but always dependent upon the 'safety net' provided by the world-character of reality. The way of negation proceeds from a more basic (though often implicit) awareness of the doctrine of creation, namely that reality receives its world-character from God, and that the world is therefore related to God as an effect to its cause. Implied within that basic intuition is a correlated primordial negation: whatever we might take God to be, God is *not* one of the effects of God.

Starting from this primordial negation, a great many further negations can be derived, each deepening the sense of God's otherness from anything that is caused. Whatever features a conceptual analysis can identify as being implicated by the status of being caused, they must be negated in the case of the un-caused cause, the God who is beyond all causality. Before unpacking the specifics of these negations any further, it is important to note the direction in which the argument moves. Although God cannot (yet) be known directly, God can be known *indirectly*, by reasoning 'upwards' from God's effects to their cause. Any perfection that we can find in the world has its origin and infinite realization in the life of God. The negative way does not give us access to a privileged divine vantage point over the world, but it is one of the tools that is embedded within the causal framework of reality. In other words, it is natural for us to look at the causal structure of the world around us and ask questions about ultimate causality. It is as if God encodes within the world the invitation to ask the deeper 'why' question that gestures towards God's infinite perfection. So the way of negation simultaneously both affirms the real causality of the world and subjects it to a critique. Knowledge of God as the uncaused causer relativizes the world of causality by exposing (yet again) its contingency, but it is only possible to reach after any knowledge that transcends the world by depending upon the world of causality it seeks to move beyond.

UNCOMPOSED

The conceptual heart of Thomas's understanding of God is the doctrine of divine simplicity.[26] God is not made up of parts, but this absolute lack of composition is not a lack but rather the pure presence of perfection. What must ultimately be denied of God is anything that could be modelled in terms of extension (meaning, roughly, conceived in terms of occupying space or time).[27] For something to be extended is to be potentially divided, since even the tiniest speck of dust can be further broken down into fragments. To have extension is to be potentially contained and to be the type of thing that might have a history, spanning a space between a beginning and an end. Moreover, to be extended is to be vulnerable to disruption or to the introduction of disorder into the relationships between the component parts. Extended things have a certain necessary lack of total self-possession and self-identity, since to have parts is to have something that belongs to the thing but is not identical with the whole. Once everything that resembles extension is removed, so too is any hint of limitation or change.[28] By negating extension, the philosopher's journey into mystery culminates in a negation of negation itself: an intellectual act that strips away any concepts or limits that would confine the infinity of divine glory.

The denial of composition in God is absolute, extending to every conceivable form of composition or extension. Most fundamentally, however, the doctrine of divine simplicity implies a negation of each layer of metaphysical composition that was identified in the previous chapter as comprising the landscape of reality: from the real distinction of essence and existence,[29] through the form-matter analysis,[30] to the limitation of substance by accidents,[31] all these forms of metaphysical composition must be found utterly inadequate to ultimate divine reality.

Of particular importance is the denial of a distinction between essence and existence. In the case of creatures, this articulates their non-necessary existence and their dependence upon an external cause (from whence they receive their existence). Since God is un-caused and exists necessarily (though perfect in freedom, God could never cease to exist), in God alone there is an absolute identity of essence and existence.[32] God simply is God's existence: to be God is to be to-be (*esse*). Put another way, God's reality is not actualized or brought into reality by anything else (note, in this apparent affirmation, the dominant negation of anything that resembles creaturehood).

For similar reasons, ultimate divine reality can in no way be understood in terms of a substance being qualified by accidents. Accidents, as qualities that exist in or through a substance, operate by bringing some potentiality within a substance to life. As God is not possessed of the imperfection of any residual potentiality, God is not liable to be 'activated' by any accident. Indeed, the synthetic role played by the language of 'substance' is equally inappropriate to God, who has no component parts that need 'holding together' in the present, and no narrative history of change and development across which substance could serve its integrating purpose. Indeed, the language of form and matter evidently implies finitude and potentiality but is also determined to a large extent by the dimensions of causality, including self-causality: precisely the residual features of the world that must be purged from any concept of the ultimate.

SIMPLICITY AND PERFECTION

The doctrine of divine simplicity establishes that God is not dependent upon any other. Taken on its own, however, simplicity does not provide an adequate account of God's transcendent primacy. In our experience of the world, that which is simple is not necessarily good on account of its simplicity: worldly simpleness might more readily be associated with incompleteness, inferiority or lack than with pre-eminence and majesty. Having removed composition from our conception of God, then, the second step is the elimination of any sense of incompleteness or imperfection.[33] This follows logically from the account of God's life as pure act (*actus purus*) that was delivered by the doctrine of divine simplicity. Since to be perfect is to be complete, that which is complete and absolute actuality must, by definition, be perfect. A complete understanding of what it means to deny composition of God requires the tethering of the doctrine of simplicity to the affirmation of God's absolute and unsurpassable perfection.[34]

If Thomas's account of simplicity corresponds to the way of knowing God through negation (*via negationis*), the question on divine perfection corresponds to that of super-eminence (*via eminentiae*).[35] Perfection is found in God without any limit or contraction. Consequently, some intuitions concerning God's life can be reached by a rendering infinite of any perfection of intra-worldly things that we know by natural reason. In place of any ability to know directly what God is, Aquinas proposes an intellectual oscillation between the ways of super-eminence and negation, both grounded within a basic awareness of God as the first cause of the world.

Simplicity and perfection are consequently the two most primitive and constellating perfections of God's life, from which Aquinas unfolds a hierarchy of perfections. God's perfection (q. 4) implies God's goodness (qq. 5 and 6). Perfection and simplicity together unfold into an account of divine infinity (q. 7), from which follows God's omnipresence (q. 8). Unchangeability (also known as immutability) follows from God's infinite perfection (q. 9) and in turn implies eternity (q. 10). Finally, immutability is unpacked into an account of God's internal unity (q. 11). The result of the coupling of simplicity and perfection, then, is a logical ordering within the divine perfections, in which the primary attributes that follow from the primordial coupling (infinity, immutability and unity) are unfolded into the secondary perfections of omnipresence and eternity, with divine goodness following directly from the account of infinite perfection.[36]

THE BIBLICAL GOD

Quite understandably, some readers of Aquinas, particularly in the modern period, have questioned whether the eternally perfect and unchangeable ultimate reality gestured to by the doctrine of divine simplicity and perfection is worthy of the name God. Is the simple God really the God of the Bible, a God who commands respect and worship, who seems caught up in the affairs of a chosen people, a passionate and often unpredictable God to whom it makes sense to pray? The utterly simple God seems utterly impersonal, so disconnected from the world as to be unknowable and unreachable, leaving God unaware of or disinterested in the sorrowing of creation. This God seems to have no need of a mother, no possibility of dying on a cross. Worshipping such a God would be nothing but an egregious waste of time and energy. In short, the God of divine simplicity seems more like a 'what' than a 'who'.

Answering these concerns is a complicated business. It is, however, a mistake to reduce the God affirmed by divine simplicity to the status of an unreconstructed Aristotelian 'unmoved mover' or the disinterested 'substantialist' God easily lambasted by critics of so-called 'classical theism'. Such a God is, in fact, a God that almost nobody – and least of all Thomists – believes in. The start of a response resides in the importance of Thomas's understanding of God as fully actual (*actus purus*). The term *actus* has two conjoined meanings. In a technical metaphysical sense, it affirms that God is purely actualized, with no residue of potentiality. In a broader sense, it can be taken to mean that God's life is infinitely in-act. The divine being is so purely actual that it can only be construed as infinite happening or an eternal doing. We will consider in a moment what the content of this doing or enactment might be, but for now the point is that the God of Aquinas – beyond all containment – is not primarily a thing, or an object, or even an abstract power. God is more like an infinite agent, with the caveat that the agent and the act (the do-er and the do-ing) are absolutely identical. As some readers of Aquinas have put it (not without provocation), the root meaning of the word 'God' is more like a verb than a noun.[37]

One of the implications of this highly dynamic and non-static account of God's ultimate reality concerns the status of the so-called divine attributes, the 'characteristics' of God such as eternity, immutability, omniscience and so forth. If God is basically verbal rather than nominal, these attributes are more like adverbs than adjectives: they function to describe one element of an infinite occurrence, rather than features of an object.[38] Two important implications can be extracted from this. First, since the agent and the act are utterly identical, the diverse adverbial perfections of God are identical with God's own self, distinguished at the level of concepts, on the part of human reflection.[39] The divine attributes are more like the ways in which a single piece of art might be described according to various perfections, each being a distinct way of capturing something that is indivisible in the work itself. The enormity of the singular divine perfection can only be understood and described through a variety of concepts.[40]

Secondly, the divine perfections are by no means abstractions, nor are they philosophical categories against which the divine life can be measured. God does not use, wield, have or receive God's perfections. God simply is God's own perfection, which forms a symphony of divine beauty in the glory of an undifferentiated plenitude. Consequently, to take just two examples, when God is said to be eternal, this does not mean that God lives 'in' eternity, as if eternity were a conceptual container. Rather, eternity captures some element of God's own life; eternity is a perfection which is ultimately identical with God. A similar point can be made when it comes to the portrayal of divine freedom. God's freedom does not indicate a world of abstract alternatives or unactualized possibilities. God does not operate within an arena of freedom; God *is* the arena of freedom. Freedom cannot be taken to represent a realm in which God could be other than God is. The freedom of God is rather a perfection of God's reality, the glory of God's actuality as uncompelled, utterly undetermined by any internal necessity or external compulsion.[41]

SPEAKING SKILFULLY

Speaking about God requires a particular skilled mode of speech: this Aquinas calls analogy.[42] Aquinas's doctrine of analogy is as familiar as it is contested.[43] At its root, the debate is twofold, concerning in the first place the extent of analogy's role as a structuring principle of Aquinas's thought and, in the second place, the precise dynamics by which religious language functions analogically. It is the first debate that has proved most entrenched. For some of Aquinas's readers, 'analogy' is a linguistic manifestation of the internal structure of the whole Thomistic world view.[44] For others, the doctrine of analogy serves merely to demarcate the distinctive features of God-talk, making no direct assertions about the structure of reality itself.[45] An assessment of why the doctrine of analogy matters, however, need not be detained by these rather intramural debates among Thomists. Even on the most deflationary readings, it is clear that Aquinas takes analogy to be correlated with his central convictions about God, the world and the relationship between the two. The way in which we speak about God corresponds to our basic intuitions about ultimate reality, and so Aquinas's doctrine of analogy invites us to interrogate the hidden assumptions that are smuggled away in the recesses of our practices of speech.

Despite the labyrinthine complexities of interpretation, the rudiments of Aquinas's theory of analogy can be outlined swiftly, provided we keep in mind the question to which the doctrine of analogy offers an answer. The basic framework for the discussion of knowing and naming God is provided by the texts of scripture, where God is described in startlingly creaturely ways. Often, this can be handled as non-literal imagery and metaphor (as when God is said to have a right hand), but other statements are clearly intended to be taken as straightforwardly true (as when God is said to be merciful, loving or powerful). In talking of God, we necessarily have to transfer terms from their everyday use in the description of the perfections of finite creatures into a theological use in naming the infinite source of perfection in God. This is unavoidable; we simply have no other resources to turn to. The process of transfer, however, raises the question of how the meanings of the transferred words differ between their natural and supernatural uses, and it is here that analogy offers an answer.

With this in mind, Aquinas turns to philosophical accounts of how the same word can be used twice (that is, how the same word can be used of two distinct realities). Famously, Aquinas locates analogy at a moderating mid-point between two more extreme ways of using the same word twice, one that emphasizes identity and the other difference. The most obvious way of using the same words twice occurs when the word is simply repeated and functions in an identical way. In this case, the same word simply means exactly the same thing in both applications (as, for instance, when we say that the sky is blue and the ink is blue). Following the grammatical tradition, Aquinas calls this 'univocity'. When it comes to theological language, Thomas's convictions about the utter transcendence of God lead him to reject the possibility of using words univocally of God and anything that is not God: 'no word when used of God means the same thing as when it is used of creatures.'[46]

An obvious alternative to univocity is 'equivocity', which stands at the opposite extreme. Words are used equivocally when the same word is used in different instances with utterly unrelated meanings, as when the word 'tap' means a knock at the door and the thing through which water flows. While equivocal language would take into account the infinite difference between God and the world, it cannot successfully model theological language, for at least two reasons. First, equivocal terms are useless when it comes to scientific demonstration: from the fact that taps are made of metal, we can say nothing meaningful of the tap at the door. If theological language were entirely equivocal it would be impossible to continue to practise theology as a science (something Aquinas vigorously defends). Equivocal language would ultimately deliver no real knowledge of God. Theological statements would make no real contact with the world of human concern. Secondly, somewhat paradoxically, in its efforts to affirm the transcendence of God, equivocity would posit the absolute autonomy of creaturely meanings. Everything we could know and understand would be so utterly discontinuous with anything that could be said of God that there would be no way for God to get into our human language. This is, for Aquinas, incompatible with the affirmation of God as the source of all meaning and creation. There is residual similarity or resemblance between the perfections we encounter within the world and the perfection of God from which they emerge, even if any similarity is always immediately qualified by an ever-greater dissimilarity.

Mediating between the extremes of univocity and equivocity lies the way of analogy. In analogy, the same word is deployed with two distinct but related meanings. One set of such uses is related to the category of causality, in which a term that is proper to the producer is transferred by analogy to the product. So, for example, the smartphone is 'clever', but in a sense quite different from the cleverness of the inventor, upon which it depends. Likewise, the bucket of urine is 'healthy' insofar as it has the hallmarks of health communicated to it by the horse whose effusion it is. In another instance of analogy, all of this might be due to the horse's regular consumption of a 'healthy' diet, but in each and every case the primary reference is the health of the horse, with the analogy drawn by way of relation to that primary reference (whether as cause or effect).

Another major category of analogy is based not upon this kind of relation to a primary non-analogous reference point, but to a similarity between two relationships, even when the related things are entirely different. An example of this is the way in which we use the language of the senses to describe the activity of the mind, as in the phrase 'Thomas's theological vision' or when we exclaim 'I see!' upon understanding Thomas's abstruse theory of the angels for the first time. Strictly speaking, the analogy is not between sight and understanding, which remain entirely different (one material, the other immaterial). Rather, the analogy is between the relationship between each activity and their fulfilment. In other words, seeing is to the eye as understanding is to the mind: it is the natural function and intrinsic fulfilment of the eye to see and of the mind to understand.

When applied to theological language, each of these forms of predication embodies a different picture of the God–world relation.

Equivocity affirms the real distance and discontinuity between God and the world. God is utterly beyond, the disinterested creator God of the Deists, who gets creation going and then stays out of it. Univocity, by contrast, would assert a basic continuity between God and the world. This moves towards a picture of God as the pantheist or panentheist deity, embroiled in the stuff of our worldly experience. The analogical, by contrast, affirms a God who is both in-and-beyond, a transcendent God who is nonetheless the ultimate horizon of our worldly experience. Learning to speak analogically is, then, not only a means of accommodating our speech to God's otherness, but also of basic fidelity to the character of reality as dependent upon God's gift of being.

THE GAPS IN LANGUAGE

Leaving to one side the various types and divisions of analogy that Thomists customarily derive, Thomas's account of how analogy enables theological language operates with a crucial but often overlooked distinction: the gap between knowing-that and knowing-how. It is one thing to know *that* something is true, but quite another to know *how* that statement is true by specifying what it is that makes it true. It is a simple feature of human life that we can readily accept something to be the truth without knowing what it is that makes it true, the way in which it acquires its truth-value. For instance, I can know that a particular liquid is an acid without knowing that this is the case because it donates H+ ions in water. Similarly, by accepting the authority of a trusted medical practitioner, I can know that it is true that a person has cancer, without knowing anything about how to diagnose cancer. In the case of theological language, we can never claim access to an explanation of how a particular truthful statement about God is true, because God is entirely self-determining and independent of external determination, so this explanation could only be provided by knowledge of God's essence (the very thing that we take to be unknowable). Notwithstanding this, we can know that certain ways in which we speak about God *are* true, not least because we are authorized to speak in this manner by God's own self-revelation in the scripture.

To put this in more concrete terms, consider the difference between saying that 'Thomas was a good teacher' and 'God is good'. Both statements are true, but in the first case we can fairly easily produce a set of characteristics by which it is possible to explain how this statement is true, outlining what made it the case that Thomas was a good teacher: he was an excellent communicator, had the capacity to enthuse his students, was patient, diligent and a competent administrator, and so forth. When we say (analogously) that God is good, we have no possible route to the generation of such a list. To put it strongly, when we say that God is good, we mean what we say, but we have no idea what we really mean in saying it. The strength of this assertion can be seen by contrasting it with metaphor, in which we do not mean what we say, but we (and our audience) know what we mean.

A straightforward appeal to the doctrine of analogy does not immediately resolve all the problems of theological language. Thomists still have to account for what it is about a word that makes it patient to deployment with various shades of meaning, and so the important task of clarifying the way in which analogous terms can operate within scientific arguments remains open. A large library of works, spanning the centuries, has taken up this theme, often with reference to the findings of contemporary theories of language (an area that has proved particularly fecund in recent years, after the 'linguistic turn' in contemporary philosophy). When it comes to assessing the contemporary significance of Thomas's theory of analogy, these debates can largely be put to one side. The enduring relevance of the doctrine of analogy only partially resides in its implied affirmations about God and human language. Analogy's most explosive significance to today's reader can be located in the distinctive method that it embodies.

The account of language with which the doctrine of analogy operates refuses to confine meaning to a single register or zone of reality. Words are porous to their contexts, dense with respect to the concepts that they embody, and versatile in their amenability to almost endless re-invention and re-use. Language is not a thin reality, merely about coupling sounds with objects, but an enormously powerful tool for the disclosure and discovery of reality. There is no sense for Aquinas that metaphor and analogy are abuses of language, as if the literal sense were automatically the purest and most unadulterated form of speech. Rather, analogy and metaphor are one of the many legitimate ways in which human beings use language to deepen their encounter with the world, reaching to recesses that the literal cannot penetrate. Though we easily take it for granted, language is deeply mysterious and explosively powerful. 'Sticks and stones may break my bones but words will never hurt me' is a pernicious lie: we would do better to become acquainted with the power of language from within than attempt to build resilience to the power of our most human asset.

THE ANALOGICAL IMAGINATION

At the macroscopic level, the doctrine of analogy is supposed to highlight that knowing how to use language well — whether rhetorically or argumentatively — is an important human survival skill. Consequently, any genuinely progressive education will involve the formation of linguistic competence and a habituation to various forms of literary genre and procedure. The university will only flourish when it is the arena of such a formation, hospitable to insights that can only be delivered by the tropological forms of analogy, metaphor, irony and so on. This demand is not satisfied by the study of the literary canon as a repository of human wisdom (important though such a study undoubtedly is). Rather, it demands that today's student acquire a competence in language by which they can fashion the categories and concepts of tomorrow, through which the problems of today can be reconceived and their solutions re-imagined.

Aquinas does not always make it clear that the theory of analogy he develops is not only (or even primarily) an account of how particular propositions function. Even while philosophers have rightly cautioned against constructing a totalizing grand 'theory of everything' out of what is basically a linguistic doctrine, analogy is (at least) both a craft and a fundamental way of orientating oneself to the world. As a craft, it is a skilled use of language that characterizes a particular community, into which the good theologian is apprenticed. As a form of 'imaginary', the analogical mindset of St Thomas embodies an attunement to the universal form of contingency exposed by the Five Ways.

After Pierre Hadot, it has become fashionable to posit philosophy as a way of life.[47] It is no straightforward accommodation to this *Zeitgeist* to suggest that analogy can be seen as being extended into a form of life configured by this analogical orientation to the world. If a univocal way of life is one confined to a single register or level of meaning (and an equivocal way of life either madness or the recluse), an analogical life is one lived in multiple dimensions, on various levels and simultaneously transgressing various kinds of boundary. To introduce a student into the analogical structure of Thomas's way of thinking is not simply a matter of unpacking various kinds of arguments but involves introducing them to various forms of discursive and bodily practice. If this leaves the educator with a feeling of discomfort, it is nonetheless inevitable: teaching abstracted arguments is just as much a matter of teaching a certain form of practice with an embedded criterion for judging the legitimacy of the intellectual procedure. It is just that the cluster of practices we teach by default are dominantly univocal. We might see in this a reason for the sense of disconnection between the academy and the broader world of human concern. If we – complex creatures that we are – inevitably live transgressive and analogical lives, then the tendency for philosophy to default to patterns of univocity can only entrench the gulf between philosophy and life that a scholar like Hadot sought to bridge.

It is here that the practice of analogy – if it were given a sustained go – would make a decisive contribution to the renewal of intellectual culture. The tyranny of univocity is well entrenched. The prioritization of univocal modes of imagination follows from the dominance of certain kinds of argumentative reasoning that, while manifestly powerful, can only accommodate the univocal meanings upon which they also depend. The power of univocity's grasp is such that unless we are woken from our univocal slumbers into the strangely familiar domain of analogy, we will remain unaware of its confines. It is possible that many experiences could bring such a change about: an encounter with poetry, a near-death experience, the need to articulate the tragedies of war and grief, and the modes of understanding mediated by psychoanalysis. But for Thomas, there is nothing that can achieve this transition as effectively or as fundamentally as the worship of God.

4

Symphony

THE TRIUNE GOD OF GRACE

There is no place of absolute silence in a world that speaks. No matter how hard we try, we could never find a point of neutrality beyond the conversation of the reality. Beyond the horizon of the world-conversation lies the abyss of divine silence, which is, in fact, not the absence of conversation but rather the fullness of an infinite conversation, unhearable only because its noise would overwhelm the senses. Thomas finds communication at every level of reality: from the smallest building blocks of life to the ultimate reality of God. For Aquinas, finding a way to tune into the symphony of divine conversation sheds light on everything else. The world presents itself to us not as a *tabula rasa* on which to unfold our own creativity but as a dynamic movement charged with the energy of divine conversation.

Aquinas locates an account of this infinite divine conversation in his doctrine of the trinity. In accordance with the doctrine of analogy, the divine conversation is radically unlike any conversation we could imagine taking place within the horizon of the world. As we will see, Aquinas invests very considerable intellectual energies in differentiating God's own communicative life from that of God's creatures. Nonetheless, the idea that God's own life is an act of communication – an event of meaning, we might say – is among the most striking elements of Aquinas's analysis of Christian faith. Although Aquinas is dealing here with what we might term 'Christian difference' – the distinctive contribution made by Christian faith – his account of the trinity is so rigorously developed – and so consistent with his broader philosophy – that it retains significance even for non-Christian philosophers.

BLISS

The oneness of God that is knowable through philosophical reasoning is an account of divine life from the outside. When it comes to the triune life of God, Aquinas speaks as one who has been admitted to the inner conversation of the divine life by God's own gracious invitation. The name for the symphony of divine perfection that comprises God's 'inner conversation' is bliss.[1] In an unusual question (incorrectly announced by Aquinas in the prologue to the section and therefore made to stand out rather acutely),[2] Thomas considers what he calls divine beatitude. The infinite bliss of God confirms, as it were, the particularity of the infinite act of divine conversation. The perfections do not hang in the air as abstractions. They are ways in which we can grasp something of a uniquely meaningful life. Bliss is no abstraction, no lifeless concept: the perfection of God constitutes the infinite joy of one whose infinity and lack of enclosure in no way reduce the particularity of God's life. Freedom, eternity, omnipotence and so on are but refractions of the utter joy of God's own life. The God who is alive and vibrant with the bliss of sheer existence is a long way from the distant and uncaring substance criticized as 'classical theism'.

The theme of bliss forms a unifying and structuring principle for Thomas's thought. The purpose of the entire theological and philosophical endeavour is to (re)gain human beatitude, to show how human beings can achieve lasting happiness and enduring meaning under the sometimes hostile circumstances of a transient world. The entirety of God's action towards the world is governed by the free decision to communicate and share the bliss of God's own inner conversation with creatures, who could claim no natural entitlement to such a participation. For one as philosophically sharpened as Aquinas, the question on divine beatitude amounts to a rather forceful claim: ultimate reality, the primordial origin and final consummation of everything that exists, is neither a chthonic chaos nor neutral impassivity, but rather identical with the bliss of divine beatitude.

Divine bliss is, of course, quite beyond (and distinct from) anything like experience, the default category by which we might parse the notion of 'joy' or 'bliss'. Aquinas's understanding of bliss as beatitude is the unimpeded flourishing of essence, the quality of life reposing within itself, of being exactly as it should be. In this way, the affirmation of divine beatitude is necessarily correlated with that of divine simplicity: to be utterly self-identical and free from extrinsic determination is *ipso facto* to subsist as bliss. Wherever there is disorder within the world we are encountering bliss that has been lost. The brokenness of suffering and evil is not the reversion to a more primitive state of existence through the loss of a higher achievement, but the fall from the bliss of sheer existence into the disorder of fullness that has been sundered.

With the consideration of divine beatitude, Aquinas takes himself to have reached the limits of what can know about God by natural reason.[3] From here on, Aquinas must have recourse to dogma, to that which is known by faith and accepted on authority. Dogmatic theology in no way nullifies what has been gained by philosophical reflection, but the knowledge given to faith does perfect and surpass mere reason. In itself, this is not an irrational move, but a profoundly sensible one that prevents us from having to make ourselves eyewitnesses to every situation. We accept authority easily and sensibly in many mundane circumstances where it would be irrational not to do so. Imagine a situation in which we are unable to go outside but can smell smoke coming through the window. From an analysis of the smoke, we would know the existence of combustion and might be able to make certain educated guesses about the nature of the fire from the particular characteristics of the smoke and the sounds that accompany it. But unless somebody who has been outside comes inside and gives us more information, we would never know why the fire had started or where exactly it was burning. Similarly, we can know certain things about God from the ways in which God leaks into our natural world, but knowing more than that requires God to witness to Godself within the world. That is precisely what Aquinas takes God to have done in the person of Jesus Christ, who grants us access to the interior mystery of God's own life as a communion of three divine persons, Father, Son and Holy Spirit.

GOD IS NO INDIVIDUAL

That there are three persons in the one God is the most important and explosive thing Aquinas learns from revelation about ultimate reality. Paradoxically, God's self-disclosure also discloses to us our lack of knowledge of the divine, deepening our awareness of God's unknowability.[4] Only by God's self-revelation do we truly apprehend the extent of our philosophical poverty. Moreover, God's self-disclosure reveals to us the reasons for our limited natural grasp over the divine. The limits placed on our natural knowledge of God are by no means arbitrary, nor are they simply determined on our side by the finitude of our minds or the brokenness of sinful humanity.[5] As we have seen, philosophical reasoning about God proceeds indirectly, from an analysis of effects to the knowledge of causes: from what God has done to God's character. Creation is a work of God's power, which is possessed by God's singular divine nature, shared by all three divine persons. Only that which belongs to the Godhead by the perfection of God's nature can therefore be known by working backwards from God's effects. Consequently, while the eyes of faith can identify certain trinitarian 'vestiges' within creation,[6] the reality of the trinity can in no way be deduced from a study of the world. The direction of movement is quite the opposite: Thomas's faith-informed account of the trinity folds back onto our knowledge of the world, allowing us to unpack a richer and more satisfying account of reality.

Thomas's account of divine simplicity and perfection has already established one sense in which God, while utterly singular and unique, is not an individual. God can in no way be conceived as a single instance of a broader type of thing; the ever-greater infinity of God implies that God does not have the 'limits' that are necessary to speak of individuation in the natural order. In knowing God as a trinity, however, Aquinas thinks we discover another sense in which God is radically non-individual. There is no reality more primordial in God than the infinite movement of God's life by which God lives as the eternal communication of love between three persons. There is no God alongside, prior to or behind this infinite communion of persons. In this deepest mystery, God is always already related, always already speaking, and always already on the move. In a supreme mystery of love, God's own life is directed towards God in a unique form of communication that in no way posits composition or division.

The primary challenge of any trinitarian theology lies in reconciling the divine triunity (the three-ness of the Godhead) with the simplicity of God (the oneness of God's being). The doctrine of the trinity must balance creedal trinitarianism with an unrelenting biblical monotheism. In short, whatever account is given of the particularity of the three divine persons, the persons themselves cannot be said to be composite, nor do they in any way compose the Godhead.

Thomas's answer to this challenge has at times been regarded as unremarkable. In recent years, however, there has been something of a reappraisal, to the extent that it is possible to speak of an ongoing renaissance of Thomistic trinitarianism.[7] In particular, the extraordinary work of Father Gilles Emery[8] has rendered the speculative genius of Aquinas's account of the trinity accessible to a new generation of students. Emery, and the Fribourg school that has developed around him,[9] are concerned to locate Thomas's work within its historical context, attending to the way in which Aquinas carefully ordered and structured his account of God's immanent perfection. Their work has shown Aquinas's account of the trinity to be one of the most uncompromising and consistent expositions available to the Christian tradition. Thomas's trinitarianism matters not only for the insights it yields into the life of God, or simply on account of the way in which it sheds light on the structure of reality, but also as an example of the reconciliation of intense intellectual scrutiny with unwavering faith.[10]

PRODUCTIVE LIFE

One route into Aquinas's understanding of God's inner life is via his account of the activity of the human mind as productive.[11] On Aquinas's account, to know something is to produce a concept of it: to allow the world to 'speak' itself within the mind of the knower by producing an echo of its speaking. Whereas many of the productions of human intelligence emerge into the outside world (like spoken words or technological products), these concepts remain interior to the mind, like an internal word spoken to ourselves. In order to handle the scriptural language of the Son and Spirit 'coming from' the Father, or being sent by him, Aquinas argues that there are two such internal productions in God, and these he calls processions.[12] Since the divine persons can in no way stand outside of the divine being, these processions must be purely internal productions: God's divine identity depends upon nothing other than the divine nature itself. These interior processions are not conceived as being distinct from the divine being, as if they were later additions to the divine life as it is supplemented by divine action. This is an easy mistake to make: interior productions do have such a status in our creaturely experience, because there is a necessary precedence of the agent over the act that is performed (we exist before we do anything else). Aquinas's sustained reflection on the divine simplicity has closed such a gap in the case of intra-divine communication. God's nature is always already identical with God's internal action. The infinite act of divine existence simply is the subsistence of divine knowing and loving.

Sketching an account of God's internal self-communication requires a careful balancing act that moves by excluding views that pit simplicity and triunity against one another. In particular, any successful account of trinitarian personhood stands between the excesses of two excluded extremes. The first, known as 'subordinationism', so stresses the individuality of the divine persons as to see the Son and the Holy Spirit as distinct products of the Father, subordinated to him not merely functionally or in terms of logical sequence, but at the level of their very being. Subordinationism treats the Son and the Spirit as if they were effects of an eternal causation by the Father. At the opposite extreme, modalism, in its efforts to emphasize the unity of the divine essence, eliminates the real distinction of the persons. Modalists tend to construe the distinction of persons either logically or purely in terms of how God relates to God's creatures, construing the persons as merely modes of divine action towards the world. Both these excluded views share a common tendency: they regard the distinction of personhood and the unity of divine life as somehow competitive or as reconciled only in paradox. Aquinas's account of divine processions offers an alternative. The production of the divine persons could only 'compete' with the unity of God if they were *external* processions, and this is the very position that Aquinas rejects.[13] By articulating an account of personal production in terms of *internal* movements, Aquinas is able to subvert the common error that underpins both modalism and subordinationism.

The first of these productions that remain internal to God can be correlated (by analogy) with the production of a concept by human knowing; the second procession corresponds to the mode of love. The first procession is easiest to conceive, in that we have a good analogy in our experience of conceptualization. When God knows Godself, however, the result is not the production of a concept – this would violate the principle of divine simplicity – but the generation of a distinct divine person. This is the Son, the Word whom scripture says 'was in the beginning with God and was God'. The more intensely something is understood, the more intimately it is known and so the more deeply interior is the concept that is produced. God's self-knowledge is identical with God's own life and so necessarily remains absolutely internal to the Godhead.

The second procession, which is productive of the Father and the Son's shared subsistent love, is more remote from our experience and so requires a little more unpacking. Aquinas takes the procession of love to produce a certain 'impress' of that which is loved.[14] At this point, Thomas runs into the poverty of terminology to designate such a production of subsistent love: while concept formation and internal speech acts provide the resources to find analogous terms for the production of the Son, Thomas acknowledges that no such terms are available to describe the procession of love.[15] It is necessary, then, to map this second procession in its natural relationship to the first. Knowing, for Aquinas, is never clinically isolated from loving. Knowledge is not pursued in disinterested detachment as a disengaged and dispassionate stance of pure observation. In knowledge, we draw the world into our minds, but we are simultaneously drawn out of ourselves towards the things that we know in acts of loving valuation of the reality we have conceived with our minds.[16] There is a logical ordering of the processions that serves a crucial function here: since there is a sense in which we cannot love what we do not know, the procession of love presupposes that of knowledge. This has two consequences. First, although knowing and loving are strictly identical with God's nature, the processions of knowledge and love can (and must) be distinguished. Secondly, the Spirit proceeds from both the Son *and* the Father, in that the procession of love presupposes the Son's procession in the mode of knowledge.[17]

The language of processions captures a sense of God's life as infinite flow and movement. It risks, however, giving the appearance of a subordinationist hierarchy *within* God, with the Father logically (or, worse, chronologically) preceding the Son and the Holy Spirit who depend upon him. Consequently, attentiveness to the importance of the processions in God needs to be balanced with a thorough consideration of two related categories: persons and relations. It is the latter category that carries the most substantial conceptual burdens within Aquinas's account of God's own life: to be eternally communicative is to be eternally relational. Relationality has become a central preoccupation of contemporary philosophy and anthropology; Aquinas anticipates these developments in his own distinctive, medieval, way.

SUBSISTENT RELATIONS

One of the challenges that haunts contemporary accounts of the trinity is the enormous conceptual overlay that the concept of personhood has acquired in contemporary intellectual culture. Intuitively, we tend to conceive of persons as individual subjects: centres of agency and consciousness, persons are bearers of rights and responsibilities, determined by their own unique and unrepeatable individuality. There is much to be said for an account of *human* personhood, which still bears the imprint of the classical medieval theology that formed it (even if, at times, the discourse of personalism has, like Oedipus, ended up slaying and supplanting its parent). When it comes to understanding what Thomas means by 'persons' in the Godhead, however, this conceptual baggage must be put to one side. Divine persons are decidedly not distinct centres of individual consciousness. They are defined not so much by their unique unrepeatable identity as by their particular relationality.

The fundamental point of contrast between divine and human personhood is located in the fact that in God persons are not prior to the things they do and relations they acquire.[18] On the contrary, the persons are constituted by the relations with which they are identical. The persons of the trinity are emphatically not individual zones of consciousness characterized by a privileged interiority that they alone can access. Like many of his contemporaries, Aquinas takes divine persons to be 'subsistent relations'.[19] That is, they are relations that exist in and of themselves, which are possessed of a real kind of endurance and perseverance of their own.

The enormous importance given to the category of divine relations is a distinctive feature of Thomas's account of God's life. While other traditions of theological reflection (including Aquinas's contemporary Franciscan interlocutors) emphasized the two processions as the basis for the distinction within the Godhead, for Thomas it is the relations alone that both distinguish and constitute the divine persons.[20] Appeal to real relationality in God helps Thomas to square the circle of trinitarian monotheism. On the one hand, the relations are identical with the divine essence and the doctrine of divine simplicity is therefore safeguarded: the relations do not in any way introduce composition, nor do they stand outside of the divine being or modify it in the way that an accident would. On the other hand, the relations are possessed of an objective reality: they are neither glosses of the singular divine perfection (as the divine attributes are), nor are they imaginary, purely mental projections. The particular status that Aquinas gives to relations within the Godhead allows him to avoid the twin pitfalls of subordinationism and modalism.

A first step in understanding Aquinas's theory of divine relationality is to note his distinction between a 'relative' and a 'relation': a relative is the thing (or word) itself, which is related to another thing. 'Relation' refers to the accident within a relative, through which it is related to another thing. Broadly speaking, Aquinas identifies two ways in which a relation can be said to belong to a relative. 'Real' relations have an enduring existence *within* the relative, quite apart from whether or not we are actually aware of it. In this case, it belongs to the very nature of the relative to be referred to another. Importantly, real relations do not hang between the entities they relate, but rather endure *within* one or both of the relatives. These real relations modify in some way the character of a relative's existence (much like any other accident does). By contrast, the second broad category of relations, logical relations, are those that do not have such an inherence within the object, but are the products of a comparing mind. That is not to say that logical relations are just mental fictions, only that they fall short of actual inherence within the relative, as, for instance, when something that is really real is compared with something that is utterly fictional.

The distinction between logical and real relations opens up a field of enormous explanatory power. In the first place, sets of relations can either be symmetrical or asymmetrical (matched or unmatched): both relatives can be related by the same kind of relation (whether logical or real), or what is logical in one relative can be real in another relative. Thomas's stock example of an unmatched set of relations is the case of knowledge, in which the knowing mind is really related to the thing it knows (it has an inherent relation that qualifies the way in which it exists), but the thing known is only logically related to the knowing mind (its existence does not change in any way by the fact that it is known).

Aquinas takes the relations that characterize the Godhead to be real and symmetrical. Since logical relations stand outside the relatives, they cannot be an adequate account of the internal relatedness of God. Nonetheless, an awareness of the possibility of merely logical relations underlines a feature of relationality that gives the category a surprising flexibility in being applied to the life of God. Every other thing we can say about a reality has some concrete enduring reality within the thing itself, and if such inherence is impossible in the case of God, must be excluded.[21] A real relation has two elements: first, it exists by inherence in some reality; secondly, it is a connection to another reality. It is this second aspect that provides the defining characteristic of relations (the principle that makes a relation a relation), since the first element is shared with every other kind of accident: a relation is distinguished as a relation insofar as it is a connection with another.[22] Aquinas argues that while this first element of real relationality has to be excluded from God in accordance with the doctrine of divine simplicity, the second aspect can be said of God in an unmodified way. When the category of relation is transposed into the Godhead, it loses everything of its accidental character, but nothing of its defining character as reference to another. This procedure follows a pathway similar to the purification of perfection-language: anything that would be accidental in creatures is substantial in God. Just as God does not *have* attributes, so God does not *have* or enter into relations. God *is* the relations of God's own life.

It follows from all of this that the application of relationality to the Godhead is achieved by eliminating a feature that inevitably characterizes our experience of relationships. In the world of creaturely realities, relations have a 'foundation' from which they emerge. This foundation is an accident that exists prior to the relation, and which serves as its enabling condition. For instance, it is a person's height that allows her to be related to another as taller to shorter. In the case of divine relations, this element of grounding by foundation does not obtain. Not only are there no accidents in God whatsoever, but there can also be nothing prior to the relations, since these are identical with God's own life. The divine persons are so thoroughly relational that they are not other than or prior to the relations that constitute them. In other words, the persons 'hold onto' nothing of their own; they are entirely and purely infinite relatedness to one another, with absolute mutuality and perfect reciprocity.

RELATIONAL OPPOSITION

The mutuality and reciprocity of the relations in God are essential to avoiding the charge of imbalance or subordinationism. In Aquinas's terms, the relations of God's own life are not only real but also necessarily symmetrical. For every relation in God there is a matching relation moving in the opposite direction: the Father's relation of paternity is paired with the Son's relation of filiation, and so on. Medieval theologians generally referred to this as 'relative opposition', 'opposition of relations' or 'relational opposition'. Aquinas shifts his terminology across his work in a way that seems frustrating to the contemporary reader,[23] but – importantly – he never refers to a 'relation of opposition' in the singular. Throughout his account of personal identity, Aquinas returns again and again to the practice of double reference, in which it is a *pair* of relations – each real in its own right – that are opposed, and that these are relations of origin. The idea of opposition does not connote competitiveness or confrontation; rather the only thing that can ground the relations is the action by which the persons are produced. The communication between the persons of the trinity is thus perfectly reciprocal. Each person 'responds' with perfect and equal correspondence to that which addresses them, with no communicative gap in the infinite exchange of meaning that would need to be bridged by one person who would have to take the initiative in order to elicit the response. As the relations are each perfectly matched by a corresponding communication, each person and each communicative relation is both absolutely necessary and utterly sufficient; there is nothing further that could be said, and nothing less that would express the divine life.

At the personal level, the principle of relative opposition emphasizes that the divine persons are both utterly distinct and entirely inseparable. Within Thomas's account of the trinity, it is crucial to distinguish between what belongs to the persons as divine, and what belongs to the persons as persons. In thinking through the implications of this distinction, it is necessary to speak with two distinct emphases, of the divine *persons* and of the *divine* persons. As such, each person of the trinity is characterized in a twofold manner. In the first place, they share everything of the perfection we attribute to the one Godhead as their common possession. Secondly, they are distinguished by their distinctive mode of relationality, according to which each of the persons is referred to each of the other persons. To put this another way, the 'what-ness' of what is uttered in the infinite 'conversation' of God's life is shared by all three persons, with the distinction emerging only at the level of 'who'-questions. By using the principle of relative opposition as the *sole* principle of personal differentiation in God, Thomas can emphasize that anything that is personal about the divine persons must relate to each of the other persons. In other words, even at the level of relational differentiation, the co-equality of each of the divine persons demands that no divine person could be constituted by a single relation (that is, by a relation to just one of the other divine persons), as if, for instance, the Son were distinguished merely by the relationship of filiation from the Father. Rather, each of the divine persons are utterly relative to each of the other divine persons.

Aquinas's use of relative opposition has the important implication of limiting the amount of conceptual work that can be done by an analysis of the two processions. Although theologians in Aquinas's day were (thanks largely to Anselm of Canterbury's arguments) agreed that the divine persons were actually differentiated by relational opposition, some of Thomas's contemporaries (particularly among the Franciscans) held that the different modes of procession (knowledge and love) would theoretically be sufficient principles of differentiation in the absence of symmetrical relationality. Aquinas rejects this view, opting for a more thoroughly relative account of divine personhood in which complete mutual referentiality is not only expressive of personhood but also determinative of it.

DIVINE FATHERHOOD

Theologians have habitually referred to the study of the person and the work of the Son and the Holy Spirit by distinct titles – Christology and pneumatology – but rather less frequently spoken of a sub-discipline of 'pateriology' concerned with God the Father. The person of the Father is perhaps the most neglected of the divine persons. That the Son and the Spirit (unlike the Father) are sent in distinctive missions to creation has bequeathed to theologians a special interest in their personal characteristics. A consequence of Thomas's prioritization of relational opposition is a uniquely helpful account of the Father's status within the Godhead.[24] Some trinitarian theologies have been haunted by a tendency to conceive of the Father as if he were the source of the Godhead, the beginning and the end of a flow of divine generosity. On this account, the Father communicates all that he is to the Son and, together with the Son, shares their common life with the Spirit. Such models of trinitarian theology have proved particularly attractive as they offer an account of the triune life as a logical sequence that can be understood by analogy with human experiences of gift exchange, albeit with the implied temporal changes subtracted. As well as appearing to insert a logical 'before' and 'after' into the Godhead, the Father risks being construed as a primordial store or source – a point of fontal plenitude – responsible for the unity of Godhead's life.[25]

In the perspective of Thomas's trinitarian imagination, the root error in such an account is the lack of double reference, which leads to a construal of the Father's divine personhood in such a way that he is a person who just also happens to be the Father. As we have seen, any such attempt inserts an illegitimate disjunction between the relations and the persons, each of whom must be constituted by a duality of opposed relations. Aquinas's emphasis on relationality excludes the possibility of such a fontal plenitude within the divine life, as the Father's personhood (no less than the Son's or the Spirit's) is derived from his relation to both the other persons. As we will see, this marks a radical point of disanalogy from creaturely Father–Son relations in which a person *becomes* a Father on account of the acquisition of a relationship to a child. In the Godhead, the Father is not the Father because he generates the Son, but the opposite: he generates the Son because he is the Father.

PERSONS: DIVINE AND HUMAN

This extensive analysis of divine relationality as real but non-accidental, allows us to see more clearly the unique contribution that Aquinas makes to trinitarian theology. As we noted above, Aquinas takes divine persons to be subsistent relations. Consequently, Thomas takes the principle of distinction within God's own life (the relation) to be identical with that which is distinguished (the person). This does not mean that the words 'relation' and 'person' are synonymous when applied to God. The language of divine personhood narrates relationality insofar as it is *subsistent* relationality. This ultimately distinguishes divine and human personhood. Human beings are both personal and relational, but we are not subsistent relations.

Aquinas provides for a limited commonality between divine and human personhood by slightly nuancing Boethius's definition of a person as 'a distinct subsistent in an intellectual nature'.[26] The essential features of personhood, then, are as follows: (1) distinction (irreducibility and un-repeatability); (2) subsistence (existing through itself, rather than within another); (3) the freedom of action that follows from the possession of an intellectual nature. By carefully substituting the language of 'distinction' in place of that of individuality, Aquinas yields a modified concept of personhood that can be used analogously in instances of divine, angelic and human personhood.

The elimination of individuality from the account of the way in which the divine persons are distinct points to the thorough reconstrual of what constitutes a 'relative'. As subsistent relations, the divine persons in no way resemble the relatives of our everyday experiences. Indeed, the persons of the trinity are not individuated in such a way that they exist independently or at a distance from one another. Since the persons of the trinity are identical in all things except their relations of origin, then at the level of their essential commonality they can be taken to dwell within one another. The Father communicates all that he is to the Son, who thus 'contains' within himself the fullness of the Father; together they communicate their life to the Spirit who thus breathes forth as the divine nature. This is known as the doctrine of mutual indwelling or circumincession (sometimes the Greek *perichoresis* is preferred, indicating the importance of this concept within the Greek patristic tradition).[27]

FOLDING BACK

Thomas's primary concern in developing such a philosophically elaborate trinitarian theology is fidelity to the Bible. The folding back of trinitarian faith into a broader and more thoroughly trinitarian understanding of created reality is a project that Aquinas inaugurates but leaves to his students to complete. These themes have been more thoroughly developed by twentieth-century Thomists, often those writing in the German language and attuned to themes from Martin Heidegger's philosophy and Edmund Husserl's phenomenology, including such important names as Ferdinand Ulrich,[28] Klaus Hemmerle[29] and Erich Przywara.[30] The knowledge of the triunity of ultimate reality that is given in faith authorizes the philosopher to see within the structure of creaturely reality a trinitarian architecture, even if that must remain unknown as trinitarian outside of faith. In short, a fully developed account of the triune God enables us to unlock a new understanding of created being and to detect within all being the vestigial traces of God's triune life.[31] The things that make our world are not mere objects littering the landscape of reality, but conceal within themselves a rich depth of being that can only finally be seen in the light of God. Trinitarian theology invites us to move beyond the thinghood of objects to an awareness of existents as centres of vitality, depth and meaning.

An account of this hidden structure of individual existents, inspired by Thomas's trinitarian theology, might look something like this. In each and every thing that exists there are three simultaneous 'moments' that coalesce within that particular thing's act of self-realization. In its 'stability' of inner integrity and distinct individuation, the existent images the paternity of the Father as the one who is not sent forth. In its interior intelligibility, the existent manifests the mysterious divine sonship, the subsistent word who proceeds from the Father by way of knowledge. In its tendency towards self-giving – making itself available to relations beyond itself in a generosity of being – each reality images the Holy Spirit, properly called Gift, the person who proceeds by way of love.[32] In this way, the imprint of God's own internal dynamism can be found in all of the various existents that make up the world, all of which speak forth something of this infinite dance of triune perfection. It is only by that infinite movement of God that we exist at all, and it is within this space of divine dynamism that creaturely possibility unfolds.

The intensity of Aquinas's engagement with the category of relation anticipates certain themes in contemporary philosophy and theology, where the vital potency of relationality and its connection to personal identity has been rediscovered. Attempts to see relationality as going 'all the way down' into the basic building blocks of our world might resonate in surprising ways with Aquinas's affirmation that there is no reality more primordial than the triune relations that are God's life. Indeed, the trinitarian theology of Aquinas opens up a conceptual space in which to re-think questions of individual difference and community of belonging. Within the Godhead, personal difference is – without any loss of distinction – never conceivable in terms of division. In God's life of relationality, diversity confirms and is secured by the common unity of being: each of the divine persons is irreducibly particular and yet utterly and non-competitively related, with each of these moments in their constitution supporting and entailing the other. In other words, Thomas's trinitarian theology offers to contemporary political and social theorists a non-competitive account of difference as diversity, which supports and presupposes the community of belonging. Thomas's doctrine of the trinity presents itself not only as an account of ultimate reality, but also as a moral and political project. The perfection of human community life lies in the perfected imaging, by grace, of this infinite divine conversation, in which inclusive embrace accommodates and requires the recognition of personal particularity.

To talk of such a 'folding back' of trinitarian insights into pre-theological conversations about the nature and character of reality – and of human existence within it – depends upon a prior 'folding out' of God's life into the world. While the infinite conversation of God's own life is entirely self-sufficient, an infinite and unsurpassable exchange of meaning, God freely unfolds it, inviting creatures into the conversation of reality through the act of creation. Humanity is given a participative share in this task of unfolding, and it is to this that we now turn our attention.

5

Frontier

THE MYSTERY OF HUMANITY

Human beings belong to the world in such a way that we make the world belong to us. To be human is, for Thomas, to be a co-creator with God in the consummation of an as yet unfinished world: we are not only habitat-occupiers, but also home-builders. We not only inhabit; we re-figure and, sadly, often dis-figure. As the history of the twentieth century showed with brutal clarity, attempts at human home-building can go disastrously wrong with devastating consequences for people, communities and cultures, not to mention the non-human world around us. Thomas's account of human nature matters because he interrogates the basis for both the power and the limitations of human home-building. Rather than jumping directly outwards to moral exhortation, Thomas takes a journey inwards, into the recesses of the human psyche, raising the question of *why* and *how* we build homes for ourselves. Only by taking this journey – coming to terms with our unique complexity, power and destructiveness – can moral formation take firm root within human culture.

NAMING LIFE

The kinds of home-building that humans engage in are radically different from the genetically-programmed nest-building that can be observed elsewhere in the animal kingdom. Although some would see this as an example of what has been called 'speciesism' – prejudice against animals rooted in a shamefully arrogant anthropocentrism – Thomas is unashamedly of the view that the existence of human beings marks the emergence of a radically new situation for the world, one that both discloses the primordial meaning of creation and opens up new possibilities for the world's completion. With the existence of human beings comes the emergence of humanity: an utterly new framework of meaning, a frontier between the material and the spiritual.

Much of Aquinas's account of the human person probes the character of this human 'extra' – the newness of possibility and actuality that humanity inserts into the world. The emphasis on human distinctiveness must, of course, be balanced by an attunement to the continuities between humans and non-human animals (and to the infinite discontinuity between humanity and God). The task of balancing human capacity and human incapacity is of paramount importance, since it is only by arriving at such an holistic account of human life – such as Aquinas proposes – that we can come to terms with both our human limitation and our moral responsibilities as powerful agents of change. Without such an account of human nature we lack the framework within which to root an analysis of how the enormous power of human potential can be unleashed in morally responsible ways.

At the heart of Thomas's understanding of human difference is rationality, manifested in the human being's unique constitution as a 'language animal'.[1] Human life is a symbolic life: we are agents of meaning, for whom truth is an essential medium in which our lives are realized. In the way analogous to the movement of a fish through water, so our bodies move through the meanings that we disclose and generate. Nonetheless, the unique character of our symbolic lives is rooted, for Aquinas, in our basic animality. The difference between our existence as language animals and other animals is largely non-contrastive. In fact, as we will see, our linguistic capacities make us *more* incarnate, *more* material and *more* animal than the mute beasts.[2]

This non-contrastive account of human difference is already indicated in the biblical account of creation. The seven-day creation myth found in the first chapter of Genesis does not grant human beings the dignity of a day of creation entirely to themselves. The creation of humanity emerges alongside the other land animals. Similarly, Adam and Eve are not granted a physical sphere of occupancy that is uniquely theirs. Nonetheless, the human person is granted admission to a unique spiritual sphere of activity: they alone are named by God and commissioned to share in God's creative power to bring order to the cosmos by naming the animals. The power of naming is the power of ordering, of placing something within the organized framework of the world. Naming can be liberative or it can be oppressive: it can situate somebody within a framework of possibility, or it can trap them within limitation. It is precisely this power of naming that goes drastically wrong, culminating in the destruction of the unity of the human community at Babel, an incident motivated – Genesis tells – by a desire to usurp God's privilege and to 'make a name for [ourselves]'.[3]

INTERIOR LANDSCAPES

A previous generation of readers located the most important contribution made by Thomas's anthropology in the positive valuation that Aquinas gives to the body.[4] Aquinas's thought was widely used to address a pervasive and yet damaging understanding of what it means to be human. This view (usually identified, perhaps somewhat unfairly, with the combined legacies of Descartes and Kant) emphasized the mind as the locus of the 'true self', consequently privileging human interiority and the capacity for abstract reasoning at the expense of the body with its emotions and patent fragility. Aquinas offered a remedy to such a devaluation of the body by stressing that the body is not only the vehicle by which the mind acts but is also entirely integral to personal identity. Bodiliness, affectivity and vulnerability were no longer to be seen as unfortunate but unavoidable encumbrances that hinder the realization of our true identities or hold us back from the realization of authentic happiness. Rather, these markers of our finitude are emphatically positive features of humanity, divinely bestowed tools for the achievement of our common human flourishing. These accounts of Thomas's anthropology exhibited great diversity of emphasis and application, but they shared a conviction that Aquinas's account of the body as availability for relationship could wean us off the philosophical views that underpinned an ambient despisal of the body.

Today, the philosophical landscape looks different. The emergence of transhumanism and the intensification of conversations around human enhancement, as well as a renewed attentiveness to material practices among scholars of the humanities, have reconfigured and complexified the ways in which we relate to our bodies. The body is now widely recognized as a contested site, a focus upon which complex and multifaceted discourses converge.[5] This is not to say that these signs of preoccupation with the body are not ultimately rooted in a deeply entrenched body-despisal – that seems plausible to me. But embodiment and relationality are themes so deeply entrenched within contemporary philosophy and theology that today's readers of Aquinas are likely to locate his distinctive contribution elsewhere. To put it bluntly: today almost everyone believes embodiment is worth talking about, but we rarely hear talk of the soul (and disciplines of introspection like psychoanalysis seem to be under threat).

In this context, two features of Aquinas's thought stand out: first, his emphasis on the multi-dimensional reality of the soul and its internal landscape;[6] secondly, his attentiveness to balancing an awareness of the complexity of human nature with an emphasis on the basic unity of the human person.[7] In reminding us that the 'body is the best picture of the soul' we have,[8] Thomas points to the importance of our inwardness – an inner spirituality that in no way competes with our body for attention – to understanding the meaning of the body as more than simply another type of animal body populating the world. By attending to the internal complexity of human experience and the rhythms and dynamisms that comprise our life as embodied souls, the unique way in which the human body is a place of meaning and communication can emerge afresh. This is perhaps the most important contribution that Aquinas can offer to today's marketplace of ideas: an understanding of human complexity, an acceptance of the essentially composite and dynamic character of human life that is both extroverted and introverted.

THE HUMAN ECOSYSTEM

Humans are relational animals not only externally, but also internally. For Aquinas, the human person is like a delicately balanced ecosystem, a whole that transcends the sum of its parts and whose flourishing depends upon the healthy nourishment of each component and the harmonious, balanced relationality of parts to each other and to the whole.

The essence of the Cartesian picture that Aquinas has often been used to oppose can be distilled into two closely related claims: first, that the body and the soul are two distinct things that are brought into some kind of conjunction or relationship (the precise character of which is difficult to determine); secondly, that it is the soul that is the seat of the highest capacities of humanity (especially such things as memory, reasoning and freedom) and therefore the principle that secures continuity of personal identity. The impact of Descartes has been so enormous that we easily talk in such terms without critical reflection. It is relatively intuitive for us to imagine ourselves as minds within biological machines, gazing out into the world through the windows of the senses. Despite this, an unmodified version of Cartesianism raises apparently intractable problems, not least of which the question of how the two radically different realities of body and soul can relate to one another. For Aquinas, these questions do not present themselves with the same force. A Cartesian soul can be imagined apart from the body it inhabits, but any such sense of the soul as lurking within the body is quite alien to Aquinas. Re-visiting what Aquinas has to say about human interiority demands an imaginative un-doing of some of our received intuitions.[9]

For Thomas, a human being is neither a body nor a soul but a body–soul composite: to be human is to be simultaneously an embodied soul and an ensouled body. More precisely, the soul is the form of the body. It is the principle that configures and energizes the body, and makes the body alive. The soul is present in every part of the body and is complete in each moment of its presence. Keeping in mind the account of reality developed in Chapter 1, this amounts – at first glance – to little more than saying that the human being is an integrated object within the world. Like all other really real objects, the human being is materiality possessed of a certain dynamic configuration that Aquinas calls form, and the dynamic form that makes a body a body is what we call the soul. As such, it is no exaggeration or provocative use of language to say that the body is what the soul looks like.

Pressed a little further, however, the significance of this claim begins to emerge. For Aquinas, the substantial form that configures a form–matter composite bestows upon the whole particular causal powers and properties.[10] As a whole (and not just as the sum of its parts), the substantial form determines the being's distinctive ways of existing and acting. From this, we can see that there is a reciprocal relationship between soul and body. On the one hand, the soul has a definite priority in that it exercises an activating and configuring role with respect to the body. On the other hand, the whole human being is more than just the soul. The complete human person can do things that a separated soul could never do (like laugh, cry and make love or poetry). Importantly, then, whatever account of human flourishing we develop must pertain to the whole human being: to be fully alive is to have a flourishing joy of both body and soul. This is an important bulwark against extreme forms of religiosity that chastise the body. The flourishing of the soul can never come at the expense of bodily well-being. On the contrary, the joys of heaven must be both the most intensive spiritual and intellectual bliss as well as a glorious bodily joy.

This view of the human being leads to some deeply counterintuitive (but powerfully insightful) conclusions. These can be seen when we consider the disintegration of human life at the moment of death.[11] Death occurs, Aquinas holds, with the separation of soul and body. For a range of theological and philosophical reasons, Aquinas holds that while the soul cannot come into existence without the body, it does endure independently of the body in the event of its separation from materiality by death. This is, for Aquinas, only a temporary (and imperfect) endurance, however, since bodily animation will be restored at the end of time in the general resurrection. Even as it enjoys heavenly beatitude, the soul is incomplete without the body. Importantly, however, the body does not endure as a body after human death. There is no such thing, for a Thomist, as a dead body. Since it is the soul as substantial form that makes the body to be the body, once the soul has departed the body, the same matter comes to be animated by a new form or forms and so becomes something distinct (a corpse or a cadaver).

THE HUMAN SYMBOL

Thomas uses the precise character of human body–soul composition to locate humanity with the cosmos. Simultaneously both spiritual and material – but reducible to neither – the human being does not belong entirely either to the realm of materiality or to the realm of spirituality, but finds her uniqueness in straddling both orders of reality. The presence of humanity within the world thus opens up 'a marvellous perspective on the connectedness of things':[12] as the material–spiritual amphibian, the human being is – in her very constitution – the 'frontier and horizon'[13] that connects the spiritual and the material spheres, while also re-emphasizing their fundamental difference. Importantly, as we will see in more detail shortly, Aquinas connects this with the 'perfect balance' of the embodied human person. It is not just that the human being possesses the dual aspects of materiality and immateriality, but rather that *within* the human person the highest reaches of the animal world participate in the lowest functions of the spiritual world. The materiality of human being is performed in an intelligent, spiritual manner, while human intellectuality is properly performed only in a material mode.

With these affirmations, Aquinas re-articulated in a distinctively Aristotelian idiom the ancient idea of the human person as a microcosm of creation, embodying in miniature the diversity of the universe.[14] The human body realizes itself within the world on account of the soul's animating and configuring dynamism, but – in an analogous way – the human being realizes the world within herself. Of particular importance here is Aquinas's account of knowledge as a profoundly intimate encounter – a matter of union with the truth of the world – in which the world's meaningfulness unfolds itself within the mind. It is important, however, to note that the account of the human being as a microcosm places an emphasis not on a function that the human person performs, but on the quality of existence that the human being *is*.

A human life, then, is significant in more than just the way in which it fashions and exchanges meanings about the world. The human person is, in its very constitution, a symbol of the world, and so an embodiment of divine gratuity. This non-functional account of the human being as symbol speaks urgently to a world that so often values human lives in terms of their performativity or productivity: whether in sound economic functioning as a productive cog in society, or artistic outputs, or even in the capacity to introduce useful transgression or resistance to oppressive political and cultural regimes. All of these goods, for Aquinas, depend upon the more fundamental good of living a symbolic life – a life that can only flourish within a certain kind of freedom and the time, space and community required to cultivate a distinctive symbolic competence that expresses the symbolic constitution of humanity itself.

HUMAN UNITY

Although much contemporary philosophy has been preoccupied with the so-called 'mind-body' problem – the question of the relationship between the experience of consciousness and the brain as the organ of mental life – the hot debate in Aquinas's day was quite different. Among the most controversial – and important – of Aquinas's claims was the idea that the soul was the *only* formal cause of the body.[15] In part, this was entailed by the strictures of Aquinas's philosophical account of reality: according to Thomas's metaphysics, a substance can only be animated by one substantial form, since it is this principle that determines both what a thing is and – in conjunction with matter – that it is one unified thing. More than one form produces more than one thing. In other words, Aquinas's view of reality dictates that if the body is a single unified object (and it clearly makes sense to see it as such) then it must have a single substantial form. The various 'parts' that make up a human existence are manifestations of the complexity of the single unifying form.

Leaving these general metaphysical principles to one side, it is important to see the theological and anthropological issues that were at stake in Thomas's then rather radical idea that the soul was the sole formal cause of human life. Thomas's opponents (most notably, but not exclusively, St Bonaventure and his Franciscan disciples) stressed the complexity of human composition by positing that distinct souls are required for each of the 'layers' that characterize human life: the plant-like soul of growth, self-nourishment and development; the reactive animal-like soul of perception, reproduction and movement; and the distinctively human soul of reason, intellect and thought. Behind this idea of multiple souls, Aquinas detected a tendency to violently fragment the human being, and to keep the higher intellectual functions 'uncontaminated' by any involvement in bodiliness. There was a resistance to the idea that the highest intellectual soul, responsible for the production of theory, mysticism, art and the riches of culture, could also take charge of the basic bodily tasks of digestion, defecation and sexual desire.

The problem for Aquinas is not just that these multiple soul theories encode a certain denigration of creaturely materiality. More importantly, they fail to capture the *unity* of the human being.[16]

We can catch a glimpse of this from our experience of distraction. It is entirely possible that sexual desire, hunger or extreme physical pain can distract us from our studies. Likewise, a gripping novel can distract us from our hunger and tiredness. Aquinas thinks this only makes sense if these are all located within a single soul, otherwise we would find intellectual pursuits had no capacity to distract us from the physical discomfort, which would belong to another quite distinct sphere. A denial of the unity of the human person has damaging – and sometimes devastating – implications when extrapolated into morality and spirituality. If the anthropology we import into our moral and theological reasoning contains an implicit bias against the body, then the spiritual and religious practices it funds will intensify this by developing disciplines that disrupt the delicately balanced unity of the human ecosystem. We can easily find ourselves aspiring to the unachievable state of angelic beatitude,[17] disciplining ourselves for the inescapable fact of our animality.

Against the tendency to fragment humanity by positing different coordinated but basically autonomous levels of functioning, Thomas stresses two important points. First, he emphasizes that it is not just the case that the body needs the soul, but also that the soul needs the body.[18] The highest powers of the soul (like understanding) depend upon the data provided by the senses, and even in its unnatural state of temporary separation from the body, the soul's intellectual life depends upon that which was laid down in bodily life – the memories and concepts acquired from our physical encounter with reality. Without the body, the soul has no 'raw material' to work with. Second, Thomas seeks to avoid any sense that human complexity implies compartmentalization. The different elements of human experience cannot be divided up and parcelled out to the provinces of different souls. The self-same soul configures and governs every aspect of human life. Thomas's argument is deceptively simple: that which is superior in a hierarchy can perform the functions of the lower rungs of the hierarchy. A consultant surgeon exercises more power than a newly qualified doctor, but can nonetheless do everything the junior doctor can do. So the rational soul has all of the lower powers of animal and vegetable souls and does not require supplementation by them.

On closer inspection, Thomas's argument yields a rather more explosive conclusion. That there is a single substantial form of the human being means we cannot understand ourselves as being only intellectual in certain respects and basically animal in other respects. Aquinas does not suggest that human beings do the whole range of animal things in the same way as other animals, and then some further and more interesting things that involve language. On the contrary, these higher linguistic functions fold back onto every aspect of human existence, changing and reconfiguring the way in which human beings perform the lower functions of animality, since these too belong to the basic structure of the human symbol. In some ways, this amounts to an obvious claim: the ways in which human beings consume food, comport their bodies and make love are always already imbued with complex webs of meaning that (most of the time) transcend the functional and the transactional. On another level, however, the claim is extraordinarily important: the highest spiritual quest – humanity's search for ultimate meaning, for God – does not require that we close our eyes and abstract ourselves from the hustle and bustle of a world that excites and arouses us. Rather, the quest for God is itself already enmeshed and woven into the fabric of daily life. There is nothing human that is intrinsically profane. God can only be worshipped in the midst of the full, rich, complexity of human existence.

SENSORY PERCEPTION

As we have already seen, one of the crucial ways in which the intellectual capacities of human life depend upon our bodiliness is the reliance of our minds upon the deliverances of the senses.[19] This is an extension of the Aristotelian principle that 'whatever is received is received according to the mode of the receiver.'[20] We are familiar with this principle in the physical world, as when containers place limits upon the manner in which something can be received (ice assumes the shape of the container into which the water flowed). Something similar occurs in the intellectual realm, corresponding to our constitution as embodied souls: that which enters our mind is received in accordance with our natural modes of receptivity to reality, namely our senses. Leaving aside potential cases of special divine action (when God might infuse knowledge directly into our minds), 'nothing is in the intellect that was not first in the senses.'[21]

When Aquinas offers an analysis of the interior landscape of our minds, it is our species-specific mode of receptivity to reality that he understands himself to be investigating. In other words, he is tracing out the ways in which we are addressable by the world that speaks. Consequently, Thomas's psychology does not indulge in speculation concerning the putative internal psychodynamic forces that swirl around within us. He is not, like Sigmund Freud and his followers, trying to unearth processes that are concealed from view. Aquinas is not an archaeologist digging down to get to the deepest and most primitive roots of our minds. In fact, the inward turn of psychology is, for Aquinas, not a turning away from external reality whatsoever. Instead, the point is to examine the various tools by which we are equipped to fruitfully negotiate a world that is not only filled with physical objects but also charged with spiritual meanings.

To use a piece of (unusually helpful) Thomistic jargon, these tools are the 'powers of the soul'.[22] These powers are distinct from the soul itself, but are the ways in which the soul acts to achieve and sustain life.[23] It is important, however, not to misconstrue the direction of movement. As we noted in the discussion of reality, the world itself speaks. We find ourselves addressed by the world, as the objects within the world bombard our senses and present themselves to us as good. The powers of the soul are, then, the capacities and tools that engage with the world as it addresses itself to us as gift and task: the powers receive and process the self-presentation of the world. As the powers are concerned with our interaction with reality, they are only co-known: that is, we come to know the powers of the soul only as we catch a glimpse of them in their engagement with reality. In considering the inner recesses of our soul, there is a painstaking and almost phenomenological analysis of the ordinary daily experiences of feeling, sensing, knowing, pondering, wondering, moving and loving.

The powers of the soul that human beings share with both plants and animals (like self-nutrition and growth) are integral and basic to human life, but the specifics need not detain us here. In short, they operate to stabilize and perpetuate bodily existence and maintain a basic biological equilibrium. It is with the sensory capacities (shared with animals and sometimes called 'sensory cognition') that the most interesting implications of Thomas's account of the soul's powers as tools for meaningful interaction emerge. We can begin to see this by considering animal movement. Non-living entities move in accordance with their intrinsic characteristics and without the need for forces acting on them from outside. Things have tendencies towards certain types of movement that will be fulfilled unless there is something blocking the path. The standard Aristotelian example (before a complete understanding of gravity had been arrived at) was that heavy objects tend to fall towards the ground. An alternative image is offered by Herbert McCabe: the needle of a compass will, unless obstructed, move to point towards magnetic north.[24] These are tendencies built into things and 'automatically' activated by their existing within the world.

Animals have these in-built natural tendencies to move on account of characteristics that they possess, but differ from plants and simple objects in that they also *receive* new tendencies to move from their environment. These are 'intentional' characteristics in that, while they stand for or mediate things that are 'out there' in the world, they are still (albeit temporarily) characteristics of the animal itself (the animal *is* undergoing some kind of sensory experience). Through sensory perception, the external object has inserted itself into the animal's framework of action and affected its tendencies to move in particular ways. In these cases, the tendency to movement is in some way mediated or activated by the senses. When a cat sees a mouse, the mouse becomes part of the cat's frame, and the cat acquires a tendency to pounce. Similar things could be said of dogs rushing towards plates of meat and cats fleeing snakes (and, oddly enough, cucumbers).

As a result of these sensory capacities, animal movements require a different kind of explanation than the falling of a rock or the movement of a compass does. These explanations reflect upon the ways in which awareness of the external environment is 'translated' into internal tendencies within the animal. Two important points should be noted. First, to analyse movement in this way introduces a primitive kind of meaning into consideration. The animal's intentional tendency to move is a product of the fact that a particular sensation means something to the animal, whether the opportunity to satisfy a desire or the presence of danger. Of course, these meanings are not present to non-human animals *as* meanings. Since non-human animals lack the discursive power of language, they cannot consciously consider or articulate the meanings they encounter in the world. Nonetheless, investigating these meanings is a necessary component of any explanation of animal behaviour. Secondly, the intentional characteristics do not *automatically* trigger a response, as if the sensation presses a button within the animal that unleashes a cascade of necessary reactions. The perception introduces a *tendency* to movement rather than simply the movement itself. The sensation, and the meaning it represents for that animal, become part of the experiential field of the animal. Whether or not the animal activates that tendency will depend upon the other elements that are within its experiential field, factors that might catalyse or impede the activation of the tendency. It is precisely this need to account for the whole that differentiates the animal from a kind of machine or biological mechanism.

HUMAN PERCEPTION

When it comes to explaining the ways in which humans receive tendencies to act from their environment, a further layer of explanation is required. The environment within which our decisions to move are located is one that we not only receive but also have the capacity to fashion for ourselves. Roughly speaking, this further kind of explanation answers to questions that seek to reconstruct the internal conversation a person might have with themselves before deciding how to act.[25] It is not necessary that a person did in fact hold such an internal soliloquy, only that they might have done and could be asked to reflect on their behaviour in such a way. It is, of course, entirely possible that an action could have emerged from longstanding habituation or even have been determined quite unreflectively. The point is that it could have been the fruit of internal discussion, and thus the person's tendencies to action emerge not only from within the manifold of their sensory experience but also from the broader way in which they talk about the world, how they symbolize it and narrate their place within it.

This has a radical consequence. Whereas the animal's tendencies to action are responsive to a segment of reality – the one that presents itself to their senses – human symbolic capacities allow us to situate our action within the much broader framework of the world as a whole. It is a result of this broadening of horizons that our actions become *moral* actions. We even locate ourselves relative to aspects of reality that transcend any kind of availability to the senses (like God). This intensifies the kind of explanatory holism that is required to account for human action. If animals differ from machines on account of a necessary explanatory attentiveness to the whole, humans might be seen to represent a further step towards explanatory wholeness and thus a passage into a more intense form of animality. Explanation of human action demands an attentiveness to the ways in which that human being symbolizes the broadest possible whole.

INTERIOR SENSES

The senses, as we have seen, are a set of powers or capacities by which we are enabled to perceive the reality of the world around us. In addition to the five 'external' senses with which we are familiar, Aquinas identifies four 'internal senses': common sense, imagination, memory and something that he calls the estimative power.[26] In almost every case, these names are misleading for the contemporary reader, as the same terms are used in quite a distinct manner by contemporary psychology.

The problem begins with the very idea of the interior senses. Thomas does not mean by this phrase that there are – alongside the external senses – interior sources that provide additional sensory data. Rather, these powers are called senses because their object is particular material objects, not universal ideas or concepts.[27] The interior senses, then, work on the deliverances of sensible perception but are *interior* because they receive their raw material not from the object in the world outside of our minds, but from another power of the soul. The interior senses receive their contents from the exterior senses: sensible reality flows into us through the exterior senses and then into the interior senses that further act upon that sense data.

Broadly speaking, the role of the interior senses is the coordination of our sensory experience, so as to render a very basic and universal form of interpretation. In our encounter with the world, we naturally harmonize and synthesize the data provided by the senses into a singular experience. We do not encounter the world through the senses as five distinct channels or pathways of information. In fact, we do not become aware of raw sense-data at all (except when conducting strange philosophical thought experiments). Instead of encountering a world of abstract shapes and sounds, we become aware of objects as the sensuous material wholes that they are in reality. This points to the operation of the *sensus communis* ('common sense'). By this, Aquinas does not mean the kind of intuitive, sound, practical judgement in everyday matters that is often found lacking in academics. Rather, Thomas means the power we have to perceive sense qualities as common. It is the common sense that forges a unity from our sense experience, by which we are able to experience sound and vision together and can know that a certain noise belongs to a certain textured object. Since the *sensus communis* unifies, it is also the power that instils order into sensory experience and thus the capacity that allows us to know that a sound is something that is heard, and so on.[28]

Among the sensations the common sense unifies and parses is the unique awareness that each of us has of our own bodies. Aquinas likens this to the sense of touch: we know the 'feeling' of our own body as it comes into contact with (and thus senses) the world around us. It is the common sense that marks the bodily registration of this difference. This form of self-perception is a rather mysterious capacity, but also rather mundane: it bestows upon us a basic awareness of where our body is within the world, and thus of our locatedness within space and time.

Like the *sensus communis*, the estimative power concerns itself with what is co-known in our knowledge of worldly objects. In this case, the matter concerned is the intuition that we hold instinctively about the value to ourselves of the things we perceive. This can be seen in the way we experience a threat. We do not perceive a snake slithering across the desk and then by a subsequent intellectual act make judgements about its dangerousness. We simply immediately perceive the snake as a threat, though we might subsequently return to that perception in our intellects and correct it or reflect upon it. In this way the estimative power goes beyond that which is sensed in a way that the *sensus communis* does not. In the same way that the visual clues are present to us as a snake, the snake is immediately known to us as something more than a snake: as a threat to our well-being.

The common sense and the estimative power both concern realities that are currently present to our senses. The two remaining interior senses concern the 'retention' of what was once sensed. The imagination is the power to recall what has been received by the senses.[29] Thomas's use of the term does not imply the introduction of something new or creative, but rather the ability to make the structures that were once known to the senses present to our minds once again. Since I was once burned, I can now recall the feeling of the flame. Although we would probably call this operation of the mind 'memory', Thomas reserves that term for another interior sense that takes us beyond the immediate perception in a way similar to the estimative power. The sense-memory indexes the retained sensory perception relative to our autobiography.[30] Memory adds to the imagination the particularities of temporal location and of narrative that are not contained within the sensory object itself, but which are an unavoidable feature of our original encounter with it. Like the estimative power, then, sense-memory connects my sensory perceptions to my instinctive valuation of their importance to me and my identity.

THE BEGINNINGS OF BIOGRAPHY

Today we are likely to see the work of these interior senses as belonging to the realm of the mind and of cognition. For Aquinas, their work takes place at the level of bodily sensibility. Aquinas does not think in terms of input–output or hardware–software, as if the hardware of the senses provided the raw input and the software of the mind did the information processing. This is especially clear in the case of memory. Thomas differentiates – in a way quite alien to our own times – a sense-based memory from an intellectual form of memory. The ability to remember a fact (that George lives in Hampstead, or that 2 x 2 = 4, or that there was a schism in 1054) is something that we can do with our minds, concerning facts that have been inserted into our intellectual memory. But while all of us should remember that there was a schism in 1054, remembering the schism itself is impossible for us. The latter form of knowledge belongs (or would belong) to the sense-memory: it is the senses, which handle the realm of particularity, that can negotiate the past as past, rather than simply as a repository of facts. This indicates a twofold dependence of the mind upon the senses: as we have already seen, a first dependence for the provision of the contents of the mind. But we can now discern the ways in which not only the concept of history, but also any sense of 'pastness' whatsoever, depend upon the combined work of the interior and exterior senses and intellectual reflection. Without sense-memory we would have an incomplete sense of what it means for an event to be a past event, and would therefore lack any complete framework for the ordering of our accumulated facts about the world.

As we have seen, the interior senses (particularly the memory and the estimative power) are intimately related to our most basic sense of self. Alongside their function in relation to the world as perceived, they provide us with a foundational awareness of where we are located within space and time, and of our bodies and ourselves as coherent realities within the world. As the interior senses are sensory powers, we cannot yet talk of the intellect's capacity for narrative formation, but it is not overly premature to suggest that there is something like 'autobiography' at play here. The development of a self-narrative will require the higher, symbolizing capacities of our minds, but these depend upon the proto-biography generated by the interior senses. Indeed, Aquinas underlines (in a way that is deeply consistent with strands of contemporary therapeutic theory) the ways in which our sense of self and our autobiographical memories are so rooted within the body that our bodies 'keep the score'. It is not just the case that the crafting of an autobiography is a profoundly bodily practice. It is also the case that to be the kinds of bodies that we are is *ipso facto* to be practitioners of autobiography.

EMOTIONAL LIFE

The amphibious character of the human being as a material-spiritual composite is acutely expressed in Aquinas's account of the emotions.[31] While the emotions are profoundly bodily experiences – someone who is 'gutted' does indeed feel it in their guts – Aquinas locates the emotions within the soul. What we would call emotions are, for Aquinas, *passiones animae* ('passions of the soul'): reactions to the world rooted in our bodily composition that are located in the powers of the soul. In calling the emotions *passions*, Aquinas stresses that the emotions are not something we can exercise complete control over or generate entirely within our minds. Rather, the passions are something we undergo, our basic reactions to our environment as it presents itself to us under the aspects of attraction (the good) and repulsion (the evil or bad).[32]

Understood in this way – and without any prejudice to the profound complexity of human emotional life – there is a basic continuity between human emotions and the reactions that animals have to their environment.³³ To some degree, the passions of the soul are involuntary experiences, located at a more primitive level than the kind of inclination towards the good we find in the higher realm of intellectual freedom. A consequence of the pre-intellectual character of the emotions is that they are basically morally neutral.³⁴ It is no sin or human failing to feel something or to be moved by one's environment. The emotions do subsequently acquire a moral character, but only from the way in which they enter into the domain of human freedom, where we fail to moderate the emotions or use them well. There is, then, no point disciplining ourselves for feeling anger, disgust or fear. The question is what we ought to do with these experiences, how we can live them in ways that integrate rather than fragment our personhood.

Aquinas's account of the emotions is especially important at a time when we are witnessing a resurgence – sometimes explicit and sometimes not – of ideas associated with ancient Stoicism. For the Stoics, the ideal state was one of undisturbed apathy. The emotions were construed as perturbation and therefore as one of the primary enemies of human flourishing. Securing happiness was a matter of subduing or overcoming the emotions, with various modes of approach ranging from bodily asceticism to the higher forces of reason and intellect. As we will see, Thomas thinks this view of the emotions is profoundly damaging to human integrity. Aquinas is, of course, well aware of the power of emotions to cloud our judgement. These he calls 'antecedent', since they are emotional reactions that jump out in front of rational judgement and so diminish the goodness of a moral act.³⁵ But there are, Thomas thinks, other emotional responses that are not only the fruits of virtue and sound judgement, but also vitalize and intensify human excellence. These emotions are essential to human flourishing.³⁶

Thomas's account of human emotions matters, then, for three reasons: first, he helps avoid emotional self-mutilation, by providing us with an account of the emotions as good, reliable and God-given; secondly, he provides us with a complex landscape of our emotional life that helps us to parse and understand our reactions to the world around us; thirdly, he offers some sage advice about how we might bring greater harmony to our interior life and so live fully affective lives, at peace with our emotional reactions to an often turbulent world.

THE LANGUAGE OF EMOTIONS

Nonetheless, the human emotions are not the unreconstructed reactions of other animals. As we have already seen, the passions arise for us against not only the backdrop of the world that is present to our sensory experience, but also the world we have partially created for ourselves in narrative and symbolization. By modifying the stories we tell ourselves about the world, we can modify our involuntary emotional reactions to it. This is an arduous process of formation that requires the application of virtue and some considerable tenacity (particularly as we get older). But this medieval insight into the interaction of the emotions and the intellect shows a remarkable affinity with the cognitive approaches to psychotherapy advocated by Aaron Beck and others.

Aquinas's account of the emotions is unusually prominent and extensive.[37] Some of his analysis is simply without parallel in the medieval world, and even today, in an era when attentiveness to affect is rather fashionable, few philosophers have treated the emotions to such extended and granular analysis, and even fewer theologians examine them as a theological category in their own right. Thomas does not directly indicate the reasons for his decision. Some speculate that the *Summa* was intended for the training of priests whose ministry would be primarily in the confessional rather than the pulpit or lecture theatre: the demands of the pastoral care of penitents demanded a deep familiarity with both the tradition of moral theology and the mysterious ways of the human heart.

However, it seems to me that more than this is at stake. Perhaps it is possible to detect here something of Aquinas's own biography, even of his spiritual struggle: there is a profound sense that Aquinas is someone who knows the emotions from the inside, who has entered into a deep analysis of the movements of the soul out of some kind of necessity. Perhaps Aquinas wrote in a theologically therapeutic way because he needed to come to a deeper and more integrated understanding of why he himself reacted in powerfully emotional ways: what we glimpse here is one of the sites at which Aquinas powerfully integrates philosophical theology and spirituality. If this is so, then those of us who encounter ourselves as occasionally burdened by sadness and irascibility encounter Aquinas not only as a teacher but also as a fellow struggler. Either way, the emotions strike at the very core of Aquinas's account of what it means to be human and are fundamental to his understanding of how human beings realize their identity as co-creators with God. To live well as a human being – in fact, to be a Saint – means living emotionally: giving ourselves permission to live fully and intensely emotional lives.

THE EMOTIONAL ECOSPHERE

Although the intricate details of Aquinas's treatment of each of the particular emotions are of great profundity, his most insightful and useful contribution lies in the structure that he discerns within our emotional life. The emotions emerge for Aquinas as a micro-ecosystem of their own, a delicately balanced economy of affectivity. The major division lies between what are called – rather unfortunately – the concupiscible and the irascible passions.[38] The terminology is so remote that it is perhaps best abandoned, and replaced with the 'reactive emotions' and the 'emotions of struggle'. The reactive emotions ('concupiscible') are the reactions that concern objects as they present themselves as present. These emotions direct us to move towards things that appear good and to move away from things that appear evil. The emotions of struggle ('irascible') are still reactions to things that are good or evil, but now insofar as they present themselves as being hard to achieve or difficult to avoid. These two distinct types of emotion correspond to two different ways in which we encounter the world. On the reactive side, the world gives itself without demanding that we seek it out; it simply affects us in the way that it addresses itself to us. On the side of the emotions of struggle, the world provokes and evokes us by a kind of demandingness: in this mode, the world presents itself to us as a project that demands our attention and requires us to grapple with its brokenness and incompleteness.

Within these two broad families of emotions, all but one of the emotions Aquinas considers belong within a coupling of contrary pairs, where one concerns the good and the other concerns evil. On the side of the reactive emotions, the pairs are: love–hate, desire–aversion, and joy–sorrow.[39] The structure of these pairings can be seen by tracing a journey through the positive emotions: love is the emotion that is a sensory registration of the perception that there is something good 'out there' in the world.[40] Love gives rise to a further emotion, the character of which is determined by whether the lovable good is present or absent.

If the good is not present, the emotional response is that of desire, which is a form of love-in-motion.[41] If and when the good is present and possessed by us, the emotional response is that of joy (a form of pleasurable delight) that can be conceived as a form of love-at-rest.[42] A similar pathway obtains in relation to the perception of evil, registered as 'out there' in the emotion of hatred;[43] aversion is the emotion of hatred-in-motion, negotiating the possibility that the evil will come into contact with us.[44] Sorrow (or perhaps better simply 'pain') is the emotion of hatred-at-rest, a result of our having been encountered by some element of reality that is destructive or unfitting.[45] In short, one pair of passions (love–hate) concerns registration; another equips us to negotiate absence (desire–aversion); a final pair is concerned with the negotiation of presence (joy–sorrow).

The passions of struggle have a similar structure, but involve two further considerations: (im)possibility and the direction of emotional movement. The first pairing (hope–despair) concerns the perception of goods under the aspect of their (im)possibility. Hope as an emotional response concerns the apprehension of a good outcome that, while difficult to secure, is nonetheless possible.[46] Despair, on the other hand is the emotional registration of *im*possibility, the recognition that a particular arduous good cannot actually be secured, that it lies outside of the realm of our capacities to obtain it.[47] While hope might propel us into motion, despair is more static, causing us to draw back from a particular pursuit or course of action. The second pairing (daring–fear) is related to evils that are hard to avoid or with which we must struggle in order to overcome. Daring is the passion of confrontation with evil:[48] like hope, it impels us to movement, functioning as an emotional determination to tackle a threat or a difficulty. The passion of fear, by contrast, emerges in the context of impossibility, when the hated outcome appears unavoidable or inevitable. If daring is something of a 'fight' reaction, fear involves 'flight', the withdrawal or retreat from an impending catastrophe.[49]

THE IMPORTANCE OF BEING ANGRY

Anger stands alone. It has no paired emotion. Anger is the emotion that equips us to negotiate the presence of an arduous evil.[50] There is no passion that corresponds to the presence of an arduous good, in that the achieved good is no longer accompanied by difficulty but can rest. Unlike sorrow, however, the passion of anger is not at rest. Rest is precisely the thing that anger refuses. Anger involves the movement towards restitution (where the restitution is perceived as some kind of good). Anger is fundamentally an emotional refusal to accept the presence of evil. It declines to rest in a state of encounter with evil and it refuses to allow our lives to be determined by the evil situation within which we find ourselves. Anger, then, is a complex passion in that while it is a reaction to an evil that is present, it is also an orientation to a good that would overcome the evil. Importantly, the emotion of anger (and the often existentially disruptive experience of moral outrage) is by no means inappropriate. There are certain circumstances of outrageous moral evil that *demand* our anger.[51] In these circumstances the absence of anger would indicate that there was some defect in our humanity. While spiritual and human maturity might require us to channel our anger in more constructive – and forgiving – ways than immediate vengeance, it does not demand that we deny or suppress the passion of anger, but only that we appropriately moderate it and use it fruitfully. Well channelled, the passion of anger can serve as the root of social improvement.[52]

The emotional landscape traced in this analysis invites us to situate ourselves according to the following questions: is the cause of any given emotion good or bad? Is it simply present, or is the world seeming to impose upon me the task of overcoming something? Does my emotional reaction push me inwards or drive me outwards? Is my emotion a matter of embrace or of resistance?

In Thomas's analysis of human emotion, a certain primacy is given to the passion of love. Not only does Thomas indulge in a particularly extensive analysis of love's character, causes[53] and effects, but the passion of love also exercises a definitive role with respect to the other emotions, which proceed from or depend upon it. Importantly, love has an intrinsically relational element: love tends towards both union with the beloved *and* communion with it.[54] Love passionately hunts out the beloved and invites the beloved to dwell within the lover's mind. Consequently, love forms an emotional bond with the goods that sustain us. The pursuit of good that love drives within us is marked by a natural form of emotional ecstasy, since the lover goes ahead of herself into the world, standing outside of herself in the pursuit of the good. Importantly, the dynamic of love involves two necessarily related powers: the love of desire, which concerns the good thing in itself, and the love of friendship, which concerns the person on whose account a particular thing is valued as lovable. These are not to be understood as mutually exclusive modes of loving (one selfish and the other altruistic), but as always already involved in any emotional movement of love. Consequently, this dual aspect of love stresses that the act of loving objects is always indexed to a person.

Love wills the good of a person – whether oneself or another. The love of a particular good is never absolute in itself, but always relative to the one for whom it is a good. The passion of love is, then, not only the root and source of all the emotions, but also the animating force that will ultimately flourish into human community and culture. Importantly, love and hatred – as the basic positive and negative emotions – are not equally primordial. Love has a definite primacy: anything that threatens the good that is loved will be the object of hatred only on account of its tendency to drive out that which is loved and lovable. Consequently, Aquinas thinks that emotional equilibrium is not achieved through the balancing of negative and positive forces, as if we are fighting a battle between creativity and innate destructiveness. Rather, emotional harmony is – through and through, from the first to the last – the unfolding of love's forceful and life-affirming dynamism.

Emotional health is ultimately not a matter of simply eliminating experiences of negativity and confrontation. The occurrence of suffering cannot finally be eliminated with any degree of certitude in this life. Without wishing to minimize the utter devastation that evil can visit upon human lives, more damage is done to humanity by the rendering impossible of pleasure. Tragically – and not infrequently because of theology gone awry – human beings craft reasons to prohibit their enjoyment of pleasure (rather than just more sensibly moderating desire-fulfilment). Here we see just one of the ways in which the legacies of bad philosophy – often parasitic upon bad theology – do enormous damage to real human lives.

Thomas's affirmation of the primacy of love must be balanced by a second, more challenging observation. The emotions of struggle belong on the same plane as the simple emotions of desire. As such, Aquinas sees a form of aggression as playing an important natural role in our negotiation of the world as it places demands upon us. This is, in certain important respects, distinct from the opposition of positivity and negativity: the movements of desire and aggression – of grappling with difficulty – relate to both the good and to the evil. The question of the human being as 'fighter' must consequently always be framed in two respects: what are we fighting *against*? What are we fighting *for*?

MODERATING THE PASSIONS

The flow of the passions has been likened to the course of the River Nile through Egypt. The river brings something vital to life and fertility, without which all would be lost. Without the emotions to drive it, a human life would be a failed project. Nonetheless, the river also represents both a potential threat and an opportunity that can be exploited. Should the river unexpectedly breach its limits, the consequences range from inconvenient but embarrassing disruption to total devastation. Human intelligence can fashion ways of mitigating the risk and preventing destruction and – more significantly – of harnessing its power to do things that lie beyond its own innate tendencies, like irrigating ground or generating electricity by turning a corkscrew. Similar things might be said of the emotions: guided and monitored, they enable us to do great things, but unchecked and uncultivated they easily get out of control, becoming unbalanced and wreaking havoc in our moral and spiritual lives.

Although the passions are part of the material constitution of the human being and have their roots in the domain of the sensitive aspect of the soul, they do not complete their course there. 'The perfection of human good requires that the passions be moderated by reason.'[55] The precise manner in which it lies within the capacity of human reason to bring our emotional lives under such 'moderation' is the subject of the next chapter. But to repeat the point, such moderation is not a matter of overriding or shutting off the emotions, but of harmonizing and balancing their movements into a dance or symphony of human flourishing.

STEPPING BACK

Essential to any account of the human 'extra' is the uniquely human capacity for truth. We not only perceive the world and react to it emotionally, but are also possessed of a further capacity to read and interpret our experience. It is this additional capacity that puts us into contact with the meanings of the world *as* meanings. To put this another way, it is the fact that our endowment with intellect renders us *capax Veritatis* that enables us to recognize meaning and to ask questions about the meanings of our experiences, and ultimately to make judgements about them.[56]

A crucial feature of our innate capacity for truth is the ability to, as it were, 'stand back' from our experience, to move from a simple presence of a phenomenon to make it the object of a different kind of intellectual presence, one that situates it within a broader realm of consideration. There are, of course, times when we become quite aware of our capacity to step back, as, for instance, when we feel an unfamiliar sensation within our body and reflect on its location, origin and possible significance, as well as the particular character of its raw feel. Talking about such a sensation requires the capacity to ask questions about it and to compare it to other similar but different experiences. In Aquinas's account, all of our knowing involves a form of 'stepping back'.[57] Without being aware of it, we are constantly abstracting from our concrete experience, constantly taking a step back so as to reflect on the ways in which the things we encounter fit in with the world in which we find ourselves.

Paradoxically, such a stepping back is also a stepping forward: in knowing, we are simultaneously performing an action that is beyond the strictures of the purely material world and driven more deeply and intimately into materiality. To see how this is true requires attention to one of the most counterintuitive features of Thomas's understanding of our encounter with reality: his account of the identity of the knower and the known.[58] To put this simply, an example from sensory perception is useful. Conscious experience of the world is, Thomas thinks, the realization of the being of the world *within* the animal, limited in accordance with the way in which we encounter reality. As we saw in Chapter 1, a substance exists as the configuration of some matter by a particular dynamic form or organizing principle. In our encounter with that substance, the same form or meaningful pattern comes to structure our sensory perception. The snake has a snake-form substantially and cannot lose that form without changing type of substance. When we see or know a snake, we 'have' a snake form temporarily, either sensibly or intelligibly (or both). So when somebody perceives the presence of a snake as dangerous, it is the same form – as received by the subject – rather than some subsequent judgement about it that gives rise to the perception of dangerousness.

For reasons of terminological clarity, Aquinas calls a form received in this way a *species*: a sensible *species* is a form received as a perception, and an intelligible *species* is a form received in the intellect as something like a concept, idea or word.[59] It is in the passage from the sensible *species* to the intellectual *species* – from the realm of sensory perception to the domain of thought – where the 'stepping back' of abstraction becomes especially important. To see how stepping back functions within our knowledge, it is first necessary to reflect briefly on how Aquinas understands the intellect to be structured. This requires a foray into some Thomistic jargon, but the journey is worthwhile for the insights it yields concerning our way of navigating the world.

POWER AND POTENTIAL

Aquinas understands the intellect to be twofold: on the one hand, it is a potential to understand and on the other it is the power to understand. The world as it is realized in the senses is not yet thinkable. The power of the intellect functions like a light that illuminates the sensible *species* so as to draw out their intelligibility.[60] Just as a lantern casts light so as to render visible those objects that are shrouded in darkness, so the light of intelligibility cast by the agent intellect renders sensory experience accessible to thought. It is here that we encounter for the first time a capacity that is utterly unique to human beings. The agent intellect is a kind of 'stepping back' in that the darkness it dispels is the particularity proper to the senses: the agent intellect steps back from the particulars delivered by the senses into the universal realm of thought. While we encounter a particular dog called Oscar, the operation of the agent intellect allows us to apprehend that Oscar is *a* dog, one instance of a particular kind (to put it in other words, that the object 'Oscar' is possessed of the character of dog-ness, which other similarly shaped objects also possess).

The operation of the agent intellect is often described in terms of 'abstraction':[61] reaching into the realm of sensory experience and pulling out the intelligibility that is latent within it. Another analogy is subtractive: the *intellectus agens* takes up sensory experience and removes from it everything that makes it this or that particular experience, so as to yield a thinkable universal. Neither of these analogies quite does justice to the creativity of the agent intellect. Its work of 'stepping back' is not merely abstractive or subtractive but also productive, yielding an intellectual *species* as the mind becomes informed by the object that is known. Whatever analogy we use to capture the work of the agent intellect, the crucial thing is to recognize that it does *work*. Knowing the world is not simply a passive experience but involves an active entanglement, a doing something *to* the world and not merely a looking *at* the world. Indeed, this activity of our minds realizes something about the world that is otherwise merely potential: the world has within it the possibility of being known that is then realized within our knowing, as the world unfolds itself intellectually within our minds (without, of course, actually changing the status of the things themselves).

Before considering the second aspect of our knowledge (the *possibility* of understanding that resides within our minds), two clarifications should be made. First, Thomas thinks that the agent intellect is a natural endowment of the human individual. The *intellectus agens* is neither God's own action within the individual nor a singular reality that is shared within the common treasury of humankind. Nonetheless, the light of the agent intellect is a form of natural, created participation in God's mind: its light comes from God and reflects something of God's power. Secondly, the agent intellect reflects the distinctive amphibious character of human life. It corresponds to the fact that we know by way of the senses and that – unlike the angels – we gradually acquire knowledge over the course of a lifetime. Thirdly, to state the obvious, the power of the agent intellect is limited on account of its finitude. Our minds can in no way exhaust the intelligibility of the world; the capacity of the agent intellect's light to illuminate is profoundly limited.

While stressing that knowledge involves an active 'doing' (and not just a looking), Thomas also recognizes that intellection has a passive dimension.[62] When we come to know something, we undergo an important kind of change, being moved from a state of ignorance into a state of knowledge. Indeed, we intuitively speak of knowledge as a mysterious process of acquisition. Whereas we are born with the capacity to see, hear, feel and taste, we are not born with a genetically given language. Instead, we gradually and painfully acquire grammar, vocabulary and syntax. In this respect, our minds begin in potential. To borrow from the language of Genesis, there is a sense in which the new-born human being's intellectual apparatus is 'formless and void'. Since we gradually accumulate knowledge, our intellects are to this extent a passive power that is acted upon as it is brought into actuality by being shaped, structured and filled. This passive element of our intellects is known in the Aristotelian tradition as the receptive intellect (or, sometimes, the possible intellect, *intellectus possibilis*). It is, as the name suggests, the role of the *intellectus possibilis* to receive the intelligible *species* that are generated by the *intellectus agens*. To adopt a very loose analogy, we might see a parallel to the two phases of the Genesis creation account, that of distinction and that of ornamentation. It is the distinctive task of the possible intellect to be the sphere in which the intelligible *species* are received, making – as it were – a 'space for thought'. The agent intellect, on the other hand, serves to 'fill' the receptive intellect, making it teem with the life of thought.

STEPPING FORWARDS

The capacity to step backwards and form universal concepts out of our particular sensory perceptions enables us to step forward into the world. Something of this can be seen in Thomas's account of higher mental activities like discursive thought. Aquinas divides these into two broad camps: the first, the understanding of simple ideas or concepts; the second, the way of understanding by composition and division. Roughly speaking, the understanding of simple ideas corresponds to the ability to use a word correctly, and thus to know in this limited sense what the word means. On the other hand, the way of understanding by composition and division concerns the relationships between things. To say 'sugar is sweet' is an act of understanding by composition not because it succeeds in placing two words alongside each other in a meaningful way, but because it affirms that sugar and sweetness belong together in reality. The work of understanding by division is to know that two things are not, in reality, close to one another.

Thomas's account of understanding, then, negotiates a delicate balance. Understanding is a thoroughly linguistic activity, but it is not *only* a linguistic activity. Understanding is not just knowing how to rightly bring words together and move concepts around within a conceptual space. Rather, understanding involves the use of language to penetrate the structure of reality itself. Our innate intellectual capacity to 'step back' is therefore the way in which we are empowered to 'step forwards' into reality. And since, as we have seen, reality 'speaks' to us in meaningful ways, language and reality are, as it were, made for each other: reality is in some ways structured like a language, and so language is the appropriate means for exploring its complexities and hidden depths.

6

Belonging

THE MORAL LIFE

Human life, as Aquinas understands it, exhibits an inescapable paradox. The unique greatness of the human person is manifested in our incompleteness, in the fact that we reach for a fulfilment beyond our own capacities to obtain. Our lives are not, nor could they ever be, self-contained and isolated little projects, but depend for their fulfilment on the relations that we forge within the world, with our fellow human beings, and ultimately with God.

Consequently, when it comes to human life, Aquinas does not separate 'being' from 'belonging': individual flourishing and learning to live well with others are not two distinct tasks set before the human being. They are simply two faces of the single reality of humanity, consequences of being the kind of symbolic animal that we are. Since human being is always already an instance of human belonging, the question the mystery of our lives confronts us with is not *whether* I belong (or even primarily *where* I belong), but rather *how* I belong, the mode of belonging I adopt as my way of being. In answering this *how*-question of belonging, we raise the question of who we are *becoming*, of how we are choosing to unfold our lives and our unique identities within the particular contexts in which we find ourselves. In other words, being implies belonging, which raises the question of becoming.

Aquinas's moral theology and philosophy matter because they propose an approach to negotiating the moral complexities of life by consistently balancing attentiveness to each of these three essential elements: the fixity of human *being*; the dynamism of human *becoming*; and the inescapability of human *belonging*. In many of today's intractable and hotly contested moral questions, Aquinas would see one of these three aspects being prised apart from the others. In the global village of the twenty-first century, questions of identity and belonging have come to assume a central importance, often being intertwined with (or even displacing) the classical questions of politics and ethics. The rise of what has loosely been termed 'identity politics' has produced a febrile and sometimes hypersensitive moral culture, in which questions of identity-based liberation have tended to displace class-based solidarity.

Thomas's work, of course, lacks many of the distinctively (post-)modern categories that are foundational to these discussions, so why bother with him? In fact, the value of Aquinas to these conversations lies in the fact that he cannot easily be assimilated to either the opponents or proponents of an identarian shift in political discourse. This is nothing new: attempting to port Aquinas into such febrile contemporary political conversations is a risky undertaking that has seldom proved productive. His social thought and political philosophy have already been forcibly co-opted into a vast array of patently irreconcilable political endeavours. Despite this, Aquinas can help us to think consistently and rigorously about the central categories that underpin these debates: identity, belonging and the delicate balance between the rights of individuals and the societies to which they belong. In particular, Thomas's refusal to separate human becoming from human being leads him to consistently root his account of the task of belonging (and the element of self-creation and self-determination) within an analysis of the types of creatures we are.[1]

Rooting an analysis of human becoming and belonging within an account of human being is not only, or even primarily, a matter of affirming (as many will intuitively suspect) that there are certain natural 'givens' that place a limit on the scope, power and importance of our self-identification. It is, however, to stress that the task of fashioning and living out an identity is a naturally human one, and that there are ways of failing to adequately take ownership of this task and responsibility for its consequences, by, for instance, living mindlessly according to a pre-given culturally determined script, or thoughtlessly living the life that our parents have planned for us. These are failures in human *being*, which lead to the de-humanizing of ourselves and the communities within which we live.[2] Thomas's point is that the tethering of human being, becoming and belonging together provides us with a way in which we can evaluate our lives with objectivity, identifying more and less free and excellent ways of establishing our individual identities.

THE INEVITABILITY OF BELONGING

In a broad sense, Thomas recognizes three ways in which human beings always already belong. The first is a matter of biology.[3] Just like any other animal, human beings belong to a species, which gives a form and direction to their lives. To put this in more contemporary idiom, human beings belong to a particular genetic community, sharing the nature that is common to all members of the species and therefore inheriting a particular evolutionary history, reflected in our powers and capacities. Each of us is the product of a relationship between other human beings (however tenuous or corrupted that might have been). To be human involves, then, the possession of a certain genetic relationship received from other human beings, and this genetic 'programming' disposes us to act and behave in certain ways (including disposing us to reproduce, thus passing on the genetic relationship we ourselves have received from our parents).

The second inevitable form of human belonging is cultural, the outworking of our distinctive constitution as linguistic animals.[4] While genetic community concerns biological exchange and fertility, linguistic belonging concerns a second aspect of our common life as human beings: our capacity to create and exchange meanings and, indeed, to fashion the linguistic media by which we do so. All of us are born and socialized into practices of communication, the vocabulary and grammar of which we receive from the community as an important tool for our individual flourishing within that community. On one level, linguistic communities are less expansive than the genetic community that we belong to simply in virtue of our being human. Importantly, however, the boundaries of linguistic communities are porous. It may require great labours of translation or symbolic ingenuity, but there is no metaphysical obstacle that prevents, in principle, the exchange of meanings between any two members of the human species. The ways in which we share meanings with one another in both what we say and what we do – the 'how' of our belonging to the linguistic community – are studied in ethics (and its sub-discipline, politics).

A third level of inevitable belonging is theological. For Aquinas, all human beings enjoy a unique 'belonging' to God: every human person is a unique child of God – a product of God's love and freedom – who consequently belongs, whether actually or potentially, within the Church.[5] This is, to today's ears, a controversial and even hegemonic claim. The theological dimension of human belonging will be explored in more detail in the next chapter. For now, two points should be noted. First, Aquinas does not believe that we can entirely anaesthetize ourselves to questions of ultimate meaning: any consideration of human belonging will ultimately involve questions of our definitive belonging.[6] As moral creatures, we live our lives before God, in the intuited presence of ultimate significance. Secondly, this theological form of belonging involves the perfection of both genetic and linguistic community. In the incarnation, God has entered into genetic solidarity with the human community, bestowing upon that biologically determined set of relations a new theological significance: henceforth, to be human is to number God in Christ among our kith and kin.[7] As the incarnate *Word*, Jesus also bestows a supernatural integrity on human linguistic belonging. Our language and practices of communication now have the capacity to perform acts of divine power (like knowing and loving the triune God).

Although each of these three domains of inevitable belonging is the subject of a distinct science – biology, moral philosophy and theology – they are irreducibly interconnected. Linguistic community is simply the unfolding of our genetic community: we are, by nature, the symbolic animal and so by nature exist within cultural and linguistic communities. Indeed, it is our status as linguistic beings that places us within the theological community, since it is language that empowers us to form ideas about the whole of reality to which we belong. Each domain proceeds from the former, but folds back upon it and radically transfigures it.

FREEDOM AND COMMUNICATION

Correlating our cultural and linguistic belonging in terms of ethics has the surprising consequence of framing the moral life as the quest for skilful and life-enhancing forms of communication.[8] This is not an uncontroversial move. Other, perhaps more obvious, accounts of morality approach the issues in terms of law or divine command (and therefore of obedience) or love, or virtue, or the avoidance of gratuitous cruelty.[9] Since the publication of Elizabeth Anscombe's article 'Modern Moral Philosophy' in 1958, the framework of virtue (indebted to Aristotle and Thomas) has witnessed a surprising renaissance.[10] Virtue ethics frames moral reasoning in terms of the quest for human excellence and the up-building of character, rather than merely in the detailed analysis of particular deeds. Understanding ethics as communication has a deep compatibility with the virtue approach, but seeks to foreground the morally significant and distinctively human element that makes human behaviour human.

In short, when human beings act in morally significant ways, they not only accomplish something within the world, they also communicate something.[11] Our actions reveal ourselves and externalize our interior desires, reasons and dispositions. In doing something that is morally significant, we communicate something of our value system, of the things that we esteem within the world and about the priorities that govern our lives, as well as our fears, anxieties and motivations. It is for this reason that moments of acute moral significance (the 'hard' problems of moral philosophy) can be spoken of as somebody being 'put to the test': not the kind of test that determines whether our moral compass is right or wrong, but the kind of 'proving' that draws out from within us otherwise concealed facets of our moral character. Moments of urgent moral decision reveal the moral fibre of our lives, often as much to ourselves as to those around us.

Clearly, not everything human beings do is equally communicative.[12] Some things, like automatic bodily responses, are not communicative at all, while relatively few things are entirely transparent to the meanings we might invest in them. Indeed, we might say that something is morally significant insofar as it is communicative. Readers of Aquinas have articulated this truth by distinguishing authentic 'human acts' from the other things human beings do.[13] Only those things that are imprinted with reason and freedom of the will are, strictly speaking, human acts. An act's humanity can be increased or diminished by factors that increase or decrease its freedom and engagement with reason.[14] The point is this: while our automatic responses are guided by the 'programming' we received from our genetic community, the ways in which we belong to the political, linguistic, community depend upon and are formed by the ways in which we communicate using our free and communicative human acts.

In previous chapters we have seen how human behaviour demands narrative explanation of the type that speculates imaginatively about what a person might have said to themselves as they deliberated about what to do. Even when such a dialogue has not entered into the consciousness of the individual, Thomas holds that all human acts emerge from a subtle dialogue or dance between the faculties of knowing and loving.[15] There are, roughly, six dialogical stages. First, our mind perceives something good and our will moves in an act of simple desire for it. Secondly, our reason makes a primitive judgement about the attainability of the good, and the will forms an intention to move towards it. Thirdly, reason deliberates about the intention and, together with the will, gives consent. Fourthly, the reason decides to act and the will joins it in electing to do so. Fifthly, reason gives a 'command' to act and the will executes that command. Finally, there is the act's 'fruition', perceived actively by the intellect and enjoyed passively by the will.[16]

Clearly, Thomas does not think we are necessarily conscious of this kind of internal dialogue going on within us, nor should we be. The analysis is supposed to help us to understand the complexities of the internal movements that emerge into intelligent action and enable us to diagnose points of failure at which our desires escape our control. Nonetheless, whenever we act in a fully human manner, we implicitly externalize this internal dialogical process. This internal process involves an imperfect (because internal) communication; the public act perfects the communication by manifesting it externally. Importantly, then, communication is not something we add to our human acts as a later supplement. Communication is an intrinsic feature of every action that proceeds from our freedom. Our moral actions communicate something of who we are and (as we will see) are the means by which we shape who we are becoming within webs of human belonging. In other words, human acts are the essential means by which we give shape to and express the story that is our lives.[17]

THE MEANING OF FREEDOM

This account of human action lends a particular character to Thomas's understanding of human freedom and its meaning. Within the communicative understanding of ethics, freedom is the ability to bring being, becoming and belonging together in a moment of communicative human action. The significance of this can be seen through a comparison with alternative accounts of freedom. Instinctively, we are likely to see freedom as a matter of having a choice: we are free if, and only if, we are able to decide which course of action to take from a number of possible options. By contrast, Thomas's account of freedom is more like having the ability to completely give oneself over to the narrative of our lives, to entirely invest ourselves in the project of becoming who we desire to be. Moral freedom means having no areas of un-freedom that hold us back from our project of becoming by tethering us to the mediocre half-lives that impede our flourishing.

This account shares a number of important features with the model of freedom-as-choice, including an emphasis on the absence of external compulsion or inner necessity.[18] Thomas's account of freedom does not, however, celebrate a stance of neutrality or indifference, but rather the overcoming of things that hold us back from the pursuit of self-realization. It is true that, in some circumstances, we can be held back from authentic freedom by the absence of viable alternatives or by the foreclosure of choice. But we are more likely, Thomas thinks, to be held back by the inability to make a rational choice that corresponds to the project of becoming our best self. The factors that hold us back from fully embracing the project of becoming are complex. They include things like fear, economic disadvantage and a lack of vision or imagination, as well as cultural (and perhaps familial) pressure to conform to dehumanizing life scripts. For Thomas, however, the chief offender is best seen as something like a lack of full self-possession, the inability to bring the whole of oneself behind a particular goal.[19]

The idea of a fragmented self that lacks this kind of unity might sound like a rare, even pathological state of affairs. In fact, Thomas is pointing to a far more ordinary reality: our sometimes shocking inability to avoid doing the things we least want to do. As anyone who has listened to a motivational speaker, or used a self-organization app, or hired a personal trainer, will readily attest, we sometimes need help to lean into the projects we have set for ourselves, even when those projects are – objectively speaking – eminently feasible. Faced with a decisive, potentially life-affirming, opportunity, the individual who lacks a certain degree of self-integration will be unable to make anything other than a half-hearted (and thus only partially free) response. The single biggest impediment to our belonging within our homes, jobs and communities turns out to be a lack of *self*-belonging, an inability to make our lives truly our own. We are haunted by the tendency to live our lives on automatic, as if some other authority were doing the living and we are merely following the script. Although such totalizing passivity is rare – and alarming – it is much more frequently observed in partial forms, where there is some element or area of an individual's life that eludes their control or determination, whether as an addictive behaviour that cannot be shed, a shameful secret that is not easily integrated into the story they tell about themselves, or a fragmented 'double life' in which the different faces of a person's life do not easily commune, lacking integration and transparency.

BECOMING FREE

Like being human, freedom is paradoxically both given and achieved. On the one hand, human beings are, by their very nature, possessed of a particular innate sovereignty over their actions: although we may be coerced and moved against our will, no power can force us to actively will something that we do not. In this limited sense, there is something inviolably free and untouchable about the human spirit, a power of self-governance that can never be corrupted or taken from us (except by the power of death). On the other hand, as we have already seen, this innate freedom often realizes itself within a framework of considerable un-freedom, the messy realities of the half-lives that hold us back from authentic self-realization. Achieving authentic freedom – the richer and more comprehensive freedom that is human flourishing – is not only a question of removing obstacles that impede our full engagement with the project of living. What is called for, Aquinas thinks, are active practices of freedom that form and shape our lives into a comprehensive whole and dispose us to consecrate ourselves entirely to the task of self-realization. In other words, establishing ourselves in freedom is not like shedding a few pounds so that we might regain a lost agility. It is more like muscular growth and organic development, in which we make more of ourselves and reach towards a state of moral and spiritual maturity. By these practices of freedom we become more substantial and robust, and belong more fully to our families, communities and world.

These practices of freedom make up what Aquinas sees as the life of virtue.[20] The virtuous life is a life of human excellence lived in accordance with reason, by which we gain a kind of existential 'weightiness' and come to leave deeper moral and spiritual footprints in the world.[21] Just as in the case of physical maturation, the growth in virtue is, in a certain sense, the growing into our identities: we become more ourselves, more robustly the person we are and want to be. In this task we can succeed or fail, or make a mixed job. We can hit or miss the mark. The 'mark' here shares in some of the paradox we have been exploring: it is both something that is given and determined by our nature, and yet one we can shape for ourselves. There are ways of living that are objectively not fitting to the human character of our lives, just as there are physical conditions (like malnutrition) that are not conducive to biological flourishing (and therefore place certain limits on the range of healthy choices open to us). Within these wide parameters, however, we are free to craft our identities by committing ourselves to various projects of becoming that correspond to our personalities, unique abilities and desires. Becoming a teacher or nurse, embracing a priestly or political vocation, or deciding to marry are all examples of particular 'projects of becoming'. By these projects we consecrate ourselves to a multitude of practical identities of human flourishing, into which we spend a lifetime (or a career) growing. Much, then, depends upon the appropriateness of the projects of becoming that we commit ourselves into.

BEING HAPPY

Thomas's understanding of virtue remains somewhat inaccessible to today's readers. The language of 'virtue' still carries a somewhat negative overtone, suggesting a rather boring or limp state of predictability, or placing a rather individualistic focus on personal character. All this conceptual baggage must be put to one side if we are to see the vision of virtuous living that drives Thomas's account of human flourishing. For Thomas, the virtues make a monochrome existence come alive in Technicolor. The virtues make us belong to the world with greater vigour and intensity. They make a human being more alive and more vibrant in their own unique identity and freedom. Their acquisition is the great and noble adventure to which each and every human person is invited. The virtues are excellences or strengths of character that make a particular person a great or iconic example of human flourishing.[22] A life lived without the virtues will not only be a tragic waste, but also a profoundly unhappy and ultimately destabilized existence. When it comes to being happy, Thomas thinks that everything hinges on the possession of the virtues.

So what exactly are the virtues? Thomas takes the virtues to be a form of *habitus*, often rendered as 'habit' in English. This terminology is not entirely helpful. Certainly, the virtues are forms of habituation – behavioural traits of character that are relatively stable and hard to change. But whereas habits might today be taken to be somewhat irrational repetitions or destructive behaviours that take us over and impede rational communication (even rather mild habits like umm-ing and err-ing during public speaking), virtues do not escape our rational control but are used and deployed by us to enhance our communicative lives.[23] Habits are, then, more like predispositions towards performing certain actions: they do not force or compel us to react in certain ways as if we were automatons, but rather make it easier for us to do the (often difficult) things we really want to achieve. If the energetic dynamism of our lives were liquid being poured onto the surface of moral action, the dispositions are like channels habituated into the surface, by which the energy of the water can be captured and directed to flow along useful paths. If the channels are well ordered and comprehensive enough, the moral and spiritual energies of our lives will be well harnessed, and tend to flow towards creative and life-giving outcomes.

Generally speaking, we acquire and maintain these dispositions through action:[24] the more intense, intentional and repeated the action, the stronger and more well developed the disposition will be. Consequently, the virtues (and their opposites, the vices) witness to the ways in which we shape, form and mould ourselves across a lifetime. As the residual traces of our past actions, they are the outcome of a degree of self-creation and self-shaping. This self-creation is limited, for an important reason: the dispositions do not touch upon the very nature of the person (the '*what*'-ness of their humanity is not modified) but rather mould the faculties by which our human nature unfolds and deploys itself.[25] Although, taken together, they are determinative of – and expressive of – our fundamental character, virtues are primarily dispositions towards action and relationship, rather than modes of existence. Consequently, they are orientated towards the future:

products of our past, the dispositions of the present mould our actions as we move into an unknown or uncertain future.

The dispositions therefore occupy a strange intermediate position between actuality and potentiality.[26] They are actual insofar as they are brought into being by intentional action of the past and really exist in the present, but they are potential insofar as they are activated in their use, brought to fruition in circumstances of the future. The need we have for the habituation of such dispositions emerges at the intersection of the uncertainty of the futures we must face and the vast open-endedness of our natural faculties. Our faculties are not constrained to unfold our lives according to the pre-programmed instincts of our genetic community, nor can we find authentic flourishing by legislating for every eventuality in advance. The unique flexibility and creativity of human existence can only be harnessed and focused through this kind of habituation.

As modifications of the faculties, the virtues can be classified according to the aspect of life's unfolding they give shape to. The intellectual virtues, for instance, are dispositions of our power to understand, serving to unfold the human capacity to penetrate the riches of truth. The moral virtues, upon which much more scholarly attention has been trained, mould the appetites, giving structure to the ways in which we are attracted to the goods of the world, disposing us to desire and move towards the world in ways that are rational rather than overwhelming or destructive.

Of particular importance for Aquinas (as for much ancient philosophy, paradigmatically Aristotle's *Nicomachean Ethics*) are the cardinal virtues: the intellectual virtue of prudence and the moral virtues of justice, temperance and fortitude.[27] Named after the 'hinge' (*cardo*), these virtues play a crucial role in holding a human personality together, with each virtue giving shape to a distinctive region of human flourishing.[28] Prudence – of pre-eminent importance to Aquinas – disposes the intellect to skilfully orchestrate the moral life by deploying the moral virtues well. Justice concerns the will, disposing us to respond well to the world as it is understood and interpreted. Temperance and fortitude are dispositions of the lower sense appetites, conforming our animal reactions and passions to the measure of reasonableness. Temperance modifies the concupiscible power's attraction to the good, so that we are not overcome by our desires and can enjoy a more moderate serenity of spirit. Fortitude in turn modifies the irascibility of life, so that we are not overcome by sensory discouragement as we face squarely the difficulties inherent in the realization of our projects of becoming. Fortitude holds us back from giving up on ourselves prematurely.

PRUDENCE

Being human is a skill. Prudence is the cardinal virtue that most closely corresponds to this overall skill of being human. As the intellectual virtue that functions to bring the moral virtues into play at the right moment, prudence plays an essential role in orchestrating and integrating our moral personality, marshalling ourselves into our projects of becoming.[29] To put this another way, by the virtue of prudence we are not just good at this or that aspect of human activity, we are actually good at being human.[30] If there were a verb 'to human' (along the lines of the idea of 'adulting'), it would be an act of the virtue of prudence.

Much like other terms of art in Thomas's account of virtue, 'prudence' does not easily map onto Aquinas's use of the term '*prudentia*'. Today's ear is wont to take prudence as a slightly excessive caution or self-protective reticence: in this contemporary usage, prudence is an inhibiting caution, basically ordered towards self-preservation by holding us back from too readily embracing the whims of enthusiasm. In this model, prudence is the laudable victory of 'head over heart', the rational control of the attractive force of romantic emotional appeal. This sense of prudence easily slips into a cool-blooded cynicism; it is remote from a wild sense of adventure.

In fact, Thomas understands prudence to be a far more resolute and determinative force.[31] Its role certainly does facilitate deliberation, but its force is decisive, culminating in a decision that is transparent to the situation and our involvement in it. Prudence gives us an intuitive intellectual 'feel' or grasp of the moral moment and its demands:[32] the skills of prudential living involve recognizing the particularity of the demands of the situation and joining this to a moral decision that best corresponds to our own individual moral identity. In other words, prudence is the skill by which we are able to answer the question: 'How does a person like me – living into the projects of becoming that I have consecrated myself into – act in this particular circumstance?' The answer might involve withdrawal from a particular project of becoming for good reasons of self-preservation, but it could equally command a radical investment of the self into a new and exciting endeavour. More often it will involve the mundane: doing the next honourable and morally indicated thing. Absent any other considerations, the prudent person pays her bills on time.

Thomas's account of prudence is closely aligned with another virtue, albeit one formally connected with fortitude: magnanimity, the virtue of being great of mind and heart, 'stretching forth' into the greatness of humanity that is open to us.[33] Among the vices opposed to prudence, Aquinas numbers an excessive form of cleverness (*astutia*), a form of 'craftiness' of guile or fraudulence, the careful manipulative pursuit of bad ends.[34] So here we find another point of differentiation from the timorous sense of 'prudence' with which we are today familiar: while anxious self-preservation involves the manipulation or control of risk, authentic prudence adopts a much more honest and open orientation to the reality that the outcomes of our projects of becoming are invariably beyond our total control.[35]

Prudence helps us face this inescapable lack of certitude.[36] The point of an authentic prudence, then, is not primarily the probability of a desirable outcome, but the determination of who I am within the particular moment or framework of moral decision. One of the chief opponents of prudence is fakeness or game-playing. The authentic exercise of prudence will demand that we embark upon the long and often painful process of overcoming self-deception about our abilities, mixed motivations and fortunes.[37] It will involve intuiting the distinction between what lies within our power to address and what can only be recognized as unchangeable fact, as well as a frank acceptance of the scope of our moral responsibility. Prudence works to fashion a correspondence between our being, becoming and belonging, ensuring that we are who we aspire to be within our communicative action. Anything that interposes conflict between these three essential facets of human existence is opposed to prudence, as is limp moral inconsistency. The hallmark of prudence is a rational authenticity and whole-hearted self-engagement.[38]

FACES OF PRUDENCE

The complexity of prudence's operation can be understood by reference to a range of complementary and overlapping metaphors. Like the conductor of a symphony, prudence works to orchestrate the moral virtues into a glory that exceeds the simple sum of the parts, summoning each at the requisite moment and, in coordination with other contributory virtues, allowing the individual skills and dispositions to make their own indispensable contribution to the whole.[39] In the flow of a life's narrative, prudence knows which word to summon next from our moral vocabulary and how to punctuate the flow with syntax. Prudence also serves as a kind of interpreter, delivering existential insight into the moral realities we encounter. Paradoxically, the skill of prudential living shows that only one who acts well can see the moral situation with acuity.[40] Finally, prudence functions like a translator, mediating between knowledge of moral principles and the situational particularities of a moment, translating from the abstract imagination of our projects of becoming into the particular concrete actions that simultaneously manifest and realize it.

Prudence is, therefore, a complex disposition, made up of a diverse range of sub-skills, each essential in themselves but lacking the overarching power of a fully developed and mature *prudentia*.[41] Alongside the capacity to draw upon a clarity of reasoning and the memory of relevant past moral experience, the prudent person needs a form of moral agility to meet new challenges, balancing a far-sightedness with a circumspection regarding obstacles that might realistically impede the attainment of objectives. Lest this description of prudence sounds too much like an intelligent form of self-assertion, it is important to note that Aquinas takes docility to be an integral element of prudence;[42] the entire virtue is strengthened by the capacity to take advice well.[43] The skill of being human is developed through trial and error, but also in apprenticeship to flourishing human exemplars, and in reflecting on one's moral experience with true friends. In all things, prudence attains to a balance between an excess of self-examination (the 'analysis paralysis' that breeds a phobia of commitment) and the unexamined life that fragments into moral anarchy.

That prudence is anything but a reductively self-referential skill is further underlined by Thomas's emphasis on the way it acquires various context-dependent faces. The prudence appropriate to the self-governance of an individual (which Aquinas calls 'monastic prudence') is distinct from the prudence necessary for the governance of the community ('regnative prudence').[44] Likewise, there are forms of prudence proper to participation in the intermediate groupings that mediate between the solitary individual and the whole political community: an economic prudence for the domestic sphere of family life; a military prudence for the soldier; the prudence of a citizen for those who are governed. In other words, the skills of being human unfold into the sorts of tactful 'people skills' that are necessary for leadership and management.[45] This points already to the intimate connection between prudence and the cardinal virtue of justice, to which we will shortly turn our attention.

PRUDENCE AND PROVIDENCE

Embedded within Thomas's account of prudence is an extraordinarily rich understanding of the power and potential of human action. In moral deliberation, we are engaged in far more than simply matching ends and means. In Thomas's analysis, there is something almost mystical about ordinary human action, especially prudent action. In our communicative acts, we are engaged – albeit in a limited way – in the project of shaping the reality of our lives, our communities and our world. By acting communicatively, we become co-creators with God in the project of consummating an as yet unfinished cosmos. In its communicative aspect, our moral action shares in the creativity of God's creative word that calls into being the reality that it declares. Only by recognizing the power inherent in human communication can we come to terms with the destructive potential that resides within us, and only then can we wield our power with moral responsibility. Nothing is gained by a refusal to face up to the power dynamics that structure our relationship to the world around us, by the well-intentioned pretence to impotence that is parasitic upon a studied denial of the power vested within our agency.

Aquinas's efforts to come to terms with the power of human agency are evident in his treatment of the 'natural law'.[46] Among Catholics of the post-*Humanae Vitae* era, Thomas's account of natural law is among the most misunderstood (and, frankly, maligned) of his theological and philosophical contributions. It is not unusual to hear reference to the natural law as if it were a list of moral principles that could be (or have been) derived from rational reflection on human nature without the assistance of divine revelation. Put simply, the idea is that by studying the natures of things we can become aware of the ends towards which they would naturally tend, and therefore the types of actions that will conduce to their flourishing (the realization of that end) and which will frustrate the unfolding of their natural dynamism. This is all good and well, and confirms the intuition that there are some deeds that are so obviously destructive of human life in society (like murder and adultery) that nobody could be invincibly ignorant of their wrongness.[47] We simply have no need of a religion or a revelation to tell us that we should not wantonly destroy life.

Nonetheless, natural law is a much richer and more radical category in Thomas's understanding. To see this, we need to zoom out so as to locate his understanding of natural law within a broader context of law as something more than laws. Aquinas famously defines law as 'an ordinance of reason in service of the common good, made by the one who has care of the community and promulgated'.[48] Applying this definition has a number of interesting and important consequences, including the principle that an unjust law (one that does not serve the common good) is in fact no law whatsoever. An unjust ordinance lacks one of the essential features of the full dignity of law and so would not demand our observance as law (though it still might be best to observe it, since one has to be prudent in deciding what battles to fight). More widely, however, the definition embraces not only 'laws' of the type that might be codified in the statute book (from the minor and somewhat arbitrary determination of the speed limit up to the proscription of unlawful killing), but also to the way in which God governs the whole of creation according to the ordinance of divine reason. This Aquinas calls the 'eternal law' and, in accordance with the doctrine of divine simplicity, is identical with Godself. 'The whole community of the universe is governed by God's mind':[49] speaking analogously, God stands in relation to the world that God governs in the way a political authority stands to the community for whom they are responsible. The eternal law is the divine mind as known by God. It is the unchanging measure of the goodness of creatures seen in God's foreknowledge and enacted within the world by providential governance (the *gubernatio* discussed in the chapter on creation).[50]

Aquinas likens the eternal law to the intellectual blueprint in the mind of God.[51] Most creatures simply passively 'reflect' this eternal blueprint insofar as they are moved in accordance with it. Human beings, however, are not merely passive recipients of divine governance. By the gift of intellectual freedom, we receive an active share in God's work of governance.[52] 'Natural law' is the name Thomas gives to this rational participation in eternal law, naming the way in which our moral action is drawn (in our freedom) to participate within God's providential governance of the world. God's eternal plan is such that God wills to achieve certain ends through the free agency of God's intelligent creatures.[53] In this, natural law shows itself to have two aspects. The first basically concerns our knowledge of the eternal law. Eternal law has been promulgated to us in accordance with our status as reasoning animals who must learn over the course of a lifetime the difference between sound and unsound moral reasoning. The second aspect concerns the way in which we enact the eternal law in our doing. Prudential action renders us small centres of providence within the world, shaping ourselves and our communities so as to reach more completely towards our divinely bestowed fulfilment.

Thomas's account of natural law matters in our febrile political times for two reasons. First, it emphasizes the importance of reason and of rational discourse in coming to know how we ought to live well together. The natural law is known as 'natural' because it corresponds to something innate and universally accessible to human beings: the capacity to communicate. No human person should be excluded from this common quest for justice and truth (though they can, of course, exclude themselves through a refusal to participate in the give-and-take of communication). Moral appeal and the exciting of the emotions certainly play an essential role in political life. Nonetheless, it is in the process of communal and personal reasoning that we gain moral insight. This is, of course, a deeply demanding principle. It involves the investment of time, the discipline of attentive listening and the intentional making of space for those with whom we have very fundamental disagreements. Nonetheless, only a community that commits itself to the discipline of communicating well with one another in the pursuit of truth can hope to escape the endless oscillation between victory and defeat. Secondly, the natural law approach reframes the significance of our action in terms of providence. The point of virtuous self-mastery is not simply self-possession or self-assertion, but rational contribution to the common flourishing of the community. The self-belonging of the prudent person allows them to give themselves away in the noble endeavour of whatever particular service they are summoned to offer to the world.

FRIENDSHIP

The prudent person's self-discovery and self-realization flow, then, from their self-bestowal in relation to others. Only when we are able to 'dispose' of ourselves in belonging to others can we discover the inexhaustible riches of being human. To put it directly, human happiness can neither be achieved nor enjoyed alone. To find rest in ourselves we must cultivate and maintain a range of friendships, suited to the different kinds of belonging that mark our existence.

Although he never wrote a single extended treatment of the theme, friendship plays a uniquely important role in Thomas's thought. For Thomas, friendship is the paradigm case of human relationality.[54] Not only does his account of friendship fund some of his most profound anthropological insights, but he also derives much of his political philosophy and account of justice from it. Even more provocatively, an analysis of human friendship provides Aquinas with the analogical resources by which to understand the relationship of the Christian to God.[55]

Aquinas's emphasis on friendship speaks powerfully to an era that urgently seeks a sense of connection and rootedness. Our age has often been described as a lonely one. The growing technologization of human relationships (social media, dating apps, the smartphone) presents the familiar paradox that while we have never been so quantitatively rich in connection, for many people the depth and quality of our friendships feel impaired, perhaps even by the quantitative increase in connection itself. Intuitively, we know that a true friend is something more than a Facebook friend. Aquinas speaks powerfully to this complex situation. On the one hand, Thomas would celebrate the possibility of new forms of friendship that technology offers. Aquinas recognizes that there are different forms of friendship, differing according to both context and intensity:[56] not every friendship needs to have the degree of intimacy and unicity of soulmates. The challenge is to build a matched and contextually appropriate pairing. On the other hand, Thomas's analysis presents a challenge in that he sees friendship not as the alliance of the like-minded (those who share a particular interest or set of opinions) but as a union of the will.⁵⁷ Moreover, friendship, for Aquinas, is not about the cultivation of a protected space of intimacy buffered away from the rough and tumble of the world. Friendship is somewhat more goal-orientated, so that a friendship is neither an action or a set of warm feelings of appreciation and gratitude. It is instead a state of affairs, resembling a virtue in its solidity and endurance even when particular 'acts of friendship' are not being made.⁵⁸

Friendship is not a nebulous bond hanging in the cosmos between two people, but rather a relation, a way of being towards another. The basis of friendship is communication, the communing in some shared element of life,⁵⁹ and involves three distinct but related aspects: benevolence (the willing of the good of the friend); beneficence (the doing of good things for the friend); and concord (the shared willing of the same goods).⁶⁰ Friendship consequently involves some basic commonality or equality, as well as the sharing of particular goals or tasks that are mutually acknowledged to be good. Importantly, Aquinas emphasizes the element of choice that marks friendship. Friends do not act out of a sense of fate or determination, but with the love of *dilectio*, a love that requires personal choice and affirmation.⁶¹ To love a friend is to celebrate their existence, to share in their own will for their good, and to freely and willingly inhabit together some sphere or shared project of becoming.

It is already clear that Thomas's understanding of friendship extends far beyond our own customary use of the term. Aristotelian-Thomistic friendship includes various forms of social bond that would now be considered matters either of civic or professional responsibility. It is a form of friendship that secures the unity of the citizens within a political community, and another that renders colleagues authentic co-workers within a business enterprise. Indeed, Aristotle already acknowledges this in identifying two imperfect forms of friendship (the friendship of utility and that of enjoyment) in which another is loved principally for what they can bring to one's life, rather than (as in friendship properly so-called) a friend being loved simply for their own sake.⁶² It is, of course, this latter form of friendship that is most cherished and rewarding and upon which our ultimate flourishing must depend.

It is, however, only a matter of realism to acknowledge that there are many imperfect – but nonetheless good – forms of friendship that pattern our belonging to the world. Most intriguingly (and perhaps more congenially to today's psychological culture), Aquinas recognizes that these other-relational friendships unfold from a basic friendship with ourselves.[63] This forms something of a virtuous feedback loop: in order to form meaningful friendships, an individual must be possessed of a degree of self-integration; in turn, the virtuous friendship strengthens their personal character and gives new lustre to their individual integrity. This is so in part because friendship presupposes a constancy (or predictability) of outlook. More significantly, friendship demands self-acceptance: the enjoyment of one's own company, the capacity to peaceably roam around one's memory and desires; the degree of self-transparency and internal consistency that allows us to recognize and accept our feelings and find them to be fundamentally compatible with a rounded sense of who we are.[64]

It is here that St Thomas offers us an important lesson for the digital age. One of the chief impediments to authentic friendship is the inability to cope with ourselves and an incapacity to tolerate solitude. It may turn out not to be the case that social media has directly banalized the sacrality and dignity of friendship, but that its relentless availability has deprived us of the space and solitude that is a prerequisite for the kind of self-acceptance that is the *sine qua non* of authentic connectedness. The problem, then, is not the availability of the technological media, but its addictiveness and its capacity to distract us from the urgent task of becoming. There is, again, a paradox at play. Without healing our *inner* fragmentation and conflict, we will not be able to form the friendships that are able to bring healing to the social fragmentation of our times. Yet we reach this inner tranquillity not through a lengthy process of introspection but by learning the art of friendship, by receiving the gift of friendship from others. For this reason, acquaintance with virtuous and wiser persons is especially valuable to one embarking on the life of virtue, since they can model friendship and its possibilities in ways that are wholesome and generous.

JUSTICE

Friendship is closely linked in Thomas's thought with justice, the cardinal virtue that perfects the human being as a social creature.[65] Justice is the skill that negotiates otherness: in our dealings with the world we encounter society not just as a whole, but rather as particular individuals who confront us as centres of moral agency and integrity, whose very existence places ethical demands upon us. Whereas the virtue of prudence enacts a form of internal correspondence or self-orchestration that can only be truly understood by analysis of the narratives we tell about ourselves, justice is somewhat easier to assess in objective terms. Justice is concerned with our external action, serving to realize and execute the good publicly.[66]

In fact, as far as Thomas is concerned, justice concerns *all* of our external action.[67] Whatever other categories we might use to analyse the things we do in the world, everything can be said to tend towards justice or injustice. Accordingly, Thomas unmasks the myth of a victimless crime. Nothing we do is so cut off from the human community that it is an entirely private action. By debasing ourselves behind closed doors – even in ways entirely unknown to our peers and with no obvious impact on anybody else – we deprive the human community of the person we could and should have been. The task of self-realization is a matter not just of self-fulfilment but also of justice: it is not only the case that we *could* become a profound exemplar of human flourishing, but also that we *should* become so, and that by doing so we contribute to the humanization of the world.

Aquinas defines justice as the stable disposition to give to each person what is due to them.[68] To put this another way, justice is concerned with a form of equality between persons.[69] This equality is not absolutizing, in that not everybody should be treated in exactly the same way, but is proportionate to the individual and their needs. Justice ensures that each person be made whole, not dispossessed of anything that is rightfully theirs, whether that be a physical, economic, spiritual or cultural entitlement (ranging from their household property to their good reputation). This definition presupposes the fundamental principle that justice depends upon something prior to and more basic than justice itself, namely the existence of rights.

Although Aquinas does not directly deploy the term 'human rights', the concept is undeniably present throughout his moral theology and philosophy, albeit in a characteristically medieval form.[70] Thomas begins his account of justice with an account of rights, and shapes his understanding of justice around this principle.[71] Justice recognizes (rather than establishes) that a debt to another has been incurred. The notion of rights operative within Thomas's thought is broader and quite distinct from today's usage. In today's parlance, rights are usually abstract principles that, unless lawfully derogated from (as by legitimate imprisonment), permit and empower a subject to enjoy freedom and determine the shape of their lives. Rights serve to protect and enhance, so that human life can be lived and not merely endured. Thomas has an equivalent starting point in his account of human flourishing:[72] each person is owed by right that which is necessary to unfold and develop their human capacities and potential. Nonetheless, Thomas's use of the category of 'rights' extends well beyond the sorts of things that we would describe as positive freedoms, but could extend to include things we would describe as responsibilities, obligations and even liabilities. The point of rights is, for Thomas, to ensure that the benefits and burdens of human society are fairly shared. Consequently, Aquinas could stretch the term to encompass the citizen's right to pay taxes, or the malefactor's right to a robust punishment.

This understanding of 'right' as the fair and proportionate distribution of the benefits and burdens of a community points to the intimate connection Thomas recognizes between justice and the common good.[73] The common good is the sum total of the 'goods' that are possessed and enjoyed in common between all members of a particular society, shared with all participants in such a way that the common good is not thereby diminished (but rather enhanced).[74] Among such goods is the cumulative social and cultural capital (the national patrimony, we might say), but also the good that is identical with the harmonious, just and peaceable life of the community itself. The common good is, then, higher and more determinative than the individual good of a particular citizen.[75] Thomas distinguishes between a 'general' form of justice, the object of which is the common good, and a 'particular' justice that concerns the rightful participation of the individual within the common good.[76] These are distinguished, however, only in their basic unity. Not only does the common good serve and protect all the members of society, but it is also a good of the individual: the glory of a winning team redounds upon all of the members and associates of the team. Inversely, the individual's good cannot be authentically pursued without an at least implicit quest for the common good. As in the organic example of a healthy body, so the individual – as a part of the whole – cannot thrive apart from the overall health of the community.

We are unavoidably part of numerous communities, from the familial up to the national, and so the adventure of self-realization cannot be pursued without an investment in the common good proper to each of these belongings.

RECALIBRATION

The need for justice emerges in the paradoxical state of dispossession: the human peculiarity that something can simultaneously be ours (by right or entitlement) and not-ours (in terms of possession or enjoyment). The primary act of justice, as Aquinas sees it, is restitution.[77] This is not intended in the sense of a mathematical calculation and repayment, but rather as a restoration or recompense that *returns* what has been unjustly taken or withheld from another. Justice addresses itself to the restoration of an imbalance in the ecology of human relations. The universality of justice – the fact that Thomas extends its scope to embrace all of our external actions – underlines the ways in which our lives constantly impinge on the lives of others, that we exist in a constant relational flux of give and take.

The presence of a debt between two people and the possibility of its payment or restoration presupposes a form of fundamental equality between persons. Justice is derived from the more basic reality of a kind of universal friendship,[78] the essential belonging of each person to the genetic community of humanity and its unfolding into linguistic society and culture. Only within such a basic equality and communicative community can an account of justice and rights avoid collapsing into a legalistic philosophy of demand and obligation.

One consequence of this view is a surprisingly strict delimitation of the scope of justice and right, which is largely limited to the human community. This limitation cuts in two directions. On the transcendent plane, God cannot be said to be just in the proper and literal sense. God is not indebted, nor could God be deprived of anything that is rightfully God's, nor could a creature ever recompense God for anything received. Perhaps the only sense in which God could be said to be just in a strict sense is in relation to Godself:[79] in the infinite communion of the three divine persons, God renders to Godself that which is due. Nonetheless, since justice primarily and properly concerns *external* actions, this remains an entirely remote analogy. In short, justice is a properly human matter, and the cultivation of particular justice is the individual's point of entry into the historic project of humanity: generating a humane society.

On a more immanent plane, Aquinas would deny that non-human animals have rights in the literal sense. This is not to legitimate cruelty or disregard for animals, something Aquinas strongly opposes (albeit for the disappointingly anthropocentric reason that cruelty to animals makes us cruel people).[80] The denial that non-human animals strictly possess rights does not in any way weaken our moral obligations towards them; quite the contrary. Thomas's point is twofold. First, the appropriate form of human relatedness to other animals will require a far more complex set of tools than that provided by the category of rights. Secondly, there is something uniquely personal and human about justice and rights, a dignity that ought not be lost through a too speedy homogenization of rights and other moral obligations. The proper context within which the language of justice operates is that of the genetic-communicative context of human solidarity, with its implications for the natural equality of the subjects. Transferring the language of rights into the sphere of non-human animals therefore requires an analysis of the type of community shared between humans and other animals, a form of solidarity that is often analogously termed friendship, but which has an important and ineliminable degree of disanalogy with friendship, not least in the disparity of communicative capacities and the great vulnerability of many non-human animals to exploitation and abuse by humans. In short, insofar as talk of 'animal rights' provides an analogical tool to help us access our moral obligations towards the non-human world, a Thomist should welcome it. At the same time, this can only provide an entry point into awareness of important moral obligations that demand further complexity and refinement.

Central to Thomas's account of human rights is his analysis of human nature. Without a robust account of what it means to be human – and thus of what the human flourishing to which we are entitled might plausibly look like – there would be nothing for Aquinas to anchor his account of rights in. One important implication of this is that legislative and political disputes can often conceal philosophical disagreements concerning fundamental questions about the nature of humanity and our place within the world. It is no coincidence, then, that a time of entrenched debate about the extent and scope of rights has coincided with a period of unprecedented neglect of academic philosophy, the discipline that is charged with thinking rigorously and normatively about such questions.

Ultimately, however, Thomas's account of rights is theologically charged. Rights do not guarantee themselves, nor do they go 'all the way down' to the most fundamental level of analysis. Instead, they terminate in human nature, amenable to rational investigation but ultimately a given, freely bestowed by God without necessity or compulsion. In other words, rights are ultimately inalienable on account of a gift given in an act of creation that is not an act of justice but the presupposition for all acts of justice that follow from it. While there is a right to life on the part of all who actually do exist, no creature had a pre-existent right to their own creation. Two implications follow from this. First, even as justice is a matter of moral obligation, this can (and should) coexist with a form of gratitude that recognizes that even the most fundamental and inalienable rights witness to a gratuity of divine gift, and to the mystery of being human. Secondly, rights follow from persons: the existence of rights is a 'symptom' of the creative personal communion of each human being with God, and the virtue of justice brings a healthy structure to the complex web of interpersonal relations that comprise the human community. Consequently, in the realm of politics, the element of the personal occupies a logical and metaphysical primacy. Attentiveness to the ways in which institutions operate to secure or foreclose human flourishing ought never to displace the personal, since the greatest evils and good are alike given and received by persons. Ultimately, politics must involve an analysis and account of the formation of moral character within citizens and their leaders. The political sphere cannot be reduced simply to economic or social management by way of policy, but is always primarily about virtuous leadership and belonging.

JUSTICE AND BELONGING

The connection between the practice of justice and human belonging becomes clear from the three basic forms that justice takes, each corresponding to a basic structural relationship intrinsic to the human community. First, the relationship of the individual to society; secondly, the relation of one individual to another individual; thirdly, the relationship of the whole society to the particular individual member.[81]

The forms of justice proper to the first two of these relationships will be broadly familiar to us. In the first case, the individual owes a legal justice to the community, the general justice of promoting the common good by, among other things, observing the laws and customs of the society and not unduly compromising its harmony. In the second case, the form of justice that rightly orders the relationship between two individuals within the community is known as 'commutative' justice (that is, involving substitution or exchange), and its principles animate today's contract and employment law.[82] In sum, leaving aside the type of gift exchange that animates friendship, whenever there is an exchange of goods between two individuals (whether intentionally and voluntarily or otherwise), there arises the obligation that the one from whom something has been taken receive a just and proportionate recompense from the one who has done the taking.[83]

Commutative justice requires not only that we ought to promptly make good our contractual obligations, but also that we must also pay a fair wage and a non-exploitative price. In fact, commutative justice ought to prevent us from entering into certain contracts – perhaps zero hours contracts are an example – and might invalidate unjust contracts (though without either party gaining an undue advantage). Commutative justice also obliges us to the restoration of non-material losses, including when somebody has unjustly been deprived of an opportunity or held back from developing their natural potential, and to compensate those whose privacy or natural right to secrecy are violated. Thomas gives extremely nuanced consideration to the ways in which unjust discourse deprives individuals of their rightful reputational goods, deploying a complex taxonomy of terms that would now all be covered by the idea of slander. 'Talebearing', for instance, is the crime of undermining an individual to her friends, and is particularly grave in that it attacks the good of friendship, one of the greatest goods of a human life, without which a person can never truly flourish.[84]

More complexity arises with the consideration of the relationship of the society to the individual, governed by the obligations of distributive justice.[85] Distributive justice unavoidably touches upon issues of power and authority, binding those in authority not only to wield the power that they have been given with fairness and accountability, but also with generosity towards those who are in situations of precarity or stand in need of protection. Those who preside over the 'treasury' of the common good have the obligation to distribute the community's goods to members of society in accordance with their individual status (including a consideration of their needs and vulnerabilities, as well as their dignity and rank, and a fitting recompense of self-sacrificing community service). This could include providing a war pension to those whose partner has been lost in combat, or the provision of financial support to those unable to work due to illness or care responsibilities, but could also be taken to extend to the provision of healthcare and educational opportunities so that each citizen has an opportunity to realize their individual capacities for human excellence.

There are two distinctive features of distributive justice that combine to make its realization in actual human societies particularly challenging. First, the debt that is owed in distributive justice is not easily calculated. In commutative justice, the debt owed straightforwardly corresponds to the value of the goods that have been taken. While the loss of non-material goods is, of course, hard to quantify, the situation is not complicated beyond the difficulty in determining the value (notional or actual) of that which has been lost. In the case of distributive justice, however, the debt owed is 'whatever corresponds proportionally to the person':[86] the principle of proportionality demands a careful consideration of the needs and status of the one to whom the debt is owed, and the question of the value of what has been lost to the individual. The situation of the beneficiary has, then, to be considered in its totality. Such an assessment cannot be undertaken by just anyone, and cannot aspire to the same kind of objectivity as the determination of a commutative obligation can. The determination of what is allocated by distributive justice can only be achieved synoptically, from the perspective of one who has authority and presides over the common good. We might, of course, find various ways to influence that decision (as by democratic means) and it might be possible to argue for a natural law distribution (those who are starving through famine are entitled to claim the stockpiled grain of another as their own), but the obligation of reallocation only arises with the determination by the proper authority.[87]

This contributes to the second challenging feature of distributive justice: its tendency towards a nascent form of totalitarianism. Distributive justice is, by its very definition, impossible to adequately enforce. As the sovereign authority alone can determine and enact the allocation, there is no higher platform of authority that can compel the delivery of what is rightfully owed. Much hinges on the moral character and prudence of those who exercise power. This points to the importance of being able to hold those in power to account and, if necessary, remove them from power by democratic or other means. Indeed, in grave circumstances, Thomas accepts that tyrannicide can be a legitimate response of last resort to the totalitarian rule of one whose vicious government is entirely incompatible with the common good.[88] Aquinas offers a timely reminder that the central concern of the democratic process is the safeguarding of rights acquired under distributive justice.[89]

MORAL COMPLEXITY

The threefold character of justice voices an account of human belonging that is multi-faceted and multi-dimensional. The complex equilibrium of our belonging requires a constant adjustment through redress of justice. Our belonging is realized in a constant tension of giving and receiving, in relation to individuals and to society as a whole. The perennial temptation of moral reasoning is to reduce this complexity by eliminating one or more of the axes along which justice operates. On the one hand, there is an individualism that sees society as nothing more than a fairly large collection of individuals, and so models all of its moral analysis in terms of commutative justice. On the other hand, the twentieth century witnessed forms of communitarianism that so expanded the scope of the public square as to entirely absorb the individual, denying that there could be any private relations whatsoever. In the end, such a system can sustain neither commutative justice nor – even as elements of distribution might be present – distributive justice: there is but one legitimate individual, whose boundaries are identical with the state, and all other difference is subsumed and consumed within it.

Aquinas's account of justice matters precisely because he systematically refuses the temptation to reduce moral complexity by eliminating any of the constitutive relations by which we belong to the world. As our moral situation is determined by those relations, so our moral decisions need to be triangulated within the perspective of each of those relations, even if one perspective inevitably dominates. In other words, the rights of individuals and the rights of the community are not competitive philosophical frameworks for moral reasoning, but complementary perspectives within an overarching moral web of relations that constantly seek a renewed moral equilibrium. We can only adequately think through the implications of our individuality by reference to society, and *vice versa*.

IN EXCESS OF JUSTICE

Notwithstanding this essential role that justice plays in fashioning our belonging, Aquinas recognizes that it cannot deliver everything. There are some debts – often, in fact, the most significant ones – that we could never repay, and which it would be inappropriate to even attempt to discharge. Indeed, it is part of moral and spiritual maturity to encounter as fully as possible the impossibility of making full restitution. For many of us who have been blessed with loving and nurturing parents, the debt we have naturally incurred to our elders could never be repaid. Others will have had deeply formative relationships with teachers or have benefited incalculably from prudential leadership of a particular public official, or been in receipt of life-saving counsel at a particular juncture. To our parents and country we owe, Thomas thinks, a form of devotion that he calls piety, and to others a form of respect that he names *observantia*.[90] Thomas thinks that such gestures, beyond mere justice, redound upon the whole community and are part of the social glue that binds a society together. An acute example of this kind of excess might be the respect and esteem that was widely felt for Queen Elizabeth II, even by those who might otherwise have been trenchantly critical of the monarchy.

For Aquinas, however, the ultimate 'debt' that we owe is to God. Our very existence is inscribed with a debt of gratitude that we could never adequately settle, since everything is received from God and nothing can be added to God's infinite majesty. The recognition that we owe God nothing less than everything, and yet that we cannot even make a beginning of an attempt at repayment, is the basis of the virtue of religion. We 'owe' God worship. Importantly, we are, at this stage, still in the realm of philosophy rather than theology (the virtue of 'religion' is annexed to the acquired virtue of 'justice').[91] In other words, Aquinas takes the need to worship to be part and parcel of our natural constitution. Indeed, the recognition of our incapacity to repay the debt we owe to God is the philosophical principle that underpins the often hyperbolic character of many religious rituals and practices. If justice is the skill of negotiating otherness and belonging in a world of irreducible difference, religion is the skill of gesturing towards ultimate otherness, infinite distance.

For our purposes, however, the religious attitude is essential to our belonging *within* the world. The question is, once again, not whether but who or what we tend to worship. Crucial to human belonging is the ability to register the profound experience of gratitude and the sense of mysterious wonder at the contingency of our existence. Without worship of that which lies infinitely beyond the world (or some kind of contemporary equivalent) all our attempts at belonging within the world will ultimately be futile.

THE VULNERABILITY OF BELONGING

The remaining cardinal virtues of fortitude and temperance address the vulnerability of our projects of belonging. No matter how well established and entrenched the practice of justice becomes, the equilibrium of belonging we arrive at is always provisional, perpetually threatened by the unexpected and unhoped for. In other words, belonging – like the project of human becoming more generally – is a constant work and not a definitive achievement (at least in this life). To belong well, therefore, also requires a set of survival skills that enable us to make it through the crises of life intact and, whenever possible, to live those crises as opportunities for self-discovery and growth. To put it bluntly: wherever we are in life, we can be sure a crisis is coming. Fortitude and temperance are the skills we ought to develop to live those crises robustly, with prudence and justice. In other words, fortitude and temperance are the skills that ensure that we do not lose our true selves in the storms of life.[92]

The virtue of fortitude and its components correspond to our vulnerability to attack from without. Authentic self-realization demands that we acquire a taste for reality, the full palate of which includes the presence of hostility and even enmity. Our projects of becoming will inevitably fail if we anaesthetize ourselves to these painful and unpalatable realities. There is no virtue to be found in living as if the world were already an entirely peaceful and harmonious whole.[93]

Externally, the work of fortitude often looks like an almost passive state of resistance or endurance in the face of extreme difficulties meted upon the individual from without. Thomas understands the character of this endurance quite differently. Endurance involves the strenuous activity of resolutely clinging to the good.[94] To be a person of fortitude, then, is to be somebody who – even when inexpedient – actively refuses to deny the truth of reality, not least the truth of who they are in their projects of becoming. Only this kind of trenchant re-consecration of the self can ultimately generate the spiritual and psychological energies necessary to sustain the externally visible aspects of endurance.

Similarly, the related virtue of patience (a necessary component of fortitude)[95] is not a matter of not doing anything – just sitting and waiting – but is the active cultivation of psychological equilibrium in the face of difficulties. As a component part of fortitude, patience involves the refusal to be inordinately dominated by difficulty at an emotional level. There are times when this internal refusal becomes manifested as an external repulsion of an evil: Thomas notes that an assault on evil with the aim of preventing it from impacting itself upon us can indeed be an act of fortitude.[96] Even then, however, the essential feature of fortitude is the refusal to allow our project of becoming and belonging to be disrupted or taken from us.

For this reason, fortitude may ultimately take the form of a preparedness to face death rather than lose oneself and compromise the essential truths around which our projects of becoming cohere.[97] This is not, of course, a casual recklessness that would rather embrace self-destruction than compromise. Instead, it is the recognition that there are occasions – mercifully rather rare – when it is entirely in accordance with reason to face death rather than deny the truth. These situations are those where the kind of denial demanded would so compromise the self that it would yield a type of existence more like death than life. Although such instances of ultimate sacrifice are rarely demanded (except, perhaps, in places of extreme religious persecution), the minor injuries we face on a daily basis are something of a foretaste of death, the impingement of negativity that will ultimately overcome us at the end of our lives. Enduring and living well through these unavoidable incursions of negativity into our lives is, then, a way of preparing ourselves for the ultimate violation of death. Fortitude is not, however, merely future-orientated. The skills of fortitude help to secure a way of belonging to the world so deeply rooted in reality that it can thrive in the face of the ever-present threat of disruption. Fortitude, then, is not developed for its own sake. Rather, it leans upon and preserves prudence, our self-consecration into projects of becoming.

At first glance, fortitude can look somewhat individualistic, and perhaps even gesture towards a toxic vision of self-assertion. Fortitude is not, however, self-reliance.[98] In fact, fortitude depends upon a frank and realistic acceptance of our own incapacities. Thomas's account of fortitude presupposes that we have to deal with forces of disorder vastly more powerful than we are, forces that genuinely elude both our control and our powers of prediction. Indeed, the authentic practice of fortitude demands that we give up the anxiety-driven attempts to control the forces of fate and providence that lie beyond our control. Much life is wasted – and much self-destruction has been wrought – by the frantic efforts of insecure human beings to falsely shore up their sense of secure belonging. Fortitude recognizes that, if we are to belong to the world as it actually exists (and not the world generated by our fantasies of control), we must give up on the idea of entirely controlling it. Indeed, we must accept – and live with – insecurity in all its relentless unavoidability.

For Thomas the religious believer, this means giving oneself over in trust to the providential care of a loving God. For the non-believer, it would indicate the need for an analogous 'entrustment' to the higher laws that elude our grasp (the 'being at one' with nature and history). In both cases, fortitude involves a complex interplay of acceptance and resistance: a steady and trenchant resistance to the forces of negation that would undo our projects of becoming, and yet a refusal to situate oneself in the perpetual stance of being at war with the world.

VULNERABILITY TO SELF

While fortitude concerns external threats, temperance focuses on internal disruptions that threaten to unsettle the inner tranquillity and harmony of the soul.[99] The internal complexity of the psyche gives human beings an unusual propensity to self-sabotage. Today, the language of temperance is often taken to be a matter of moderation: a negative, restrictive praxis that serves to constrain our appetites for the life-preserving goods of the world (especially sex, food and alcohol). It is better to see Aquinas as invoking the ideal of an evenness of 'temper': the well-tempered body is one that is harmonious, well-tuned to rational responsiveness to the world. Seen in this way, temperance is not about calculating the right quantity of pleasure to allow ourselves, or even primarily about moderating what we ingest. It is true that temperance will sometimes hold us back from the self-destruction of indulging one desire at the expense of others. Temperance does this, however, not by a violent clash of forces but by an emotional orchestration of the concupiscible powers into a rationally structured whole. Among the fruits of temperance is serenity and an emotional tranquillity.[100]

Temperance has a uniquely self-referential quality.[101] Whereas fortitude issues in forms of self-bestowal – even the giving up of life in the service of greater truth – the acts of temperance are ordered towards authentic self-preservation. Indeed, temperance points the way to a non-selfish form of self-love, foregrounding the moral obligations we have towards ourselves (and even the extent to which our perpetration of injustice against others does profound damage to ourselves). Crucially, however, temperance is the skilful (and not overly indulgent) use of the powers of self-control.[102] The point is paradoxical, coming closed to fortitude's emphasis on relinquishing control so as to achieve freedom: the excessive or unrestrained use of our powers of self-control will ultimately lead only to self-destruction. To take one example, the self-preserving instinct towards self-assertion is harnessed into self-realization by the temperance of humility. Without this inner orchestration provided by temperance, the life-giving forces of the appetites fail to deliver that which they promise: the unfolding, preserving, enriching and fulfilling of life.

The connection between temperance and belonging can be seen most clearly in Thomas's account of its orchestration of our natural desire to know. By nature, we thirst for knowledge and for sensuous experience of the world's beauty. The disordered indulgence of that desire results in what Aquinas calls *curiositas*.[103] Curiosity is not, in this sense, the simple interest in unveiling truths currently hidden from us, nor is it the desire to crack a difficult conundrum or find the most elegant solution to a problem. In fact, curiosity is an obstacle to the kind of focused attention that is necessary to achieve new insights or knowledge. Curiosity is the intellect perpetually on the move, a 'roaming unrest of spirit' (*evagatio mentis*)[104] that issues in an insatiable desire to encounter the new and the flashy.

The insatiable thirst of curiosity results in a form of intellectual restlessness that precludes the patient and ponderous forms of attention necessary to achieving significant depth of thought. The description of curiosity is alarmingly close to the addictive experience of 'doom scrolling', the semi-mindless perusal of social media, including vast swathes of information we really did not want to see. Such scrolling briefly satisfies our attention only by propelling us into further such scrolling. Indeed, the speed with which novelty can be found on the internet pushes us in the direction of curiosity: we easily succumb to the quest for information that is unstructured by wisdom and seldom commended to memory.

The experience of losing an hour to 'doom scrolling' (or flicking the channels on the TV) points to one of the central features of intemperateness more generally: we are 'taken over' by something that seems to come from outside of ourselves, but which is in fact elements of our desires that are not integrated into our overall sense of self. Intemperateness generates a sense that we are not acting from the centre of ourselves, with a broader feeling of rootlessness within the world. In extreme cases, the intemperate are unable to live within themselves, seeking their total sense of self in external things. The virtue of temperance holds us back from this squandering of ourselves by which our belonging *in* the world becomes an enslavement, a belonging *to* the world. By so doing, it enables us to enjoy the world.

7

Consummation

GOD'S GIFT OF SELF

Thomas's world that speaks, and the whole communicative life that unfolds within it, converge upon the life of Jesus Christ, in whom God speaks in a definitive and unsurpassable way. In the life of Jesus of Nazareth, the God who first 'spoke' reality into being now speaks as a man, to re-create, to perfect and re-figure the world of communication. In the life and death of Jesus – true God and true man – Aquinas sees the drawing together of the world of creaturely words as they are united in the primordial and uncreated Word of God.

So, at the climax of the *Summa Theologiae*, the question of what the world says (and of what we are saying within it) becomes the question of *who* the world bespeaks, and how we are to live in the spaces of meanings that are framed by the events of Christ's life, death and resurrection. Thomas's theology matters not only because he repeatedly re-frames the world of human communication in such irreducibly personal terms; many theologians and philosophers have attempted to do exactly that. Thomas's theology matters because of the uniquely non-violent manner in which this re-framing is accomplished. The re-framing is ultimately a work that is performed by God in the incarnation of Christ, so it is by attending to the ways in which God reframes the world in Christ that we can intuit a way to reframe our lives in God.

CHRISTOCENTRISM?

For different reasons, the claim that the entirety of Thomas's thought converges on a non-violent figure of Christ is likely to discomfort many contemporary philosophers, who would prefer to keep the religious and philosophical aspects of his thought distinct. In a pluralistic world, the unapologetic particularity of such a focus on Jesus is extraordinarily stark (and perhaps intrinsically violent). For Aquinas, it was in the first century (and at no other time) in the life of a Jewish carpenter (and in no other life), and in the events that unfolded around him in the relative obscurity of Galilee (and at no other place), and in particular in his death, that we find the unrepeatable expression of the meaning of every other human existence (and, indeed, of the world).

This is not just to claim a unique moral exemplarity or significance for the life of Jesus of Nazareth. It is to claim that every life – and every creaturely communication – is really touched by Jesus's life (whether that is known or not) and finds within that life a key to unlocking the mystery of its own existence. In every creature, the act of self-realization by which they insert themselves into the communicative tapestry of reality speaks their own unique 'name', but within that self-actualizing speech there is an echo (perhaps silent) of the name of that crucified man. In encountering Jesus – in hearing within themselves the echo of his uniqueness – the creature speaks their own unique name in a more intense and full-bodied roar.

The life of Jesus is, then, no mere historical artefact, nor an event confined to an ultimately irretrievable past. It is not enough to see Jesus's life as a source of theologically or philosophically interesting information. Nor is it enough to say that the *legacy* of Jesus's life continues to unfold itself in the Church and in the great human struggle for justice. The actuality of Christ as a perfect divine-human (and human-divine) communication is ever-present as the pregnant possibility (and promise) of the perfection of our own communicative futures. The particularity of Jesus, then, sustains our present communicative lives and guarantees that the stories we have crafted into our biographies have a certain permanence and fixity; that, when we are no longer here to sustain them, they will not simply fade away into the nothingness of chaos.

For today's theologian, the idea that Thomas gives the figure of Jesus Christ such a central place in his theology may not be immediately apparent.¹ In fact, theologians have not infrequently criticized Aquinas for not giving *enough* attention to Christ, with some contending that he developed a doctrine of God's trinitarian perfection in a way that was unduly disconnected from sustained attentiveness to the self-disclosure of God in Christ. Modern theologians (largely under the influence of Karl Barth) have given much greater prominence to Jesus, both formally and materially. In contrast to such avowedly Christ-centred theologies, Aquinas's decision to structure the *Summa Theologiae* in accordance with a God-centred focus has seemed to relegate his account of Christ's life and work – his Christology – to the end of his work, not (it must be acknowledged) as an appendix but without granting it any decisive role in shaping the overall shape of his theology. Thomas's Christology, in other words, is not a structurally determinative locus in its own right. By the time we get there, the major theological decisions have long since been made.

There are some signs that contemporary theologians are rediscovering the value of a God-centred theology. The Barth-influenced Katherine Sonderegger has adopted the refrain that 'not all is Christology.'² Either way, there are some indications that Aquinas was uncomfortable with the deferral of Christology to the final volume of the *Summa Theologiae*. As we have seen, over the course of his lifetime Thomas experimented with a number of thematic configurations of his theological writings; the order of presentation in the *Summa* is determined by best *pedagogical* practice, rather than by the relative primacy of various theological principles. Far from indicating an intentional displacement of Christology, Thomas's decision to locate Christology in the concluding part of his *Summa* corresponds to God's pedagogical preparation of Israel for the coming of the messiah. Just as God gradually prepared Israel for the fullness of God's self-revelation in Christ, so Aquinas gradually prepares the student to receive the highest truth of the Christian religion, and to experience the resolution it brings to the tensions inherent within theological reflection.

We might, then, read Aquinas's discussion of the timing of the incarnation as an *apologia* for the deferral of his Christology. Should Christ not have come earlier in the history of humanity, or perhaps even have been the very last word of human history? The timing of the incarnation was supremely fitting, Thomas says, because it was necessary for humanity to recognize and experience our need of redemption and for us to be left with time to encounter its effects and have its consequences unfold in our lives. Like the incarnation itself, once Christology has been explicitly introduced, its implicit (but no less determinative) presence can be seen in everything that has gone before.

In both directions – from those who seek a greater prominence for Christ, and those who seek a more inclusive or pluralistic approach – the dispute touches upon what has been called the 'scandal of particularity': for the pluralist, there is too much endorsement of particularity; for the Barthian, the unique particularity of Christ is inadequately registered in the overall texture of Thomas's theology. In fact, these critiques register the poles of a fundamental tension that Thomas's Christology actively maintains. On the one hand, Thomas is unequivocally (and unapologetically) committed to the uniqueness of Christ and its salvific necessity. On the other hand, Thomas does not posit this particularity as being a competitive force that excludes and annuls all other sources of truth, overriding the diverse philosophical insights of human culture. The truth of Christ is not an 'inclusive truth' in the sense of being a truth among others that leaves other truths standing alongside it as alternative routes to enlightenment. Rather, it is an inclusive truth in the sense of being a receptive truth, drawing all the world's truths into itself and purifying them so as to enable them to be more intensely the truths that they were partially. As Thomas put it in a more poetic moment, 'truth himself speaks truly, or there's nothing true.'[3]

GRACE

This non-violence is crystallized in the most famous of Thomas's theological axioms: 'grace perfects nature and does not destroy it.'[4] Theological textbooks generally define grace along the lines of 'unmerited divine favour'. Since all attention from God is unmerited (nothing that we can do can attract the infinite perfection of God in our direction), this almost invariably ends up collapsing the definition of grace into a contrast with nature.[5] Whereas there are some things that God gives us to possess in accordance with the kind of beings that God makes us (the gratuity of creation), there are other gifts (like salvation) that are even more gratuitous in that they take us beyond anything we might have anticipated our nature receiving. While this is a reasonable enough working definition, the risk is that it trains us to think we are dealing with two distinct categories of 'thing', one natural and the other supernatural. In the reality of the Christian life, no such parcelling up makes sense.

Indeed, Aquinas has a far more vibrant, holistic and dynamic understanding of grace. To reduce his lengthy and intricate treatise on grace to a single sentence, grace is the name given to the 'newness' introduced into a believer's life by Christ. Grace, then, is the difference made by Jesus; grace is to the individual's life story what the incarnation is to world history. To put things the other way around, grace is the non-identical repetition of the incarnation in the life of the individual believer. It is not only the experience of something new, but an utterly new experience, one that reorientates and recalibrates our whole existence. The utterly new experience of grace leads to an utterly new and renewed encounter with the oldest realities with which we are familiar.

Taken as a non-identical repetition of the incarnation, it becomes clear that Thomas does not say what many have been taught he does: that grace 'builds upon' nature. While it is true that grace presupposes nature, grace does not 'sit on top' of nature like the icing on the top of a cake, but rather percolates through to the depths of our being, regenerating and healing it without doing it violence or violating its essential structure. After all, grace is the grace of the creator, whose world stands open to divine communication. Grace and nature exist in a kind of metaphysical marriage. They are only truly comprehensible together, they are bound together by divine will, and yet they retain their own particular character and distinctness.

The various categories and scholastic distinctions Aquinas uses to qualify and specify the operation of grace risk distracting us from the fact that grace *is* itself an operation. The difference grace makes is not simply the introduction of a new reality (as a kind of new creation) but the bestowal of a new mode of existence, a new and supernaturally charged way of being alive. As Philip McCosker has suggested, grace is more like a divine adverb that qualifies the human verb than it is an adjective giving content to the kinds of effects produced by God within creation. Grace actually makes us graceful (or, to be more precise, it empowers us to exist gracefully, to be little instrumental causes of en-gracement within the world).

The quality of life grace bestows upon us is that of living a fully human life in a divine manner. Without changing the nature of the human verb, it is empowered to operate on a divine level, to exist within and towards those ends that are buried within God's own life. This matters, because it shows the human-sparing character of God's dealing with the world. Thomas is concerned to emphasize that there is nothing authentically human that is overridden, annulled or removed by divine grace. Indeed, the human is only enhanced by the removal of all that holds it back from the realization of authentic humanity (namely the de-humanizing character of sin and its effects, including death).

If God is a respecter of full human integrity, then God's work of redemption provides a paradigm for the judgement of all religious activity and theological truth claims. Any religious devotion that does not safeguard the human – which demands that some portion of human nature or experience be eliminated and denied – does not correspond to God's dealings with humanity and can be discarded as a pseudo-religious aberration (or else purified of its violence through an encounter with the gospel). The question, of course, upon which the paradigm hinges is that of the nature of 'authenticity'. In what does full, authentic humanity consist? At this point the paradoxical circle is closed by Christ. All philosophical speculation about human nature is consummated in Christ, who is the personal revelation of what it means to be human, of a life lived fully alive.

AT HOME IN GOD

Among the graces bestowed upon humanity, Thomas reserves a special place for the theological virtues of faith, hope and charity. If the cardinal virtues are (as I suggested in the last chapter) the means by which we belong to the human cultural-linguistic community, the theological virtues are those God-given dispositions by which we belong to the divine community. The theological virtues are called *theological* because they utterly index a human life to the divine. They are produced within us not by repeated habituation, but directly by God. They orientate us to God who is the ultimate object upon which they converge, and the means by which their acts are accomplished.

Even more than this, God is in a certain sense also the 'context' (the 'culture') within which the theological virtues belong. The life of the theological virtues is lived not only *towards* God as an external object, but *into* God as into a new place of belonging. In other words, the acts of the theological virtues draw our human faculties into the communion of divine persons that is the Godhead. Despite this rather lofty and transcendent character, the theological virtues are also deeply rooted within the material realities of our world and religious lives. The theological virtues do not move us to overlook the struggles of life by appeal to an external future life in which all sorrows and the difficulties of this world are dissolved and forgotten. This would be an instance of the sort of dehumanizing violence that Thomas trenchantly opposes.

As authentic *virtues*, faith, hope and charity cannot be an anaesthetic but rather the opposite, an anti-anaesthetic, enhancers of our perception that strengthen and refine our focus, so that we see more and not less than we do by our natural capacities. We see here another hallmark of Thomas's understanding of authentic religiosity: if a religious practice makes us less attuned to human realities, we are dealing with a false religion, an idolatry that it is theology's task to expunge. Nonetheless, the theological virtues do situate the struggles (and the joys) of life within a broader context: their place within the great drama of God's dealings with humanity.

It may be that only this horizon, opened up by the theological virtues, can help us to resolve some of the most intractable conflicts of our times. Thomas's account of the miracle of divine re-contextualization that takes place in faith, hope and charity in fact focuses on rather more mundane matters, the types of practice a less attuned scholar would be liable to overlook as intellectually irrelevant or embarrassingly vulgar, even superstitious. The theological virtues (together with the natural virtue of religion) express themselves in the myriad of ways by which the Christian makes ultimate sense of their surroundings, the ways in which they carve meaning out of context: crossing oneself, rubbing a holy picture, going to Mass, reading the Bible, asking St Anthony to find the car keys and writing a systematic theology. All of these ordinary human activities now have an infinite significance as they bear upon eternity. The life of the theological virtues is the life of saints who were variously martyrs and mothers, but who found their own way to non-identically repeat the incarnation in their lives, 'enfleshing' the Word in the loving and suffering, the doings and the un-doings, of their lives.

It is by faith that a Christian recognizes the sacraments as divine assistance for our journey, and can apprehend the true horror of sin and injustice as it offends the God of infinite love. It is by hope that we are empowered to face and tackle the most overwhelming (and the most mundane) challenges of the hour. And it is by charity that we are able to do with God's help (and for God's sake) that which we would never do for money or calculated human reward. These virtues, taken together, orientate us to the provisionality of the world, without minimizing the real significance and seriousness of the contingent. They are the tools of a pilgrim, a spiritual wayfarer, equipped by God for the journey into God.

THE TOOLS OF THE PILGRIM

The gifts of faith and hope have a particular orientation to the provisionality of life. The condition that makes faith and hope possible is that of incomplete or absent fulfilment: their very presence indicates circumstances of frustration. Faith compensates for the frustration of the intellectual desire for the knowledge of ultimate truth, while hope sustains our desire for ultimate fulfilment, for the absolute Good. This can be seen most clearly in the case of hope, since it is, by definition, a movement towards a future that has not yet been achieved. When it comes to ultimate, theological hope (and Aquinas thinks that this is the only authentically *virtuous* form of hope there is), it moves us towards a state of ultimate fulfilment beyond our human capacities to achieve for ourselves. The fulfilment of hope could, by definition, never be liable to future dispossession or diminution. Hope will ultimately be fulfilled when both the necessity and the possibility of its acts have passed away.

Likewise, faith negotiates the absence and invisibility of God on the intellectual plane. Something that is seen directly is known not by faith but by vision. There is no merit to be found in believing something that is utterly manifest or self-evident. On the other hand, there is skill (and virtue) in deciding who or what to believe in circumstances where, by necessity, we depend upon witnesses, unreliable (and sometimes conflicting) as they are. This, indeed, is the work of juries and judges, but also of scientists who can reach certain realities only through phenomena that witness to their presence. Part of the prudential wisdom of the judge and the scientist involves a tacit assessment of the credibility of witnesses, especially when their indications appear to be outlandish, surprising or conflict with other witnesses. Judging who or what to believe (and the extent and intensity with which they are to be believed) is an important human skill. One of the challenges of reaching human maturity is allowing the naïve idealism of youth to mature into a prudential realism, without collapsing into the easy comfort of pessimistic cynicism.

When it comes to the theological virtue of faith, the situation is quite different. Theological faith is not a question of calculated plausibility or a managed uncertainty. Theological faith is, in fact, certain: it depends upon the 'witness' of God – the one who can neither deceive nor be deceived – to Godself. Consequently, theological faith retains its meritorious character without yielding any of its certitude. The essential characteristic of faith, then, is the identity of the witness and the object witnessed to. God 'testifies' to us about Godself. The technical terminology here distinguishes between the material object (the thing which is known) and the formal object (that by which it is known). Both the formal and the material object of faith are God, albeit under distinct aspects. The material object of faith is God as God is in Godself (rather than simply the effects of God); the formal object of faith is God as the first truth revealing God's inner life to the world. As a result, the act of faith is motivated not by the intrinsic believability of the contents of the faith, but on the unique sovereign authority of God. Consequently, while faith remains a free and meritorious act, it is also obligatory. To deny that which God teaches about Godself is, for Thomas, an act of culpable disobedience, an implicit refusal of divine authority – daring to think we could teach God something about Godself.

The obligatory character of faith and the stark moral framework it produces is, for Thomas, somewhat less important than the conditions that give rise to it. The important point is that faith is a relationship, a communication between persons, divine and human: to 'have' faith is in fact to be taught directly by God, and to refuse – or deny – the faith is to distort or terminate that relationship. This is not a matter of getting our facts about God right. To model theological faith as just a particularly certain species of belief, as if the unique reliability of the divine self-witness alone determined theological faith's uniqueness, would be to entirely mischaracterize Thomas's understanding of the extraordinary character of faith properly so called, which is enveloped on every side by the creative love of God. As grace, the theological virtue of faith is both an experience of the new and a radically new experience. Faith makes our minds capable of a new kind of intellectual experience: to know God by God.

CONSENTING TO GOD

To say that God is the formal object of faith gives the ordinary life of believers a deeply mystical character. The theological virtue joins the human mind to God, so that we acquire a very limited share in God's own self-knowledge. The simplest act of faith has an expansive value and significance that even the most intense mystical visions or extraordinary experiences of God could never acquire. Three important consequences follow from this. First, faith is not only knowledge *about* God, it is knowledge *within* God. Faith is fundamentally an intimate affair, the adherence of our mind to the ultimate truth. Secondly, although by faith we accept certain truths about God, faith is principally orientated to the *reality* of God rather than to any facts about God.[6] Without diminishing the importance of propositional knowledge, faith is always more than that. Thirdly, faith is not the precondition for a relationship with God, but is itself relational. It is not the case that we must first have some abstract knowledge of divinity and later taste experientially the goodness that we first knew about. The person of faith does not talk about God as if God were absent. Rather, God is known only as we give ourselves over to an intellectual relationship – initiated not by us, but by God – that is consummated in love.

Faith is unique among the theological virtues in that it perfects the intellect (rather than the will). Nonetheless, its operations are far from the cool detachment of disinterested rationalism. Faith is a fully personal act, one in which the desires of the will are always already entangled. As the work of Judith Barad has shown,[7] faith involves for Aquinas both assent to a set of facts and the freely given consent to the presence of God. There is, here, in microcosm an instance of a paradox that characterizes all of the theological virtues. To assent is to find oneself in agreement with something or someone else. The emphasis here is on alterity – otherness – since assent can only be given to something that has a certain distance from us. That to which we assent must, in other words, confront us and stand over-and-against us, at least to some degree. On the other hand, consent means feeling-with and involves a sensing-along-with another. Consent, therefore, emphasizes proximity to – even connection with – the other to which we give our consent. While assent moves our minds outwards towards the things we know, consent operates in the opposing direction by inviting those things into communion with ourselves.[8]

Thomas acknowledges that the words 'consent' and 'assent' have often been used interchangeably, but the dynamics they represent are important aspects of faith, corresponding to the objective reality of God's presence in-and-beyond the world, and the subjective reality of the theological virtues as tools for negotiating the presence within the here-and-now of the world of the future reality of God's Kingdom. This, indeed, is a common feature of all the theological virtues. While they are intrinsically future-orientated, propelling us into God as our future consummation, they are nonetheless embedded within the present, forming us into a pilgrim community in the here-and-now.

TRUST AND AUTHORITY

Although theological faith has a unique character and purpose, Aquinas recognizes the extent to which human culture and the common welfare of society depend upon the ordinary and everyday 'faith' by which we believe things based upon the testimony of others. We simply cannot be an authority on everything, and while modern media has undoubtedly extended the possibility for eyewitness testimony, advancements in technology have ushered in the possibility of 'deep-fake' and manipulative editorial framing. We are more aware than ever of the extent to which our experience of the world is mediated by algorithms, and of the power of gaslighting to lead us to call into question even those things of which we do have first-hand knowledge and experience. With new forms of deception, the importance of interrogating our reliance upon mediation is only intensified.

This is not to say that we should aspire to eliminate trust from our intellectual biographies. This would be both a Promethean desire to usurp the unique intellectual standpoint of God and dehumanizing; it would also be impossible. We cannot think through every situation from the ground up. We are, whether consciously or not, constantly investing 'faith' in the authority and benevolence of others: who is to say the capsule contains antibiotics and not a toxin? Who is to say the vaccine is safe and adequately tested? Who can confirm the reality of the climate emergency beyond all doubt? There are obvious cases when – absent any other indicators or intuitions – even the attempt at verification would be indicative of pathological anxiety. The question is not *whether* we should trust (that much is inevitable), but to make friends with our dependence on trust by interrogating *who* we trust and *how* we entrust ourselves to them. Thomas's theology matters because it faces up to that question and offers a characteristically non-violent solution.

Authority is not the dirty word for Thomas it is for many of our contemporaries. This does not mean that Aquinas embraces or endorses an uncritical reverence for authority. Quite the opposite: Thomas regards appeal to authority as the weakest (but still necessary) form of argument, except in the case of theology (where divine authority is taken to be uniquely infallible). Here we see another instance of the non-violent character of Thomas's thought. The acceptance of something on *good* authority is not an abrogation of our rational faculties. On the contrary, authentic authority always operates to enable further thought and enhances our insights. Even when an authority operates to foreclose a possibility or definitively reject an error (as it must sometimes do), it does not leave us only with the task of faithfully repeating what has already been said. The acceptance of an authentic authority will leave our intellectual horizons wider and more expansive, the avenues of forward movement more numerous and exciting. This stands as another litmus test for the quality of any theology: does it foster or subdue thought?

FAITH'S SCIENCE

Locating the account of the role of trust in human culture within a discussion of some of the most explicitly theological elements of Thomas's thought might appear strange. In fact, understanding the role that trust plays in forming the community of the human sciences (the amassed learning of human civilization) is crucial to understanding how Thomas understands the non-violent and non-hegemonic, but utterly vital and formative, role theology plays within the community of human inquiry. Aquinas's starting point is the *Posterior Analytics* of Aristotle, with its account of the sciences as differentiated by the distinct sectors of reality into which they inquire, which determines the distinctive methods and concepts that are appropriate to that domain. The fresh reception of Aristotle posed a number of significant challenges to theology. First, if theology was to remain an intellectually credible discipline within an Aristotelian universe, it was no longer sufficient for it to be regarded as a 'wisdom' (as it had been for Augustine). Rather, it would have to be conceived as a science (that is, shown to produce certain knowledge, derived – ultimately – from self-evident first principles).

This 'pinched' theological self-understanding in two directions. First, theologians cannot point to one discrete area of inquiry as their unique domain of competence. Theologians study *everything* and *no-thing*: in the first place God in God's own life of infinite perfection (which is no thing); derivatively, all other things as they relate to God as creator and consummator. Secondly, theology was understood to be the sovereign discipline – the Queen of the Sciences – and not merely as a titular honorific but as the architectonic science that had authority to provide shape and structure to the whole body of sciences. The *Posterior Analytics* seemed to usurp theology's role by bequeathing an independent self-determination to the distinct sciences.

The possibility of a clash between the sciences offended Thomas's intuition for non-violence, but the brute assertion of the sapiential primacy of theology was no less hegemonic, and risked denying the fairly obvious ways in which experimental method had an intellectual power of its own. Indeed, the Aristotelian problematic was, for Aquinas, not really about the dignity and legitimacy of theology (Thomas was not one to concern himself with such trivia). Rather, the stakes are much higher: the unity of the sciences is an intellectual correspondence to the unity of the world that speaks coherently (and not conflictually) because it is the world that is spoken into being by God in God's eternal Word. The point, it seems to me, is that the sciences are not united by anything as tenuous as academic method, but by the very structure of the world they investigate. In fact, although he does not quite put it in such polemical terms, Thomas is fighting for the very essence of science and the possibility of human learning. If the world were a conflictual place – if the university faculties must fight for their rightful place within the academy – then it would be possessed of a fundamental unpredictability that would render intellectual inquiry futile.

It is at this point that 'trust' becomes a vital element in knowledge, corresponding to the communicative 'givenness' that holds the world together as a coherent whole. To see how this operates, it is necessary to return to Aristotle (and to the *Posterior Analytics*) once again. While some sciences start their work on self-evident principles (either logical truisms or direct sensory experience), there are other ('higher') sciences that get started with the conclusions of other sciences. These sciences are characterized by a basic receptivity: they cannot provide their own starting point, but necessarily receive their foundational principles from others. The standard example given by Thomists is the relationship of optics to geometry. Optics receives the principles it needs from geometry and uses them – relies upon them – to do something distinctive and new.

In some respects, the geometry-optics example is an excellent one. The foundational principles include not just packets of information or theoretical conclusions, but also skills and practices (like the competent use of measurements). Less clear in the example, however, is the real distinction of the two sciences, since both are plausibly performed at different times by the same person. The point is that optics – insofar as it is optics – is not self-starting; it cannot provide its own starting point. The individual optician may very well be able to do so, but only by becoming (temporarily) a practitioner of geometry. With the growth of complexity and intense specialization of academic life – and the ever-greater degrees of granularity the sub-disciplines of empirical science produce – it is easy for us to imagine scenarios in which the same person cannot perform the necessary functions of the two neighbouring sciences. In such cases one can only make a provisional assessment of the received principles, based on their plausibility in the light of the consensus of the scholarly community and the way in which those principles 'work' when applied in the higher science. At this point the element of trustful accreditation of that which is received, based upon the authority of another science and its practitioners, can be seen more clearly. The name Thomists give to this relationship of reception is (rather unfortunately) 'subalternation'.[9]

Thomas salvages the scientific character of theology by demonstrating that it too is a receptive, subalternated, science, receiving its first principles from the 'science' of God's own mind. Like other sciences, theology only exists within a relationship of trust and dependence. Unlike the other sciences, its first principles are known by God's self-revelation, received in faith. Built into theological science, then, is this anti-hegemonic principle, a necessary intellectual humility that recognizes its own internal incapacity. A similar degree of humility is found in Thomas's account of theology's relationship to the other sciences. These sciences are not subalternated to theology: physicists and chemists do not ultimately receive their first principles from theologians. Consequently, theology cannot claim a right to interfere with the work of the empirical sciences, nor can it directly determine the questions they are to pursue. Nonetheless, theology *does* have an architectonic service to render to the academy. This relationship Thomas sees not as subalternation but 'subordination' (another unfortunate choice of words). Subordination is the surveying of another science's domain from a higher vantage point to provide a more comprehensive perspective (in theology's case, the *highest* vantage point of the first and creative cause).

The Thomistic understanding of theology has enormous significance for contemporary theologians seeking a non-hegemonic account of a robustly and unapologetically theological theology. Thomas yields nothing of theology's intellectual rigour, while intensely opposing a pure rationalism. Importantly, the *apologia* for scientific theology Thomas develops should not be ported into arguments simply defending theology's intellectual credibility. Rather, theology's status within the academy is the rendering of a particular and vital service to the disciplines. Where theology's status is threatened, it is often because theologians have failed to render this service to their colleagues, or have rendered it with an uncritical lack of humility. Theology's capacity to unmask, expose and interrogate the dynamic relations of trust that form the complex web of the sciences has the potential to make a contribution to the academy that is desperately needed.

The kind of 'trust' that theology has the power to unmask is not only (or necessarily) a psychological phenomenon; it also refers to a metaphysical reality upon which life depends. It indicates the ways in which we take ourselves to be making intellectual contact with reality, entrusting ourselves to modes of intellectual belonging within a world that discloses itself to us in basically reliable and trustworthy ways. As Thomas tried to indicate in the Five Ways this kind of entrustment to a world that speaks coherently is ultimately dependent upon the first stirrings of faith, the tacit intuition of the horizon that binds the world together. The ultimate basis for this trust is given and communicated to us in the person of Jesus Christ.

LEANING INTO GOD

Faith turns out, then, to have a hidden correspondence with the world-character of reality. A similar correspondence to the inner structure of reality can be found in the case of the theological virtue of hope. Hope is to the will and the concupiscible powers what faith is to the intellect, perfecting and raising it beyond its natural powers. By hope, we 'lean into' God, and depend upon God's unique divine goodness. Like faith, hope's object is – both materially and formally – God. Hope, in other words, leans into a future in which we live nothing less than the life of God.

Strictly speaking, we do not hope for the resolution of our present sorrows and difficulties (at least not directly). This is implied in what we *do* hope for: the possession of God and the enjoyment of God's bliss.[10] Hope as a 'lean' into that future is orientated towards its own destruction in a time when the leaning character of hope will be replaced with the stability of being an utterly and immovably rooted citizen of heaven. Although anticipatory, the lean of hope is not one of precarious instability, as if we are slightly off balance, precipitously leaning over the edge of a great abyss. Equally, hope does not demand a wager on an uncertain future (just as faith is not a gamble on the outcome of the available facts).[11] Rather, precisely because it is a lean into God, it is a weight-bearing lean, one that brings certainty and surety (much like the divinely guaranteed certitude of faith). The lean of hope is corrective, in that it brings about the rebalancing of the human person in a world that has become a hostile and unpredictable environment on account of sin. Hope's lean has a compensatory force that helps us to retain balance as we are battered by stormy seas. Like faith, however, hope is not an anaesthetic – nor can it provide *false* comfort. The Godwards lean of hope places us full square in the force of the world's storms, even if its certainty guarantees that the storm will never actually overcome us. Paradoxically, the assurance of hope equips us to feel more fully the brunt of the storm.

Hope has received a surprisingly negative assessment from many philosophers and theologians, especially in the years since 9/11.[12] For some, the exhortation to hope seems incalculably brutal as a response to the seemingly endless cycles of violence and misery that perpetually engulf the world. All too often, hope has been an additional spiritual burden imposed upon the poor and the destitute by the very structures that oppress them. Hope is easily invoked to appeal to a heavenly 'making right' so as to displace onto God our human obligations to work for a more just society. Indeed, the analogy of a future-orientated Godward lean captures only one dimension of Thomas's account of hope. Hope, for Thomas, is fundamentally movement. It is both gift and discipline, in that it involves a systematic refusal to give up moving towards the hoped-for future. Hope is not simply an affirmation of a good that lies ahead, but also an active refusal – a negation – of the forces of disorder that swirl around us.

This can be seen in Thomas's analysis of the two principal vices against the theological virtue of hope: despair and presumption.[13] Both of these are, in different ways, refusals to move. Despair gives up on the journey because of its intrinsic difficulty. Presumption demands that the new world come to meet us without any investment or change on our part. Many of the forms of pseudo-hope that contemporary critics are concerned to reject are either what Thomas would term presumption or – at best – an audacious form of belief in the power of progress: nowhere near anything that Thomas would find worthy of the status of a theological virtue. Indeed, precisely as a theological virtue, hope refuses any form of premature foreclosure; it will not cease from movement until it reaches the ultimate and definitive realization of justice and peace. God alone can know what hope will look like in the period between now and that final consummation, but certainly it will involve resistance, struggle and, above all, prayer.

Hope plays an indispensable role in human flourishing, not only in its orientation to a theological consummation, or in its capacity as a constellating principle of our loftiest social endeavours. Hope – as a conjunction of Godward lean and insistent refusal of false utopias – is also a virtue of homebuilding,[14] a way in which we make ourselves at home (at least provisionally) in a world of rapid and bewildering social change. Hope is one of the ways in which we make sense of our innate feelings of homelessness and dislocation, in which we make peace with our congenital restlessness as an asset rather than a liability.

Hope enables us to indwell life as a *movement*; it gives us some sense of what move to make next in the dance of becoming.

It is here that, despite its radical and gracious novelty, hope – like faith – corresponds in an unexpected way to the basic structure of reality. As we have seen, reality itself is a movement proceeding from God in creation and returning to God in redemption. The theological virtue of hope equips the believer to live within this flow of reality, to thrive in the resonant frequency of that creaturely tension between creation and redemption.

DIVINE FRIENDSHIP

Thomas's account of charity is one of the most distinctive and innovative elements of his theological synthesis.[15] Space does not allow more than a mere glance at the surface of these deep waters. The core of the theological virtue of charity is the utterly astonishing idea that we become friends with God. The astonishment resides not in the fact that God is utterly – indeed, infinitely – lovable, but in the possibility that that love could take the form of a *friendship*.[16] After all, friendship presupposes a certain minimal level of equality between the friends, and a particular community of life, a sharing in concerns and realities. These conditions are beyond our capacity to generate for ourselves, but are established on our behalf by God in the incarnation. By dwelling among us as a human being, coequal in humanity with all other human beings, God places Godself *into* the human community, creating the possibility of that divine-human friendship by establishing the perfection of such a friendship in the person of Christ. Importantly, God does not create the abstract possibility of divine-human friendship. This friendship becomes a possibility only as it is made actual – and perfected – in the life of Christ. Friendship with God is, therefore, always a sharing in the mysteries of Jesus's life and thereby enjoying a participation – by the power of the Holy Spirit – in the unique relationship of the eternal Father and eternal Son.

Perhaps even more clearly than either faith or hope, charity concerns a radical – and distinctively Christian – novelty. Nonetheless, there is a decided complexity to Thomas's thought on this point. Aquinas does not take the rather obvious strategy of identifying charity with the indwelling of the Holy Spirit (as had become customary in medieval theology).¹⁷ Rather, for all of its utterly unique character, charity does not entirely introduce the possibility of a preferential love of God. There is, it seems to Thomas, something quite natural – and certainly rational – about loving God above all other things. It is this natural love that is elevated in charity and given the new dignity of friendship in Christ. In finding some natural analogue even for the theological virtue of charity, we again catch a glimpse of Thomas's fundamentally non-violent religious instincts. Even the most astonishingly new elements of the Christian religion are found to correspond with created actuality, to be both humane and humanizing.

Charity discloses to us the extraordinary reality of our natural capacity for love. In the case of hope, there was a perfection of the concupiscible elements of our desires, of our tendency to love things insofar as they are valuable to ourselves or essential to our flourishing. Charity elevates our desire of benevolence, the things and people we love for the good of the other (as in friendship). In other words, by charity we love God not on account of what God could do or has done for us, but rather we love God for God's sake. The love friendship requires (or, perhaps, creates) is a certain community of desire: to love a friend is also to love what they love, and to desire for themselves the good that they desire for themselves. Consequently, charity involves an alignment of our will with the divine will. Charity is not only the love of God, but also the love of all that is lovable for God's sake. The theological virtue of charity is, therefore, central to the fulfilment of the dual-aspect 'golden commandment' that lies at the heart of Christianity: to love God and to love one's neighbour. The theological virtue of charity loves God and neighbour with one and the self-same love.

Given the essential role that charity and friendship play within the human community, the twofold character of charity is important for two reasons. First, it reminds us that the relevant kind of 'love' is not a matter of cultivating warm feeling or vague positive sentiments towards an abstract other. There is an objectivity to the love of charity, which depends upon the willing of that which is objectively good for the other, despite the sometimes frustrating (and, frankly, unlovable) ways in which the other might confront us. Secondly, this account of charity shows the immense importance the love of ultimate values (for Thomas, God) plays in constellating our charitable and benevolent attention to others. Without such firm and objective grounding in respect for the absolute, the particular instances of charity risk becoming disconnected, vulnerable to the emotional whims of individuals and the ephemeral moods of the community. The love of charity ensures that we do not appoint ourselves as the arbiters between the worthy and unworthy poor.

EVER MOVING REPOSE

As is already evident, the friendship of charity is not a relationship that is within our power to create, nor is it simply natural to our created natures. It exists in us as an echo of what was established in Christ; it is a response to the friendship God extends to us in the person of the redeemer. In Thomas's account, Christ has no need of the theological virtues of faith and hope, as he is always in possession of divine beatitude, even as he willed to enter into the state of the wayfarer. Nonetheless, faith and hope are also made possible by the divine Word's assumption of a human nature. It is Christ who is personally the self-revelation of God, to which faith responds. Although God has spoken historically through prophets and patriarchs, in Christ alone we encounter the one who speaks with God's own authority, in whom messenger and message are united in perfect identity. In other words, Jesus does not bring a message of redemption; he himself *is* our redemption. It is in Jesus, then, that the chain of trust that defers authority from one person to another comes to an end. As the entrustment of God to humanity, Jesus is self-referentially trustworthy in an absolute way, the only human life that can depend upon its own divine authority. In this way, Jesus in his personal identity is the objective point of dependence that makes faith's certitude possible, and (as the Word through whom all things were made) secures the whole of reality's web of trust.

Central to Thomas's Christology (and indeed to his personal 'spirituality', insofar as it is possible to reconstruct it) is the 'cyclical' movement of Christ out from the Godhead in incarnation and back to the Father (now with his assumed human nature) in the resurrection and ascension. Indeed, Thomas establishes an intimate link between the movement of incarnation (together with the sending of the Holy Spirit into the world) and the most intimate eternal 'movement' of God's own life, the twofold procession of Father and Son. The 'sendings' of Son and Spirit into the world, and the internal processions of the third and second persons of the trinity, are, in fact, not to be conceived as distinct movements. The sendings (or the 'missions', to use Thomas's terminology) are simply the processions with the addition of created effects.[18] When we see Christ's human nature, then, we glimpse the created effect that is intimately united with the very movement that makes up the intimacy of God's own inner life. Christ is, therefore, not only the forerunner, cutting the pathway of ascent to God that those who are baptized into his life will follow. Even more than this, Christ is himself the very movement into which the theological virtue of hope leans. By the work of the theological virtues within us, we are caught up with Christ into the slipstream of the triune God.

SOVEREIGN GRATUITY

At the heart of Thomas's understanding of Jesus's identity is the utter gratuity of God. It is this gratuity that forms the core of Aquinas's non-violent account of religion. Before even considering the nature of the incarnation (though of course presupposing an awareness of it in faith), Thomas considers its radical non-necessity. The incarnation is not, for Thomas, an inevitability, either as the finishing-up of creation or as the necessary means for fixing a world that has gone off the rails.[19] The point here is not to abstract from the reality of what God has done, but rather to emphasize that God's power is such that it can in no way be enclosed within the logic of a cause-and-effect necessity.

That Thomas holds the incarnation to be possessed of a unique kind of gratuity does not mean that he takes it to be arbitrary.[20] Thomas is at pains to demonstrate the supreme beauty and fittingness of the incarnation within the divine plan of creation and redemption. Above all, the incarnation is a work of sovereign wisdom and intelligence. Although not logically determined or demanded by anything other than God's own freedom, Thomas acknowledges a certain, very loose, sense in which we might say that the incarnation has a kind of 'necessity'. The village of Cuddesdon is delightful but miles from the nearest post office and supermarket; bus services are limited. Somebody living here might very well say that they 'need' a car. Of course, in an absolute sense, they do not. There are other modes of transport available and even if the options were drastically limited, survival is still perfectly possible. The point of claiming the necessity of the car is to indicate the radical and virtually life-changing difference it would make. It transforms a way of existing into a much more viable mode of living. It makes it vastly easier to achieve the ends of our flourishing. It is this kind of necessity that might worthily be said of the incarnation: given the ends that God freely wills to achieve, the incarnation is not only the most expedient means of bringing this about, but also a life-changing, horizon-opening 'means' that makes the world teem with possibility. The incarnation is 'necessary' in that it makes a new way of living possible.

Thomas's account of the incarnation's supreme fittingness further exemplifies the non-violent character of God's dealings with the world. In the first place, the incarnation does no violence to God's own identity but corresponds to the freedom of God's love. As love has an innate tendency to spread itself around ('the good is self-diffusive'), so God giving Godself over to humanity in the incarnation 'fits' with the supreme perfection of divine love. Likewise, Thomas stresses that there is no violence against the dignity of God perpetrated by God's entry into materiality.[21] Here Thomas is addressing the concerns of Manichaeism, with its denigration of materiality in general and bodiliness in particular, against which the first generation of his Dominican confreres laboured. Thomas next turns to deny the common objection of Islamic philosophers and theologians that an incarnation imperils the surpassing transcendence of God by embroiling God in the murky affairs of the world. Thomas's responses are unsurprisingly non-violent, but surprising in that his avoidance of violence pushes in two directions. On the one hand, Thomas argues that God's assumption of human nature in no way 'contaminates' the dignity and perfection of the Godhead: the incarnation does not, in other words, pull God down to our level, but raises us to the divine level. On the other hand, Thomas can – with the help of a full-blooded account of the incarnation – push back against two embedded presuppositions: the uncritical association of finitude with degradation and corruption, and the intuition that God is not *already* involved in the affairs of the world. As Thomas repeatedly emphasizes, God's transcendence is non-competitive and non-contrastive. God and the world are so utterly distinct – and yet so intimately related – that their unification in the person of Christ could never pit one against the other. The fact of the union, far from compromising the distinction, *requires* the distinction be maintained. Indeed, it is not the divine incarnation that seeks to undo the division between God and the world, or eliminate or undo the world-character of reality. On the contrary, this is the futile aim of sin and evil, against which God acts decisively and definitively in the incarnation.

THE END OF VIOLENCE

At this point, it might seem that there is a paradox. The incarnation does no violence, except a violence against violence itself. This is, in fact, almost the opposite of what Thomas teaches. For Aquinas, violence is not to be afforded the dignity of being a reality. Violence and peace are not the same sorts of things, two competing states of affairs or clashing forces. This is not a naivety. Living at a time of acute violence and civil hostility, Thomas knows very well the dangers of violence and the painful depths of sin's consequences. Rather it is to say that violence is the devastating absence of a perfection that should be in its place. Violence cannot be removed by subtraction, because violence is a 'hole' or a 'tear' in the fabric of reality. God's action in redemption is better modelled as a healing or a restoration than as a violent conquest that subdues all the forces of violence that have invaded the world. If the incarnation is to be seen as any kind of violence, then it can only be as a negation of negation: an utterly positive affirmation, the ultimate divine 'yes' to creation, merely incidentally negative in that the infinite 'yes' whose fullness drives out emptiness.

All of this, together with the natural resonances of the incarnation, might appear to sit in a certain degree of tension with one of Thomas's most famous (and contentious) Christological claims: that it was the fall of Adam (rather than the order of creation) that motivated – Thomas rather daringly uses the term 'merited' – the incarnation. In fact, as we will see, the claim ought to be restated in far less contentious terms, as an emphatic – and rather simpler – assertion that the incarnation is redemptive.

Today, the idea of original sin might appear to be the mythological vestige of an older and less enlightened form of Christianity. The complexities and nuances of the traditional doctrine are easily reduced to a crude caricature, and some considerable scholarly attention has been invested in demonstrating (not unconvincingly) that the full texture of the doctrine can be reconciled with the deliverances of contemporary natural science.[22] Nonetheless, evolutionary science has called into question the plausibility of a literal 'first sin' along with the singularity of the first parents Adam and Eve (not, of course, that theologians have ever been unduly inclined to take Genesis 1 literally). Likewise, the idea that innocent babies are infected with an inherited moral disease transmitted across the generations by sexual reproduction offends some of our most basic instincts. Even as these depictions of the classical doctrine can be acknowledged to be reductive caricatures, the force of the criticism continues to bite.

Paradoxically, the era in which original sin has been widely rejected has simultaneously been more aware than ever of intergenerational trauma and the ways in which our moral lives are shaped and determined by the sinful structures of the world into which we are born and from which we can never fully extricate ourselves. It is easy to accept the idea that we are in a constant process of negotiation or even moral compromise with societal and economic forces not of our fashioning and into which we are seemingly habituated from birth.[23] Moreover, we seem to have little choice but to make peace with these structures if we are to have any fruitful belonging within society. So pervasive are these structures that they delimit our moral grammars, making it almost impossible for us to imagine any alternative world.

In many ways, these forces operate in ways that are similar to the operation of original sin for St Thomas: circumstances external to ourselves inherited as an internal reality which determine our moral lives and appear natural to us, but were far from inevitable. Original sin is not the most intensive of moral evils according to Aquinas (the more voluntary, the more culpable, the more intense), but it is the most *extensive*, in that it has the widest and most encompassing effects.[24] Original sin marks the corruption that forms the backdrop to our moral lives; it names the simple fact that the world is not yet as it should be, and we are not yet the people we want to be. The world is often hostile and challenging; we have to reckon morally with our natural habitat and grapple with our own lack of transparency to ourselves. Yet despite all of this, the world is still the place where God can be – and actually is – found (or, more precisely, where God has found us).

ANOTHER POSSIBLE WORLD

Thomas's treatment of the notoriously vexatious question of the motives for the incarnation is appropriately tentative.[25] Helpfully, Thomas frames the question in terms of another possible world.[26] The whole scheme of the question is contained by faith. It is not idle philosophizing, but a question that emerges only within faith responding to the self-revelation of God in Christ. Thomas asks whether, given what we know about what God has done in the actually existing world, there would have been an incarnation in a world in which there had been no sin. Would God still have done what he actually has done? The truth – as Thomas readily acknowledges – is that we cannot really know. The mind of God is unknown to us, except as it is revealed to us in scripture. Clearly, God does not tell us about other possible worlds, and so we are left to speculate probabilistically based upon what God does give us to know. The answer is tentative, shrouded in qualifications and marked by provisionality. Aquinas is more convinced by the legitimacy of the question than the validity of his answer.

By raising the question in terms of possible worlds, Thomas (paradoxically) keeps his response grounded in the actual world. To see how this works, an architectural metaphor is helpful. When we ask whether there is another possible world in which a particular house exists without a particular column, we are really raising the question of whether the column in the house that really exists is weight-bearing or not. This is the only real knowledge it delivers, because the other possible houses are in non-existent worlds, and so there is nothing to know about. In this way, counterfactual scenarios help us to shed light on complicated factual scenarios. So, Thomas's question amounts to an interrogation of the weight borne by Jesus of Nazareth: was this incarnation that is given us to know in faith willed by God to redeem us from sin?

Later theologians (largely influenced by the Oxford Franciscan, John Duns Scotus) would frame the question in a subtly different way, by inquiring about the logical priority between various aspects of God's will. Although there is no chronological sequence in God's mind, we can see certain logical relationships. For instance, we can say that God willed to create human beings 'before' God permitted sin, since it would not correspond to God's goodness for God to create human beings in order to fulfil a prior decision to allow sin. In this scheme, the question of the motive of the incarnation becomes the question of whether God willed to allow sin to enter into the world 'before' or 'after' God willed the incarnation. If the incarnation is logically prior to the fall, it would have occurred in a sinless world; if the incarnation is logically after the fall, its motive is redemption.

At first glance, the Scotist way of framing the question seems to do away with hypotheticals: the focus is on the way God willed things in the world that we actually have. In fact, the logic pushes in the opposite direction: the actual world is used to illuminate possible worlds. The Scotist formulation of the question has not by any means been a fruitless avenue for theological reflection, but for a Thomist it strays too far in the direction of undue abstraction and inquires into truths that are not given us to know. Thomas's approach, by contrast, models three important intellectual virtues. First, he shows the importance of exercising tight conceptual control over the questions that animate our inquiry, since it is these questions that determine the kinds of insights that can be generated. Secondly, Aquinas shows how abstraction and counterfactual speculation can be used to shed light upon the world as it presents itself in reality. Thirdly – and especially importantly for the theologian – Aquinas shows enormous restraint in refusing to extend his speculation beyond the data made available to him in revelation. Thomas's restrained honesty and circumspection about what cannot be known enables him to direct his energies in a fruitful, reality-orientated direction, yielding valuable insight. This is an important example to an interdisciplinary world in which the blurring of boundaries between the sciences is very much encouraged: fruitful interdisciplinary engagement actually demands a relentless fidelity to disciplinarity itself. Theology can only be relevant to the academy insofar as it is resolutely theological, faithful to its defining subject matter and distinctive methods. Only by acknowledging what it can know and what is beyond its power can theology embrace the avenues of communication that emerge from within the discipline itself.

CULMINATION

The long and convoluted history of the development of Christology, particularly the intense first five centuries of Christian theology, can be read as the Church's efforts to find an intellectually credible and philosophically robust way of looking at the figure of Jesus and saying, 'This man is God.' In particular, the crucial challenge lies in giving each of those four words their most complete and undiminished meaning:

not only that Jesus is *fully* God and *fully* human (with neither mixture and confusion, nor division and separation) but that he is possessed of a radical uniqueness ('this') and an enduring significance ('is' and not 'was'). Notwithstanding the particular accent that he puts on his account, Thomas's Christology is a continuation of this trajectory.[27] As Thomas puts it in his commentary on John's gospel, 'the good theologian professes the true faith in both the humanity and the divinity of Christ.'[28] Aquinas seeks fidelity to the witness of the Bible and Church teaching (particularly that of the ecumenical councils) rather than conceptual innovations.

There are two principles that Thomas's Christology (like all Christologies) must hold in a creative tension:[29] on the one hand, the singular unity of Christ's person; on the other hand, the full and uncompromised integrity of the two distinct natures, human and divine. One impulse seems to push in the direction of synthesis, the other is suggestive of fragmentation, pushing in the direction of dialectic. Clearly, any effort to harmonize such competing tendencies invites elements of paradox, and the logical coherence and theological appropriateness of Thomas's particular attempt at a resolution has been – and will continue to be – contested. A full assessment of Thomas's Christology lies well beyond the scope of this book. Its importance for contemporary theologians and philosophers lies in the fact that Thomas did not believe that the holding together of natural difference within personal unity was impossible: we are not, ultimately, left to choose between fragmentation and synthesis. Both, in different directions, constitute the type of violence Thomas's work is thoroughly opposed to. The non-violent account of Christ's being, then, unfolds itself in the non-violence of Christ's life, and the task of philosophical theology is to unpack these foundations.

Of particular importance in the task of securing a non-violent Christology is the analogy Thomas adopts to narrate the relationship between the human nature of Christ and the divine person that assumes it.[30] Thomas rejects any analogy suggestive of an impermanence to the union: the divine Word does not 'clothe' itself in a human nature like a set of clothes that can be put on and off, discarded at will. Likewise, Thomas shows discomfort with any analogies derived from the kinds of natural union we find in the realm of philosophy (such as the body–soul unity): these show precisely what the incarnation is *not*, the union of two parts of a single nature. Similarly, the relationship of indwelling or the moral unity of a common purpose (like the coming together of human beings in a club or political party) are simply inadequate, insofar as they show only how things can become functionally adjacent to one another while remaining entirely distinct in their individual identity.

The most important analogy Thomas does adopt is that of the human nature becoming an 'organ' of the divine nature, a concept Aquinas receives from John of Damascus (who is often the voice that mediates Eastern Orthodox theology to Aquinas).[31] To develop the analogy into more contemporary terms, we might consider organ transplantation. The image is, of course, imperfect (there is always in analogy an ever-greater element of dissimilarity). In particular, the eternal son – the 'recipient' – is not strictly receptive and does not undergo change. Similarly, the human nature of Jesus does not exist prior to its being assumed by the Word. Nonetheless, in the case of an organ transplant we have an example of something external to a person's identity being assumed into their person in such a way as to become internal, being drawn to participate in their causal pathways and processes and being sustained by their own personal energy rather than a life-force of their own.

To put this another way, Thomas holds that the human nature of Christ – as an organ of divinity – has become an instrument conjoined to the Godhead. In other words, the human nature is joined into the life of the Godhead in order to fulfil a function; it is used by God to achieve some end. Just as the hand is joined to the body and used to perform certain intelligent tasks that take it beyond its merely physical capacities (like writing), so the human nature of Christ is raised above its own innate power by its status as a conjoined instrument of the Godhead. Here we see another reflection of the overall non-violence of Thomas's Christology: God not only assumes a complete human nature, but also reverences that nature by opting to relate to the world *through* that human nature. This has profound significance for the spiritual and mystical life. The grace of God we receive in faith is not an ethereal quality of unknown provenance – like a medieval ectoplasm – but 'runs through' the human nature of Christ and bears its imprint. In the same way that water contains the mineral traces of the rock it passes through *en route* from the source, so all of God's dealings with us have the 'taste' of Jesus of Nazareth.

REVEALING THE HUMAN

This leads to a second important feature of Thomas's Christology: its reverence for – and detailed analysis of – Jesus's human experience. Indeed, the full and integral humanity of Christ is itself an article of faith, which 'regards Christ's Godhead and humanity, for it is not enough to believe the one without the other'.[32] As we have seen, the genius of Aquinas's Christology lies in his ability to structure his account so there is no conflict between the two natures, as if an emphasis on the divine would downplay the human. On the contrary – to revert to the organ analogy – the human nature has no existence prior to, outside, beyond or alongside its existence in the divine person of the word. Prior to the 'transplant', there was nothing to transplant. As far as Jesus's humanity is concerned, there is no before or after the incarnation. To investigate the human life of Christ, then, is always already to investigate (even unknowingly) the divine person in which that human nature subsists.

Indeed, so intimate is the connection Thomas establishes between the two natures that he takes Christ's human action to be the actions of the second person of the divine trinity.[33] Each and every communicative action of Christ is a theological mystery, a self-disclosure of the divine word as human life. There is, therefore, no great cleavage of the historical Jesus from the Christ of faith (as would appear in later post-Enlightenment theology). Everything of the life of Christ is theologically significant. The earthly history of Jesus, enacted in individual acts of communication, is simultaneously a revelation of God and the accomplishment of human salvation. The human experience of Christ is the embodiment of divine wisdom, taught in words and manifested by deeds. The whole identity of Jesus is marked at every level by his sending from the Father and redemptive mission to humanity. The eternal generation of the Son in the infinite recesses of the divine life is not only the pattern but also the very dynamism by which the life of Jesus unfolds in time, by communicative word and deed.

Thomas's commitment to articulating the fullness of Christ's human experience can be seen clearly in one of the developments in Thomas's Christology that he himself emphasizes. Like most medievals, Thomas held that Christ possessed – from the very first moment of his conception – the immediate vision of God, which is usually reserved to the saints in heaven. This beatific vision is the seeing of God as God is, in an unmediated way: an intimacy of encounter not attained in this life by even the most exalted and loftiest of mystics. Early in his career, Thomas argued that this direct knowledge of God provided *all* the knowledge that Christ relied upon in his earthly life. Since Christ already possessed the infinite vision of God, Christ knew all things through God, and so did not learn from his ordinary human experiences. At the end of his career, Thomas had adopted the opposite view. Without diminishing his commitment to the view that Christ possessed the direct vision of God, Thomas holds that Jesus *did* learn experientially, and thus acquired knowledge in much the same way that we do. The exact mechanism by which these two apparently antithetical truths are reconciled is complex and debated. Fundamentally, however, it is a matter of the will confining the unfolding of certain joys and perfections passing into Christ's human nature (on a temporary basis). Jesus did not necessarily *need* to acquire knowledge in the usual manner in order to fulfil his divine mission, but rather wills to know things by recourse to the senses – and even to experience ignorance – so as to enter more fully into human experience, reverencing the integral role played by sensory experience within human life. More broadly, Thomas holds that the Word assumed not only a full and complete human nature, but even also co-assumes various defects of soul and body (like ignorance, sorrow and the capacity to suffer), insofar as they enable the accomplishment of his saving mission.[34] That is to say that although Christ does not assume the state of sinfulness itself, he does assume – and suffer – many of the effects of sin.

MYSTERIOUS LIFE

The extent of Thomas's reverence for the fullness of Christ's human experience is manifest in his lengthy, detailed and entirely unprecedented integration of a theological interpretation of the events of Christ's life into his systematic Christology.[35] Given the notable novelty – and conceptual density – of this treatise, its relatively comprehensive neglect by Thomists is surprising. Gladly, the work of the French Dominican, Father Jean-Pierre Torrell, has done much to rectify the situation.[36] Having established the robust contours of a metaphysical Christology, the treatise on the mysteries of Christ's life supplements this with a narrative Christology. This constitutes a 'second reading' of the Christ event: in the same way that reading a story for the second time (once a firm grasp of the identity of the main characters and a sense of the arc of the narrative has been achieved) allows much of the significance of the story, buried in the detail, to be unfolded, so the more narrative approach to Christ's life allows the implications of the metaphysics to be seen more clearly and developed more comprehensively.

Unsurprisingly, the theme of Christ's full and integral humanity is repeatedly stressed, albeit now with an emphasis on the 'believability' of the incarnation. The co-assumed defects like hunger and sorrow not only establish a deep solidarity between the Word and the whole experience of humanity, but also serve to make faith in the incarnation credible by providing marks of verification. A similar logic applies in the opposite direction: Christ's life manifests a unique perfection so as to provide motives of credibility for belief in his divine nature. Throughout this analysis, Thomas – we might even say relentlessly – returns to the category of fittingness, showing how the beauty of divine wisdom is played out in every aspect of Christ's life. The fittingness of the incarnation is not just the rational coherence of an abstract idea, but the beauty of a life well lived.

The particular genius of Aquinas's account of Christ's life lies in the organizational framework he adopts. The life of Jesus is divided into four phases or moments: his entrance into the world (27–39), the progress of his earthly life, culminating in his public ministry (40–45), his departure from the world in the events celebrated at Easter (46–52), and his subsequent exaltation in the Godhead (53–59). The life of Jesus, then, maps directly onto the overall structure of the *Summa Theologiae* in its tracing of the movement of creatures from God (*exitus*) and back to God in Christ (*reditus*). This implies an extraordinary claim. It is not only that the treatise on the life of Christ is a kind of *summa* of the *summa*, capturing in miniature the essence of Thomas's theology. It is also to make a claim about the nature of reality: the life of Jesus discloses the essential structure of reality as a movement from origination, through progress, to return and ultimately consummation. The essential non-violence of Jesus's life – his visible non-violent response to aggression – corresponds to a deeper non-violence of his very being: the life of Jesus corresponds to the journey of reality, to the basic principles of reality. Or perhaps it doesn't. Perhaps the structure of reality corresponds in anticipation to the life of Jesus, in whom is the consummation of all that is real.

However strongly we interpret the treatise, two essential lessons can be drawn from Thomas's account of the mysteries of Christ's life. The first is that metaphysics and narrative belong together. The structure of reality – including our human freedom – unfolds itself in a narrative history, and historical narrative is grounded within – and discloses in a general way – the structure of the world. A good philosopher cannot overlook the history in which they are enmeshed and embedded. While philosophy rightly has abstractive moments, thought is in no way contaminated by 'stooping' to the particularity of examples or historical questions. Indeed, Aquinas can sometimes select almost embarrassingly historical examples drawn from basic encounters with the materiality of the world, even when describing the most spiritual of phenomena.[37] This is internal to Thomas's philosophical method: the ultimate meaning of time can only be found by detecting the ways in which it sheds light within the meanings of our own times. Inattentiveness to the latter will overlook the presence of the former.

The second lesson is directed to theologians, especially those working in a philosophical or systematic key. By today's standards, Thomas shows incredible audacity in reading universal truths off the historical particularities of the life of Christ. For Thomas, this is a necessity. The Christian claim to find in Christ the ultimate meaning of history requires a sustained attention to the detail of Christ's historical life, including his relationships with others, his religious and moral teaching, the miracles of feeding and healing, and above all his prayer. There is no sense in which Thomas's speculative Christology is post-biblical. The fruitfulness of the treatise invites today's philosophical theologian to return to the 'strange new world of the Bible' (as Barth later put it) and to close the gap between biblical scholarship and dogmatic theology.

FINAL ACT

Nothing in the life of Christ is more particular (or biblical) than the brutal way in which he died and the glorious manner of his rising. Unsurprisingly, Thomas gives sustained attention to this central mystery of the Christian faith. His account of the salvific power of Christ's death and resurrection is well known, but remains underexplored by contemporary theologians.[38] Elements of Thomas's account may appear unappealing and even hyperbolic to today's theologian, not least his insistence that the sufferings of Christ are the worst – most intensively experienced and most objectively extreme – pains that can be experienced in this life.[39] There is nonetheless a compassionate humanity to Thomas's central intuitions around redemption, evidenced in his resistance to allowing any single model of the atonement to exclude or dominate any other scriptural motifs that shed light on the holistic reality of this mystery (sacrifice, ransom, satisfaction, substitution, and so on). Thomas's consideration of the paschal mystery is multi-modal: he uses different lenses and complementary frameworks to draw out different aspects of the saturation of meaning that can be found in the cross.[40]

Given the emphasis I have laid on the non-violent character of God's dealings with humanity in Thomas's theology, it is necessary to confront head on the intensely violent manner in which the story of our redemption culminates. Thomas suffers no denial whatsoever about the gruesome realities of the crucifixion. There is no impulse within his theology to mythologize the reality of Christ's death. Indeed, on account of Christ's unique perfection, Thomas holds him to have been possessed of a uniquely acute sensitivity to bodily experiences, which would have intensified his sufferings to an unimaginable degree.[41] There is no doubt that this is violence of a most extreme kind – Thomas takes it to be violence to an unparalleled degree – but it is not the violence of God, or of Christ, but rather the violence of human sinfulness meted out upon the innocent victim.

Thomas (by now predictably) returns to the principle of non-necessary gratuity: the violence of the crucifixion is not a necessary outcome of the direct will of God. Jesus does not goad the authorities into murdering him so that he might, by dying, fulfil some law of necessary atonement or establish an otherwise unachievable gain for his mission. In keeping with the principle of non-violence, the sufferings of Calvary are willingly accepted. The cross simultaneously manifests both the intrinsic violence of sin and the gratuitous, absolutely non-violent, love of God. In embracing the violence of sin within the embrace of an infinite and non-violent love, Christ's passion marks and manifests the limits beyond which violence can never transgress.

Although Thomas holds that all the communicative acts of Christ's life are both revelatory and salvific (as we have seen), this is true in an intensified and concentrated form of his death and resurrection. The passion of Christ is an act of infinite divine–human communication. Thomas views the cross from two directions. In the ascending direction, the cross is the infinite efficacious act by which Christ intercedes on behalf of humanity to God, and exposes the dire neediness of the human situation. In the descending direction, the cross is a public act of divine loving reconciliation, and a testimony to the seriousness with which God takes the shipwreck of a fallen world. In the passion of Christ, God embraces the turbulence of the world in the infinite communion that is God's inner life.

To be sure, there is something conflictual about the cross, as Thomas sees it. Within the non-violent embrace of Christ there is a confrontation: the inward experience of the full horror of human evil is met with the most intense and perfected act of pastoral charity, and thus the most complete and sorrowful contrition. The forces of worldly violence try to force into Christ's person the moral evils that are meted out upon him, but they are instead confronted and absorbed by love, and so offered to the Father in a perfect act of worship. It is this sense of Christ's suffering, death and resurrection as an act of communication – both in the sense of a transfer and in the sense of a shared communion – that, it seems to me, holds together all of the other metaphors and images that cash out the hidden depths and encompassing breadth of that which is communicated between God and humanity in the three days that changed the world.

RESURRECTION

All this is vindicated by Jesus's rising from the dead on the third day. Nonetheless, the impact of Christ's resurrection cannot be reduced to the level of knowledge, as if the real 'work' were completed on Good Friday, with Easter Sunday simply putting right the injustice. Certainly, Thomas acknowledges that the resurrection vindicates Christ's life, confirming the authenticity of his teaching and further disclosing the true character of the cross.[42] Indeed, the two events (together with Christ's descent into hell and his glorious ascension into heaven) belong together as moments within the journey of Christ into the depths of abjection and upwards into the heights of divine glory. If the cross can be said to cast a shadow across human history, then it does so in the light that emanates from the resurrection.

The resurrection, for Thomas, is performative communication.[43] It brings about the reality that it announces, and is irreversibly indexed to the personal 'I' of Jesus Christ, the one who announced himself to *be* the resurrection and the life. As such, the resurrection does not correspond to any previously established category, or realize any previously existent potentiality within the world. The resurrection is not the resuscitation of a corpse, it is a completely different kind of event. The resurrection of Christ must be distinguished from the raising of Jesus's friend Lazarus.[44] Lazarus rises not by his own power, but by the divine power of Christ, and though his raising is a prefigurement of Christ's own resurrection, it does not move Lazarus beyond the realm of death's tyranny. Lazarus will die again. Likewise, the body of Lazarus was not brought by his raising to share in the glorification of the resurrection body manifested by the risen Christ. There can be no doubt that Lazarus's life is changed by his rising, but what lies before him is essentially more of the same, albeit an unexpected 'more'. The life of the raised Lazarus is conditioned by the same framework of possibilities that lead to his first death.

In short, Jesus's rising leads humanity forwards, not backwards. The resurrection of Jesus is not the restoration of life by way of a reversion to the way things were before death. The resurrection life is not one that could be imagined within the horizon of pre-resurrection existence. It is not more of the same, but a new experience of the radically new, a total recalibration of life as it is reframed within the eternity of God. The most basic experiences of our life – even our indwelling of space and time – are transfigured so as to be beyond all possibility of fragmentation or disruption. In comparison to the sheer vitality of the resurrection, our current lives are a mere half-life, almost a living death. It is the resurrection of Jesus that creates the possibilities that Christ offers to his disciples, and the power of Jesus's resurrection that will cause our own.[45]

The non-violence of God is found in every aspect of Thomas's account of the resurrection. By a special prerogative, on account of Jesus's perfection in holiness, the physical mortal remains of Jesus are held back from the physical violence of corruption and decay.[46] Indeed, the death of Christ means – as for all of us – the separation of body and soul. While the soul of Christ descends to the underworld, his cadaver languishes in the tomb. Since a human being is a body–soul composite, Thomas makes the arresting claim that in the period between his death and resurrection, Jesus is not a human being.[47] The starkness of this claim is balanced with the equally stark assertion that brings Thomas's anthropology together with the principle of non-violence. Although it lies within the power of the forces of creaturely violence to kill – to separate body and soul – no creaturely violence can undo the union of human and divine natures God has established in the person of Christ.

So even as the body and soul of Christ are separated, both remain united with the second person of the Godhead.[48] Consequently, there is a moment of non-violence inscribed into the very moment of the resurrection itself, cloaked though this moment is in silence, without any known human witness (a silence, indeed, that creates the possibility for the speech acts of faith). Thomas does not hold – as we would intuitively be inclined to think – that the soul of Christ returns to resume and re-animate his body. The resurrection is an act not of Christ's human nature, but of the power of his divine person, still united to *both* body and soul. Consequently, at the moment of the resurrection the body and soul of Christ mutually resume one another in a peaceful and re-creative embrace. The non-violence of Christ's 're-birth' into resurrection life is mirrored in the non-violence of his birth: Thomas holds that, by an unparalleled miracle, the physical birth of Jesus did no harm to his virginal mother's body.[49] It is to this degree – utterly implausible even to many committed Christians – that Thomas takes his commitment to the radical non-violence of God's saving self-communication to humanity.

In keeping with the non-violent character of God's dealings with the world in Thomas's thought, there are continuities between the risen life and the pre-mortem life. The resurrection does not annul personal biography, but rather transfigures it into glory. Jesus still has and displays the wounds of the crucifixion, though not now as signs of painful defeat and humiliation, but as marks of triumph, indicators of what has been overcome, 'trophies of his power'.[50] The wounds of Christ were inflicted in the process of terminating a relationship; in the risen life – as seen in the case of 'doubting Thomas' – they signal Jesus's availability for communion, are used by Christ to restore relationship. So it is with our own resurrection, patterned after Christ's: we too will rise into glory, marked by our particular biographies – our own wounds and places of humiliation. They too will be manifest on the public stage in our rising, but not as ugly and shameful memories but marks of our journey, signs of Christ's victory in us and thus opportunities to rejoice in the surpassing generosity of God.

THINKING AS THANKING

Having reached this point of consummation, there is a sense in which Aquinas does not matter. Or rather, he no longer matters in the same way he once did matter, because he has rendered to us the greatest service of all: tuning us into the presence of ultimate meaning within the conversation of reality. The final act of that service was to underline the ways in which he himself does not matter, to demonstrate how the truth of which he has spoken is not an idea or a thing but the divine-human person who ought to consume our lives. So, Thomas's work gradually recedes into the mystery of the resurrection, leaving us within its movement to contemplate everything in the existential space that has been opened for us by the infinite act of divine-human communication in Christ.

The *Summa Theologiae* – Thomas's great masterpiece whose journey we have been tracing – remained incomplete. It trails off into silence at the point where the last completed treatise was the one on the Holy Eucharist, the sacrament in which Thomas believed Christ communicates himself to believers under the appearances of bread and wine. Like all of the sacraments, the eucharist is the efficacious sign that extends Christ's saving work in our direction, a way in which Christ wills to communicate his life to us who live in the period between his ascension and his glorious return. As in all of the sacraments, God shows us by visible signs what he is doing, and does invisibly the things that he shows us in signs. The sacraments are, then, communicative actions willed by God and instituted by Christ to prolong his communication of life to his disciples.

Unlike the other six sacraments, in the case of the eucharist there is a gap between the moment when the sacrament is confected (at the celebration of Mass) and when it is received (in Holy Communion, whether at Mass or not). Such a distinction is possible, on Thomas's reckoning, because of the unique status of the eucharist among the sacraments. Whereas all the other sacraments embody and communicate an aspect of Christ's saving power, the eucharist embodies the whole personal reality of Christ, the personal unity that holds together all of the communicative actions of his life (and thus the whole communicative life of the world).

The Mass is, for Thomas, not only a sacrament but a sacrifice, making present once again in our times (re-presenting) the great communication of Christ's passion. It was God's plan and not Thomas's, but if the *Summa* had to remain incomplete it is hard to think of a better place for it to finish. It seems supremely fitting (to use one of Thomas's favourite phrases) that, having laboured to build the extraordinary cathedral of philosophy and theology, the last act he performs within its confines is the celebration of Mass. What more could be said than this act of making present, by human speaking, the divine Word through whom the world speaks? Perhaps 'thank you', to God and to Thomas, but that is the very meaning of the word 'eucharist'.

8

Postlude

THE THOMAS OPTION

Only the full-blooded communication that Thomas's work teaches can overcome the spectre of alienation that haunts our world. Our journey into the wilderness of Thomas's *Summa Theologiae* has shown that overcoming alienation matters not only for the 'big picture' – the climate emergency, the crises of culture and society, challenges of politics and peacemaking – but equally in the domain of the personal. Aquinas shows that we cannot escape the communicative significance of our lives: our humanity is given to us not only as a gift, an established fact, but as a project, task and obligation. We can only become fully human – fully alive – by taking responsibility for how we communicate with and to the world around us. How we answer the unavoidable and inescapable question of the meaning of life necessarily determines how we belong within the world, and the impact that we make upon it.

The journey into the *Summa* has spanned the large and the small. We have glanced down the Thomistic microscope at the smallest micro-elements of reality, and gazed through the Thomistic telescope up to the infinite horizon of God's own life. We have caught glimpses of the vast expanses of Thomas's cosmos and the unfolding riches of the landscapes of our interior wilderness, the surprising recesses of our souls. Above all, Thomas has shown us the value of seeing things with imaginative eyes renewed by wonder and gratitude. As one of John Steinbeck's characters puts it, 'it doesn't matter whether you look down or up – as long as you look!'[1]

POSTLUDE

AFTERLIVES

Thomas's work immediately caused controversy, and continues to be a cause of contestation to this day.[2] Thomas has seemed to live multiple afterlives[3]: for some a bulwark against the changing tides of relativism, for others an exemplar of open, dialogical, progressive thinking. Readings of Thomas vary wildly, and even the early modern commentatorial tradition – often parodied as the essence of an arid hair-splitting scholasticism – exhibits an extraordinary and generative diversity.

There are no signs that interest in Aquinas's thought is waning. The tradition of Thomas Aquinas is a living and constantly evolving world. Paradoxically, as Thomas has been gradually dethroned from the place of prominence he once enjoyed in the curricula of Roman Catholic seminaries, so Thomas's work has become a more socially acceptable and intellectually credible resource for those beyond the theological and philosophical worlds. This renaissance of interest in Thomas is both ecumenical and international. Theologians from the Reformed tradition increasingly turn to Thomas for inspiration and guidance,[4] not least for Thomas's characterization of theology as *sacra doctrina*. Among the most interesting and fruitful conversations in contemporary theology is the critical dialogue between Thomists and students of Karl Barth,[5] who – for some, at least – might well have been the most trenchant critic of 'institutional' Thomism in the twentieth century. Likewise, while many of the dominant centres of Thomistic research remain in the traditionally Catholic countries of Europe and in North America, there has been an explosion of interest in Thomas in China and the global south, notably including the Thomas Centre at the University of Wuhan.

Many of the most lively centres of interest in Aquinas are associated with Thomas's sisters and brothers in the Dominican Order, where Thomas's thought remains a privileged and indispensable guide. Distinctive brands of Thomism can be found in the Order's centres of study at Oxford, Fribourg, Toulouse, Washington DC and – most notably – the Pontifical University of St Thomas Aquinas in Rome. The global work of the Thomistic Institute (based out of Washington and Rome) has taken an accessible form of Thomistic philosophy and theology onto the internet and university campuses worldwide, and continues to sponsor advanced, often interdisciplinary research.

It is hard to predict what shape this living tradition of Thomism will take in the years to come. Undoubtedly, the existing projects that place Aquinas into conversation with the natural sciences promise to yield much fruit. As the threatening advances in so-called artificial intelligence lurk around the corner (or are they already here?), Thomas's account of what it means to be a rational animal promises to play a crucial role. Perhaps today's 'thinking software' is like Aquinas's angels: the greatest threat is not that they exist, but that we are tempted to imitate them. Taking a broader, institutional, view, the next century of Thomism will probably be less clerical and ecclesiastical than the last.

As I have argued throughout this book, Thomism – both philosophical and theological – has great potential to speak to many of the binds we currently find ourselves in. Thomas could – and should – be less of a niche academic interest and more of a common reference point for all intellectual inquiry. This will only happen, however, if those who dedicate their scholarly lives to the interpretation of Aquinas can resist the temptation to be gatekeepers of authentic Thomism, and allow the space for fresh, creative and challenging interpretations to emerge from surprising directions. It sometimes feels as if Thomas has fallen among the Thomists, lost amid the crowd of commentators. But his work ought always to retain its capacity to confront us with its decadent strangeness.

READING AQUINAS NOW

Thomas ought not be left alone, as if he is a fiendishly complex thinker who can only be mediated to us mere mortals in a dumbed down, pre-digested and diluted form. We ought to feel free to drink directly from the source of Thomas's teaching. Aquinas is not, however, the type of thinker whose work you can pick up and read from cover-to-cover. Attempting to do so will likely inoculate even the most dedicated of readers against the idea that Aquinas could ever be interesting. Those seeking to engage directly with Thomas for the first time would do well to digest a sustained introduction to his thought, and carefully select their starting points. The conventional wisdom among Thomists is that readers should familiarize themselves with both Thomas's biblical commentaries and his systematic works, so as to avoid losing sight of the fact that the major undertaking of Thomas's professorial life was the exposition of scripture. This is probably good advice to anyone who seeks admission to the guild of professional Thomas scholarship, but it does not serve well those who are embarking on their Thomistic adventures or want only a flavour of what Thomas can offer. Much of the material in the commentaries is unremarkable. Thomas's distinctive insights are diffused more widely through the text than is helpful. The tightly focused and intensely distilled arguments of the *Summa Theologiae* offer a more promising (if somewhat sparse) starting point. After all, the *Summa* was, as we have seen, crafted with the concerns of pedagogy in mind.

Reliable translations of the *Summa* are widely available online, but for those with access to a good theological library, the 'Gilby Summa' – a 61-volume work of multiple specialist translators, under the leadership of the principal editor Thomas Gilby – includes extremely useful (and occasionally provocative) explanatory appendices. Useful commentaries on the entire *Summa* have been produced by Walter Farrell[6] and Brian Davies[7] (who has produced a similar volume spanning the entirety of the *Summa Contra Gentiles*.[8] Various thematic overviews of Thomas's thought have been produced, including one devoted exclusively to Thomas's theology,[9] and the *Oxford Handbook of the Reception of Aquinas* surveys in astonishing detail the reception of Thomas both historically and thematically.[10]

Deep familiarity with the rhythmic structure of the *Summa* will greatly assist newcomers to acclimatize to the *Summa*'s wilderness. This is best developed by starting with texts that cover broadly familiar territory, or which avoid an excess of Aristotelian technicality. For those who have some familiarity with Christian theology, the questions on Baptism and Confirmation,[11] or on the mysteries of Christ's earthly life,[12] are a good starting point. For those with more philosophical inclinations, the questions on the general character of law and on the human character of habits are good points of familiarization.[13] For those seeking an entertaining (even surreal) introduction, the final two questions of the first part of the *Summa* (on human reproduction)[14] are so implausible in the light of contemporary biology that they allow the contemporary reader to easily foreground the argumentative structure of the text.

One perennial temptation ought to be resisted from the outset: that of skipping the arguments to reach Thomas's own 'answer'. The journey into truth is necessary to the joy of possessing it.

THOMAS'S MOMENT

Alasdair MacIntyre famously concluded his critique of contemporary moral philosophy, *After Virtue,* by suggesting that our cultural moment 'is waiting not for Godot, but for another – doubtless very different – St Benedict.'[15] MacIntyre's work is not lacking in Thomistic resonances. Nonetheless, departing from MacIntyre and developing the idea in his own way, Rod Dreher proposed what he termed the 'Benedict option':[16] that Christian existence in a post-Christian world can only really flourish in the form of a quasi-monastic withdrawal. Recognizing what Dreher takes to be the catastrophic cultural abandonment of virtue, he argued that the survival of human flourishing demands the intentional formation of counter-cultural enclaves, pockets of community life that can foster the life of individual and communal virtue.

Whatever the strengths of Dreher's proposal, the framework of virtue-in-exile tarries dangerously with a kind of alienation that is incompatible with Thomas's communicative universe. Aquinas offers us an ambitious alternative to the Benedict Option. The Thomas Option calls not for withdrawal but for a deeper and more confident (if also humbler) engagement with ambient culture, even (and especially) when that culture is deeply hostile to Christianity. Aquinas matters now because it is only by doing what Aquinas did, by cultivating new modes of social engagement, supported by institutions in which the free thinking and rational inquiry that Thomas exemplifies is possible, that we can move beyond today's impasse.

Is this naïve optimism? After all, they once laughed at the 'dumb ox'. Maybe. But Thomas would call it hope.

Notes

CHAPTER I

1. Martin Heidegger, *Basic Concepts of Aristotelian Philosophy* (Bloomington: Indiana University Press, 2009), p. 4.
2. Jean-Pierre Torrell, *St Thomas Aquinas: The Person and His Work* (Washington DC: Catholic University of America Press, 1996), pp. 75–96.
3. Ibid.; Jean-Pierre Torrell, *Saint Thomas Aquinas: Spiritual Master* (Washington DC: CUA Press, 2003); James A. Weisheipl, *Friar Thomas D'aquino: His Life, Thought and Works* (Oxford: Blackwell, 1974).
4. See especially the editorial introduction and annotations in: Simon Tugwell, *Albert and Thomas: Selected Writings* (Mahwah, NJ: Paulist Press, 1988).
5. Marie-Dominique Chenu, *Toward Understanding Saint Thomas* (Chicago: Henry Regenry, 1964), pp. 11–69.
6. Torrell, op. cit., p. 6.
7. Chenu, op. cit., pp. 18–24.
8. For a broader account of pedagogical developments, see Alex J. Novikoff, *The Medieval Culture of Disputation: Pedagogy, Practice, and Performance*, (Philadelphia: University of Pennsylvania Press, 2013), especially pp. 133–71.
9. Particularly important – though obviously hagiographic – are the witnesses called at the canonization proceedings, and, especially, the early biography of Tocco.
10. See, for instance, the *De unitate intellectus contra Averroistas*. On which, see Chenu, pp. 337–40.
11. L. Gregory Jones, 'The Theological Transformation of Aristotelian Friendship in the Thought of St Thomas Aquinas', *New Scholasticism*, p. 61 (1987).
12. *ST* II-II, q. 91, aa. 1-2. See also the appeal to musical categories in *ST* II-II, q. 180, a. 2.
13. *ST* II-II, q. 83. See also Paul Murray, *Aquinas at Prayer: Bible, Mysticism and Poetry*, (London: Bloomsbury, 2013).
14. Even allowing for the view of those who see this incident as having been somewhat elaborated in the re-telling, see Jacques Maritain, *The Angelic Doctor: The Life and Thought of Saint Thomas Aquinas* (New York: Dial Press, 1931), p. 6.
15. *Commentary on Job*, prologue.

16 Bartolomeo de Capua, *Processus*.
17 Cornelius Ernst, *Multiple Echo: Explorations in Theology* (London: Darton, Longman Todd, 1979), pp. 7–12.
18 Antonia Fitzpatrick, *Thomas Aquinas on Bodily Identity* (Oxford: Oxford University Press, 2017).
19 Paul M. Rogers, *Aquinas on Prophecy: Wisdom and Charism in the Summa Theologiae* (Washington DC: Catholic University of America Press, 2023).
20 Nicholas E. Lombardo, *The Logic of Desire: Aquinas on Emotion* (Washington DC: Catholic University of America Press, 2011).
21 Herbert McCabe, *On Aquinas* (London: Burns and Oates, 2008).
22 Eleonore Stump, *Aquinas* (London: Routledge, 2003).
23 Chenu, op. cit.
24 G. K. Chesterton, *St Thomas Aquinas* (London: Hodder and Stoughton, 1933), p. 119.
25 Josef Pieper, *The Silence of St Thomas* (London: Faber & Faber, 1957).
26 For more, see Kellie Robertson, 'Medieval Nature and the Environment', in *Cambridge Companion to Christianity and the Environment* (Cambridge: Cambridge University Press, 2022), pp. 134–49.
27 I am indebted to Rachel Muers for the idea of God 'hearing creation into speech'. See: Rachel Muers, *Keeping God's Silence: Towards a Theological Ethics of Communication* (Oxford: Blackwell, 2004).
28 *ST* I, q. 74, a. 3; *SCG* II, c. 23.
29 On the historical/speculative divide and its overcoming, see Giovanni Ventimiglia, *Aquinas after Frege*, (London: Palgrave Macmillan, 2020), pp. 8–12. See also Gerald A. McCool, *From Unity to Pluralism: The Internal Evolution of Thomism* (New York: Fordham University Press, 1992). For somewhat typical (and negative) assessments of neoscholasticism, see Philip Gleason, 'Neoscholasticism as Preconcilliar Ideology', *Catholic Historian*, 7 (1988); Fergus Kerr, 'A Different World: Neoscholasticism and Its Discontents', *International Journal of Systematic Theology*, 8 (2006).
30 Marie-Dominique Chenu, *Nature, Man and Society in the Twelfth Century* (Chicago: Chicago University Press, 1968).
31 Roger Scruton, *Fools, Frauds and Firebrands* (London: Bloomsbury, 2015), p. 175.
32 Peter M. Candler, *Theology, Rhetoric, Manuduction: Or Reading Scripture Together on the Path to God* (London: SCM Press, 2006). See also Fáinche Ryan, *Formation in Holiness: Thomas Aquinas on Sacra Doctrina* (Utrecht: Thomas Instituut/Peeters Leuven, 2007).
33 Chenu, op. cit., pp. 91–93.
34 Marie-Dominique Chenu, 'Le Plan De La Somme Théologique De Saint Thomas', *Revue Thomiste*, 47 (1939). See also Jean-Pierre Torrell, *Aquinas's Summa: Background, Structure, Reception* (Washington DC: Catholic University of America Press, 2005).

CHAPTER 2

1 W. Norris Clarke, *The One and the Many: A Contemporary Thomistic Metaphysics* (South Bend, IN: University of Notre Dame Press, 2001), p. 31.

NOTES

2 Frederick D. Wilhelmsen, *The Paradoxical Structure of Existence* (London: Routledge, 2017), pp. 1–24.
3 *SCG*, I, c. 43.
4 *De Potentia*, q. 7, a. 2.
5 *De Ente et Essentia*, c. 2.
6 *SCG*, II, c. 79. *De Potentia*, q. 2, a. 1. For influential interpretations, see Jacques Maritain, *Existence and the Existent* (Mahwah, NJ: Paulist Press, 2015); W. Norris Clarke, 'Action as the Self-Revelation of Being', in *Explorations in Metaphysics* (South Bend, IN: University of Notre Dame Press, 1994), pp. 45–64.
7 *Quodlibet*, 8, a. 2.1.
8 For an interesting re-articulation of the concept of 'form' along these lines, see Timothy McDermott, *How to Read Aquinas* (London: Granta Books, 2007), pp. 7–18.
9 Michael J. Dodds, 'Unlocking Divine Causality: Aquinas, Contemporary Science and Divine Action', *Angelicum*, 86 (2009).
10 I am grateful to Simon Oliver for a discussion of Thomistic teleology during a *Widening Horizons in Philosophical Theology* workshop in Vienna, January 2023. See also Clarke, op. cit., pp. 199–212.
11 Herbert McCabe, *On Aquinas* (London: Burns and Oates, 2008), p. 8.
12 John Berkman, 'Towards a Thomistic Theology of Animality', in *On Creaturely Theology*, eds David Clough and Celia Deane-Drummond (London: SCM Press, 2013), pp. 21–40; McCabe, op. cit., p. 8.
13 Jean-Pierre Torrell, *Saint Thomas Aquinas: Spiritual Master* (Washington DC: CUA Press, 2003), pp. 252–76.
14 Clarke, op. cit., pp. 290–303.
15 *De Veritate*, q. 1, a. 1.
16 For an extended argument to this effect, see Umberto Eco, *The Aesthetics of Thomas Aquinas* (Cambridge, MA: Harvard University Press, 1988), pp. 20–48.
17 Jan A. Aertsen, 'The Philosophical Importance of the Doctrine of the Transcendentals in Thomas Aquinas', *Revue Internationale de Philosophie*, 52 (1998).
18 *ST* I, q11, a1.
19 *De Veritate*, q. 1, a. 2. See also: 'Jan A. Aertsen, Truth as Transcendental in Thomas Aquinas', *Topoi*, 11 (1992).
20 Josef Pieper, *Living the Truth* (San Francisco: Ignatius Press, 1989), pp. 29–50.
21 *De Veritate*, q. 1, *passim*.
22 *ST* I, q. 14.
23 Eric David Perl, *Thinking Being: Introduction to Metaphysics in the Classical Tradition* (Leiden: Brill, 2014), pp. 151–88.
24 *ST* I, q. 12, a. 7.
25 *ST* I, q. 39, a. 8. See also Thomas Joseph White, 'Beauty, Transcendence, and the Inclusive Hierarchy of Creation', *Nova et Vetera*, 16 (2018).
26 See for instance *ST* III, q. 1, a. 1.
27 I am grateful to Lexi Eikelboom for many enriching discussions concerning the place of rhythm in a theological ontology. See Lexi Eikelboom, *Rhythm: A Theological Category* (Oxford: Oxford University Press, 2018).

CHAPTER 3

1. *ST* I, q. 2. For background, see Victor White, 'Prelude to the Five Ways', in *Aquinas's Summa Theologiae: Critical Essays,* ed. Brian Davies (Oxford: Rowman & Littlefield, 2006), pp. 25–44.
2. The diversity of ways of engaging with this single question of the *Summa Theologiae* is explored by Fergus Kerr, *After Aquinas: Versions of Thomism* (Oxford: Blackwells, 2002), pp. 52–72.
3. Rather the task is to 'go on' speaking about God, see: Cornelius Ernst, *Multiple Echo: Explorations in Theology* (London: Darton, Longman Todd, 1979), p. 74.
4. *ST* I, q. 1.
5. On the significance of *ST* I, q. 1, for the broader tapestry of the *Summa Theologiae*, including the Five Ways, see the provocative proposal of Victor White, *Holy Teaching: The Idea of Theology According to St Thomas Aquinas* (London: Blackfriars Publications, 1958).
6. G. E. M. Anscombe and P. T. Geach, *Three Philosophers: Aristotle, Aquinas, Frege* (Oxford: Blackwell, 1961), pp. 112–13.
7. See Aquinas, *Commentary on the Posterior Analytics.* II. 8.
8. *ST* I, q. 12, a. 12.
9. For a complementary reading of *ST* I, q.2, a. 2, see Frederick Christian Bauerschmidt, *Thomas Aquinas: Faith, Reason and Following Christ* (Oxford: Oxford University Press, 2013), pp. 91–106.
10. Cf. *ST* I, q. 2, a. 3, *ad.* 1.
11. *ST* I, q. 2, a. 1.
12. *ST* I, q. 2, a. 2.
13. *ST* I, q. 13, a. 1.
14. *ST* I, q. 12, a. 12.
15. *SCG* I, cc. 13 and 14.
16. Aquinas does not use the terms 'transcendence' and 'immanence', which enter the standard lexicon of theology and philosophy some centuries after his death. See, however, *ST* I, q. 7, a. 4.
17. *SCG*, I, c. 25; *ST* I, q. 3, a. 5.
18. Stephen Mulhall, *The Great Riddle: Wittgenstein and Nonsense, Theology and Philosophy* (Oxford: Oxford University Press, 2015), pp. 42–60.
19. Cf., on the scope of affirmative knowledge of God, *ST* I, q. 13, a. 12. Brian Davies, 'The Summa Theologiae on What God Is Not', in *Aquinas's Summa Theologiae: A Critical Guide,* ed. Jeffrey Hause (Cambridge: Cambridge University Press, 2018), pp. 47–67. See also the Herbert McCabe-inspired reading of Aquinas's negative theology offered by Simon Hewitt, *Negative Theology and Philosophical Analysis* (London: Palgrave Macmillan, 2020).
20. This is essentially M. Polanyi's version of the ancient paradox of *Meno*. See Michael Polanyi, *The Tacit Dimension* (London: Routledge, 1967), p. 4.
21. A point famously made by Josef Pieper, *The Silence of St Thomas*, (London: Faber & Faber, 1957).
22. *ST* I, q. 86, a. 2.
23. *ST* I, q. 84.

24 *ST* I, q. 12.
25 *ST* I, q. 12, a. 7.
26 *ST* I, q. 3; *SCG* I, c. 18.
27 *SCG*, I, cc. 16–27; ST I, q. 3, a. 7.
28 *SCG*, I, c. 16.
29 *SCG*, I, c. 22; *ST* I, q. 3, a4.
30 *ST* I, q. 3, a. 2.
31 *ST* I, q. 3, a. 6; *SCG* I, c. 23.
32 *De Ente et Essentia*, 89 *et passim*; *SCG*, I, c. 22. For a helpful analysis of the *De Ente et Essentia* argument, see Gaven Kerr, *Aquinas's Way to God* (New York: Oxford University Press, USA, 2015).
33 *ST* I, q.4.
34 *SCG*, I, c. 28.
35 *ST* I, q. 13, a. 8; *SCG*, I, c. 28, 7.
36 Rudi A. te Velde, *Aquinas on God* (London: Ashgate, 2006), p. 83.
37 *ST* I, q. 13, a.8. Unfortunately, Thomas's arguments here are based upon a rather discredited etymological analysis proffered by John of Damascus. For comment, see Kerr, op. cit., p. 187.
38 *SCG*, I, c. 38. Cf. *ST* I, q. 13, a. 4.
39 *ST*, I, q. 13, a. 4.
40 *SCG*, I, c. 31.
41 *SCG*, I, c. 88.
42 *SCG*, II, c. 23.
43 George Peter Klubertanz, *St. Thomas Aquinas on Analogy* (Chicago: Loyola University Press, 1960); Ralph McInerny, *Aquinas and Analogy* (Washington DC: Catholic University of American Press, 1996); Battista Mondin, *The Principle of Analogy in Protestant and Catholic Theology* (The Hague: Nijhof, 1963); Bernard Montagnes, 'La Doctrine De L'analogie De L'être D'après Saint Thomas D'aquin' (Thèse Louvain, 1963); John R. Mortensen, *Understanding St Thomas on Analogy* (Rome: Gregorian University, 2010).
44 Laurence Paul Hemming, 'Analogia Non Entis Sed Entitatis: The Ontological Consequences of the Doctrine of Analogy', *International Journal of Systematic Theology*, 6 (2004); James V. Zeitz, 'Przywara and Von Balthasar on "Analogy"', *Thomist*, 52 (1988).
45 Herbert McCabe, 'A Note on "Analogy"', in *Summa Theologiae: Volume 3, Knowing and Naming God: 1a. 12–13*, eds Thomas Gilby and Herbert McCabe (1975), pp. 106–7; McInerny, op. cit.
46 *ST* I, q. 13, a. 5, *sed contra*.
47 Pierre Hadot, *Philosophy as a Way of Life: Spiritual Exercises from Socrates to Foucault* (Oxford: Wiley-Blackwell, 1995).

CHAPTER 4

1 *ST* I, q. 26.
2 Jean-Marc Laporte, 'Beatitude in the Structure of Aquinas' Summa: Is Ia 26 a Stray Question?', *Toronto Journal of Theology*, 18 (2002).

3   See Thomas Joseph White, *Wisdom in the Face of Modernity: A Study in Thomistic Natural Theology*, (Naples, FL: Sapientia Press, 2009).
4   On the unknowability of God in Aquinas, see Brian Davies, 'The Summa Theologiae on What God Is Not', in *Aquinas's Summa Theologiae: A Critical Guide*, ed. Jeffrey Hause (Cambridge: Cambridge University Press, 2018), pp. 47–66; Simon Hewitt, *Negative Theology and Philosophical Analysis* (London: Palgrave Macmillan, 2020); Victor White, 'The Unknown God', in *God the Unknown* (London: Harvill Press, 1956), pp. 16–25.
5   Denys Turner, 'One with God as to the Unknown', in *God, Mystery and Mystification* (South Bend, IN: Notre Dame University Press, 2019), pp. 25–44.
6   On the differentiation of these 'traces' from the image of God, see *ST* I, q. 93, a. 6.
7   Herwi Rikhof, 'The Trinity', in *The Theology of Thomas Aquinas,* eds Rik Van Nieuwenhove and Joseph Wawrykow (South Bend, IN: University of Notre Dame Press, 2005), pp. 26–57; A renewed appraisal of Thomas's trinitarianism has been identified as a central feature of the theological movement known as 'Thomistic Ressourcement', see Thomas Joseph White, 'Ressourcement Thomism', in *The New Cambridge Companion to Christian Doctrine*, ed. Michael Allen (Cambridge: Cambridge University Press, 2022), pp. 352–70.
8   Gilles Emery, 'Theologia and Dispensatio: The Centrality of the Divine Missions in St Thomas's Trinitarian Theology', *Thomist*, 74 (2010); Gilles Emery, *The Trinitarian Theology of St Thomas Aquinas* (Oxford: Oxford University Press, 2007); Gilles Emery, *Trinity in Aquinas* (Ypsilanti: Sapientia Press, 2005).
9   See, for instance, Dominic Legge, *The Trinitarian Christology of St Thomas Aquinas* (Oxford: Oxford University Press, 2017).
10 For broad accounts of the trinitarian theology of Aquinas, see J. T. Paasch, 'The Trinity', in *Aquinas's Summa Theologiae: A Critical Guide,* ed. Jeffrey Hause (Cambridge: Cambridge University Press, 2018), pp. 68–86.
11 *ST* I, q. 27, a. 3.
12 *ST* I, q. 27, a. 5.
13 *ST* I, q. 27, a. 1.
14 *ST* I, q37.
15 Emery, op. cit., pp. 62–69.
16 *ST* I, q7, a24.
17 Eugene F. Rogers, 'Trinity', in *The Cambridge Companion to the Summa Theologiae*, eds Philip McCosker and Denys Turner (Cambridge: Cambridge University Press, 2016), pp. 117–28.
18 *ST* I, q. 29, a. 1.
19 John Lamont, 'Aquinas on Subsistent Relation', *Recherches de théologie et philosophie médiévales,* 71 (2004).
20 On this as a distinguishing feature of Thomistic trinitarianism, see Russell L. Friedman, *Medieval Trinitarian Thought from Aquinas to Ockham* (Cambridge: Cambridge University Press, 2010).
21 *De Potentia*, 8, a2.
22 *ST*, I, q28, a1.
23 *De Potentia*, q10, a5; *ST* I, q39, a1; *SCG* IV, Ch 24.
24 Emery, op. cit., pp. 96–103.

25 John Baptist Ku, *God the Father in the Theology of St Thomas Aquinas* (New York: Peter Lang, 2013); Oliver James Keenan, 'Divine Antecedence and Pretemporal Election', *New Blackfriars,* 98 (2017).
26 *I Sent,* d. 23, q. 1, a4.
27 Thomas Joseph White, 'Essence and Existence, God's Simplicity and Trinity', in *The New Cambridge Companion to Aquinas,* eds Eleonore Stump and Thomas Joseph White (Cambridge: Cambridge University Press, 2022), pp. 57–84.
28 Ferdinand Ulrich, *Homo Abyssus,* (Washington DC: Humanum Press, 2018).
29 Klaus Hemmerle, *Theses Towards a Trinitarian Ontology,* (Brooklyn: Angelico Press, 2020).
30 Erich Przywara, *Analogia Entis: Metaphysik,* (München: Kösel, 1932).
31 *ST* I, q. 45, a. 7.
32 White, op. cit.

CHAPTER 5

1 For the development of this theme in a more contemporary mode, including engagement with the tradition of German Romanticism, see Charles Taylor, *The Language Animal: The Full Shape of the Human Linguistic Capacity* (Cambridge, MA: Harvard University Press, 2016); Robert Pasnau, 'Aquinas's Thoughts on Linguistic Nature,' *The Monist* 80, no. 4 (1997).
2 This point was often made by Herbert McCabe OP. See, for instance: Herbert McCabe, *On Aquinas* (London: Burns and Oates, 2008), p. 31.
3 Genesis 11:1–9. See the extended meditation on this in Jean-Louis Chrétien, *The Ark of Speech* (London: Routledge, 2003).
4 For two quite different approaches to Aquinas along these lines, see Jean-Pierre Torrell, *Saint Thomas Aquinas: Spiritual Master,* trans. Robert Royal (Washington DC: CUA Press, 2003), pp. 252–75; Nicholas Lash, 'Are We Born and Do We Die?,' *New Blackfriars* 90, no. 1,028 (2009).
5 For indicators of this trend, see Chris Boesel and Catherine Keller, *Apophatic Bodies: Negative Theology, Incarnation and Relationality* (New York: Fordham University Press, 2009); Ola Sigurdson, *Heavenly Bodies: Incarnation, the Gze and Embodiment in Christian Theology* (Grand Rapids: Eerdmans, 2016); Michel Henry, *Incarnation: A Philosophy of Flesh* (Evanston, IL: Northwestern University Press, 2015); Paul J. Griffiths, *Christian Flesh* (Stanford, CA: Stanford University Press, 2018).
6 The number of questions dedicated to unpacking this interior landscape is vast. See, for instance, *ST* I, qq. 77–102; I-II, qq. 6–85, not to mention other texts such as the *De Anima*.
7 See Therese Scarpelli Cory, 'The Distinctive Unity of the Human Being in Aquinas,' in *The Oxford Handbook of the Reception of Aquinas,* eds Marcus Plested and Matthew Levering (Oxford: Oxford University Press, 2021).
8 This is, in fact, from Ludwig Wittgenstein's *Philosophical Investigations* (178). Wittgenstein's philosophical therapeutic has assisted more than a generation of students to access Aquinas's anthropology. See Fergus Kerr, 'Ansombe, Ernst and McCabe: Wittgenstein and Catholic Theology,' *Josephinum* 15, no. 1 (2008).
9 Fergus Kerr, *Theology after Wittgenstein,* 2nd ed. (Oxford: Blackwell, 1997).

10   *ST* I, q. 75, a. 5.
11   *ST* Suppl., q. 69.
12   *SCG* II, 68.
13   *SCG* II, 68. See Gerard Verbeke, 'Man as Frontier According to Aquinas,' in *Aquinas and Problems of His Time*, eds Gerard Verbeke and Daniel Verhelst (Leuven: University Press, 1976).
14   *SCG* IV, 55.
15   *ST* I, q. 76, aa. 3–4; *SCG* II, 58.
16   Torrell, St Thomas Aquinas, 187–190.
17   *ST* I, q. 62, a. 6.
18   *ST* I, q. 78, a. 3.
19   See the lesser-known *De Sensu et Sensato*.
20   *SCG*, I, 43
21   *De Veritate*, q. 2, a. 3, 19.
22   The powers are explored in *ST* I, qq. 77–83.
23   *ST* I, q. 77, a. 1.
24   McCabe, *On Aquinas*, 29.
25   *ST* I-II, q. 9.
26   *ST* I, q. 78, a. 4.
27   *ST* I, q. 78, a. 4, *obj.* 3.
28   *ST* I, q. 78, a. 4, *respondeo*.
29   *ST* I, q. 78, a. 4, *ad.* 3.
30   See McCabe, *On Aquinas*, op. cit., 149–52.
31   For a magisterial explication and analysis of Aquinas on the emotions, see Nicholas E. Lombardo, *The Logic of Desire: Aquinas on Emotion* (Washington DC: Catholic University of America Press, 2011).
32   *ST* I-II, q. 22, a. 2.
33   *ST* I-II, q. 22, a. 3.
34   *ST* I-II, q. 24, a. 1, *respondeo*.
35   *ST* I-II, q. 24, a. 3, *ad.* 1.
36   *ST* I-II, q. 25, a. 1.
37   Torrell, *Saint Thomas Aquinas: Spiritual Master*, 259–62.
38   *ST* I-II, q. 23, aa. 1–2.
39   *ST* I-II, q. 25, a. 1.
40   *ST* I-II, q. 27, a. 1.
41   *ST* I-II, q. 28, a. 1; q. 27, a. 1, *ad.* 2.
42   *ST* I-II, q. 31, a. 3.
43   *ST* I-II, q. 29, a. 1, see also a. 2.
44   *ST* I-II, q. 26.
45   *ST* I-II, q. 35, aa. 2–3.
46   *ST* I-II, q. 40, a.1, *respondeo*.
47   *ST* I-II, q. 40, a. 4. In comparison to the passion of hope, the examination of despair is notably thin and truncated.
48   *ST* I-II, q. 45, a. 3.
49   *ST* I-II, q. 41, a. 1, see also q. 45, a. 1.

50 *ST* I-II, q. 23, a. 3.
51 *ST* I-II, q. 46, a. 2.
52 For a more cautious assessment see *ST* I-II, q. 48.
53 *ST* I-II, q. 25, a. 4.
54 *ST* I-II, q. 28, aa. 1–3.
55 *ST* I-II, q. 24, a. 3, *respondeo*.
56 *ST* I, q. 79.
57 ST I, q. 79, a. 3.
58 ST I, q. 85, a. 8.
59 *ST* I, q. 85, a. 2.
60 *ST* I, q. 85, a. 1, *ad.* 3.
61 *ST* I, q. 79, a. 3.
62 *ST* I, q. 79, a. 2.

CHAPTER 6

1 *ST* I, qq. 75–89. For a detailed examination of Aquinas's account of the human person, see Robert Pasnau, *Thomas Aquinas on Human Nature: A Philosophical Study* (Cambridge: Cambridge University Press, 2008).
2 *ST* I-II, q. 6., a. 6.
3 The tension between biological belonging and spiritual unity is evident in *ST* I, q. 72. Cf. *ST* I, q. 92, a. 2.
4 Herbert McCabe, *On Aquinas* (London: Burns and Oates, 2008), 51–57.
5 *ST* III, q. 8, a. 3 (and *cf.* a. 4).
6 *ST* I-II, q. 2, a. 8.
7 This theme has been explored very powerfully in the teaching and preaching of Richard Conrad OP.
8 The most sustained exploration of this idea can be found in Herbert McCabe, *Law, Love and Language* (London: Sheed & Ward, 1968).
9 See also Alasdair MacIntyre, *Three Rival Versions of Moral Enquiry* (London: Duckworth, 1990).
10 G. E. M. Anscombe, 'Modern Moral Philosophy,' *Philosophy* 33, no. 124 (1958); See also Alasdair MacIntyre, *After Virtue: A Study in Moral Theory*, 3rd ed. (London: Bloomsbury, 2007).
11 *ST* I-II, q. 6, a. 1.
12 Joseph Pilsner, *The Specification of Human Actions in St Thomas Aquinas* (Oxford: Oxford University Press, 2006), 9–28. See also, ST I-II, q. 6, a. 3.
13 See, for instance, Ralph Matthew McInerny, *Aquinas on Human Action: A Theory of Practice* (Washington DC: Catholic University of America Press, 2012).
14 See the comments on the 'mixed character' of some human actions at *ST* I-II, q. 6, a. 6 and a. 8.
15 See *ST* I-II, qq. 8–10.
16 Cf. *ST* I-II, q. 11, a. 2.
17 McCabe, *On Aquinas*, 79–86.
18 *ST* I, q. 83, especially a. 1.

19 I am grateful to the insightful discussion of Aquinas's account of *akrasia* provided by Bonnie Kent, 'Aquinas and Weakness of Will', *Philosophy and Phenomenological Research* 75, no. 1 (2007).
20 A useful introduction to the theme of virtue in Aquinas's mature thought is offered by James F. Keenan, 'Virtues,' in *The Cambridge Companion to the Summa Theologiae*, eds Philip McCosker and Denys Turner (Cambridge: Cambridge University Press, 2016).
21 *ST* I-II, q. 55, a. 4.
22 *ST* I-II, q. 54, a. 3. See also, Denis J. M. Bradley, *Aquinas on the Twofold Human Good: Reason and Human Happiness in Aquinas's Moral Science* (Washington DC: Catholic University of America Press, 1997).
23 *ST* I-II, q. 56, a. 3.
24 *ST* I-II, q. 51, a. 2, see also a. 3, *respondeo*.
25 *ST* I-II, q. 56, a. 2, especially the *sed contra*.
26 *ST* I-II, q. 49, a. 3.
27 *ST* I-II, q. 61. An introductory presentation of Aquinas's treatise on the cardinal virtues has been provided by Christopher Kaczor and Thomas Sherman, *Thomas Aquinas on the Cardinal Virtues* (Washington DC: Catholic University of America Press, 2020).
28 *ST* I-II, q. 61, a. 4.
29 *ST* II-II, q. 47, a. 5.
30 *ST* II-II, q. 47, a. 14.
31 *ST* II-II, q. 47, a. 8.
32 On prudence and practical reasoning, see *ST* II-II, q. 47, a. 2.
33 *ST* II-II, q. 129, aa. 3 and 4. A similar set of connections are explored by Michael Keating, 'The Strange Case of the Self-Dwarfing Man,' *Logos* 10, no. 4 (2007).
34 *ST* II-II, q. 55, a. 4. The translation of *astutia* is notoriously contested. The Shapcote translation opts for 'guile'.
35 *ST* II-II, q. 49, a. 7 and a. 8.
36 *ST* II-II, q. 47, a. 1, *ad.* 2; *ST* II-II, q. 49, a. 6.
37 *ST* II-II, q. 48 (a single article). See also the presentation in Josef Pieper, *The Four Cardinal Virtues* (South Bend, IN: University of Notre Dame Press, 1966), 3–42.
38 *ST* II-II, q. 56, a. 1.
39 *ST* II-II, q. 51, a. 1; *ST* II-II, q. 48 (a single article).
40 The 'right estimate' about matters that Aquinas called 'shrewdness', *ST* II-II, q. 49, a. 4.
41 *ST* II-II, q. 49 and q. 51 explore the various facets and internal dimensions of prudence.
42 *ST* II-II, q. 52 explores the corresponding gift of taking counsel, see also *ST* II-II, 49, a. 3;
43 *ST* II-II, q. 51, a. 2.
44 *ST* II-II, q. 50, a. 1. See also the other articles of q. 50.
45 *ST* II-II, q. 50, a. 2.
46 For a survey of approaches to Thomas on natural law, see Fergus Kerr, *After Aquinas: Versions of Thomism* (Oxford: Blackwell, 2002), 97–113. For various contemporary receptions of natural theory (including those that go beyond the

NOTES

strict limits of Aquinas's thought) see John Finnis, *Natural Law and Natural Rights* (Oxford: Oxford University Press, 2011); Russell Hittinger, *Critique of the New Natural Law Theory* (South Bend, IN: University of Notre Dame Press, 1988); Anthony J. Lisska, *Aquinas's Theory of Natural Law: An Analytic Reconstruction* (Oxford: Wiley-Blackwell, 1998).

47   *ST* I-II, q. 49, a. 6.
48   *ST* I-II, q. 90.
49   *ST* II-II, q. 91, a. 1.
50   *ST* I, q. 103, a. 8, and q. 104, a. 2.
51   *ST* I-II, q. 93.
52   On the theological framework that underpins Thomas's account of natural law, see Craig A. Boyd, 'Participation Metaphysics in Aquinas's Theory of Natural Law,' *American Catholic Philosophical Quarterly* 79, no. 3 (2005).
53   *ST* I-II, q. 94, a. 1.
54   An excellent study of this theme in Aquinas can be found in Daniel Schwartz, *Aquinas on Friendship* (Oxford: Oxford University Press, 2020). See also Jean-Pierre Torrell, *Saint Thomas Aquinas: Spiritual Master*, trans. Robert Royal (Washington DC: CUA Press, 2003), 276–308.
55   *ST* II-II, q. 23, a. 1.
56   See Walter H. Principe, 'Affectivity and the Heart in Thomas Aquinas' Spirituality,' in *Spiritualities of the Heart*, ed. Annice Callahan (New York: Paulist Press, 1990).
57   Eth. IX, 6. See *ST* II-II, q. 29, a. 3, *ad.* 2.
58   Eth. VIII, 1.
59   *SCG* III, c. 151, 3.
60   *ST* II-II, q. 80.
61   Schwartz, *Aquinas on Friendship*, op. cit., 1–21.
62   L. Gregory Jones, 'The Theological Transformation of Aristotelian Friendship in the Thought of St Thomas Aquinas,' *New Scholasticism* 61, no. 4 (1987).
63   Aquinas, *De Regno*, c. 11.
64   *ST* II-II, q. 29, a. 3.
65   For helpful treatments of Aquinas on justice, see John Finnis, *Aquinas: Moral, Political and Legal Theory* (Oxford: Oxford University Press, 1998), pp. 132–80; Pieper, *The Four Cardinal Virtues*, op. cit., pp. 43–75; McCabe, *On Aquinas*, op. cit., pp. 143–56; Eleonore Stump, *Aquinas* (London: Routledge, 2003), pp. 309–38.
66   ST II-II, q. 123, a. 6.
67   ST II-II, q. 58, a. 1.
68   ST II-II, q. 58, a. 11.
69   *ST* II-II, q. 58, a. 2, *respondeo*.
70   The relationship between natural right and natural law has been explored widely by Thomists. I am grateful to Robert Ombres OP for discussions on this point. See also Ralph McInerny, 'Natural Law and Human Rights,' *American Journal of Jurisprudence* 36, no. 1 (1991); Finnis, *Natural Law and Natural Rights*, op. cit.
71   *ST* II-II, q. 57: the question on '*ius*' (right) that precedes the formal account of justice (*iustitia*).
72   *ST* II-II, q. 57, a. 2.
73   Finnis, *Aquinas: Moral, Political and Legal Theory*, 113–23.

74 *ST* I-II, q. 90, a. 2.
75 *ST* I-II, q. 90, a. 3.
76 *ST* II-II, q. 58, a. 6. Note the extent to which the material here oscillates between the account of law in *ST* I-II and the account of justice in *ST* II-II.
77 *ST* II-II, q. 62.
78 *ST* II-II, q. 58, a. 2.
79 Pieper, *The Four Cardinal Virtues*, op. cit., p. 57.
80 *ST* I-II, q. 102, a. 6, *ad.* 1, see also a. 3, *ad.* 8.
81 This provides the structure of *ST* II-II, q. 61.
82 *ST* II-II, q. 61, a. 1.
83 *ST* II-II, q. 62, a. 2.
84 *ST* II-II, q. 74. For its severity, see a. 2.
85 *ST* II-II, q. 63, a. 1.
86 *ST* II-II, q. 61, a. 2.
87 *ST* II-II, q. 61, a. 1, *ad.* 3.
88 II *Sent.* 44.2.2.
89 *ST* II-II, q. 29, a. 1.
90 *ST* II-II, q. 102 on *observantia*, and q. 101 on piety.
91 *ST* II-II, q. 81.
92 *ST* II-II, q. 123.
93 *ST* II-II, q. 123, a. 5.
94 *ST* II-II, q. 123, a. 6.
95 *ST* II-II, q. 136, a. 4.
96 *ST* II-II, q. 126.
97 *ST* II-II, q. 124, a. 3.
98 *ST* II-II, q. 128, in a single article.
99 *ST* II-II, q. 157, a. 1.
100 *ST* II-II, q. 155, a. 3.
101 *ST* II-II, q. 141, a. 8, *respondeo*.
102 *ST* II-II, q. 142.
103 *ST* II-II, q. 167, a. 1.
104 *ST* II-II, q. 167, a. 2; see also *ST* II-II, q. 166 (on *studiositas*).

CHAPTER 7

1 Fergus Kerr, 'Christ in the Summa Theologiae', in *After Aquinas: Versions of Thomism*, (Oxford: Blackwell, 2002), pp. 181–206.
2 See, for instance, Katherine Sonderegger, *Systematic Theology 2: The Doctrine of the Holy Trinity, Processions and Persons*, (Minneapolis: Fortress Press, 2020), p. 91.
3 From Thomas's private prayer *Adoro te Devote*, now commonly used as a hymn. See Paul Murray, *Aquinas at Prayer: Bible, Mysticism and Poetry* (London: Bloomsbury, 2013), Chapter 10.
4 *ST* I, q. 8, ad. 2 (and elsewhere).
5 For an examination of 'nature' as a theological category in its own right, see Steven A. Long, *Natura Pura: On the Recovery of Nature in the Doctrine of Grace* (New York: Fordham University Press, 2010).

NOTES

6. See *De Veritate*, 14.2.
7. Judith Barad, *Consent: The Means to an Active Faith According to St Thomas Aquinas* (New York: Peter Lang, 1992).
8. Ibid. p. 13.
9. For Thomas's account, see *ST* I, q. 1, a2.
10. *ST* II-II, q. 17, a. 2.
11. ST II-II, q. 18, a. 4.
12. See, for instance, Miguel A. De La Torre, *Embracing Hopelessness* (Minneapolis: Fortress Press, 2017).
13. ST II-II, q. 20 and 21.
14. I am grateful to Amber Bowen for helpful discussions on this point.
15. Michael S. Sherwin, *By Knowledge & by Love: Charity and Knowledge in the Moral Theology of St Thomas Aquinas* (Washington DC: Catholic University of America Press, 2005).
16. See *ST* II-II, q. 23, a. 1.
17. See the consideration at *ST* II-II, q. 23, a. 1. This view is often associated with Peter Lombard. On Aquinas's engagement with this view, see Nicholas Ogle, 'Trinitarian Charity: Aquinas and Lombard on Charity and the Holy Spirit', *Scottish Journal of Theology*, 74 (2021).
18. *ST* I, q. 43.
19. *ST* III, q. 1, a. 2 and 3.
20. *ST* III, q. 1, a. 1, and *passim*.
21. *ST* III, q. 1, a. 1, *ad*. 4.
22. Daniel W. Houck, *Aquinas, Original Sin, and the Challenge of Evolution* (Cambridge: Cambridge University Press, 2020).
23. See Herbert McCabe, 'Original Sin', in *God Still Matters* (London: Bloomsbury, 2002), pp. 166–81.
24. *ST* III, q. 1, a. 4, *respondeo*.
25. Two excellent recent volumes explore the debate and make creative contributions (and retrievals) of their own: Justus Hunter, *If Adam Had Not Sinned: The Reason for the Incarnation from Anselm to Scotus*, (Washington DC: Catholic University of America Press, 2020); Dylan Schrader, *A Thomistic Christocentrism: Recovering the Carmelites of Salamanca on the Logic of the Incarnation* (Washington DC: Catholic University of America Press, 2021).
26. *ST* III, q. 1, a. 3. The brevity of the article stands in stark contrast to the volumes of commentary written on it.
27. For detailed scholarly introductions to Thomas's account of the incarnation, see Sarah Coakley, 'Person of Christ', in *Cambridge Companion to the Summa Theologiae*, eds Philip McCosker and Denys Turner (Cambridge: Cambridge University Press, 2016), pp. 222–39; Joseph Wawrykow, 'Hypostatic Union', in *The Theology of Thomas Aquinas*, eds Rik Van Nieuwenhove and Joseph Wawrykow (Notre Dame, IN: University of Notre Dame Press, 2005), pp. 222–51.
28. *In Ioan*, 20.6. See also: *ST* III, q. 52, a. 2.
29. Michael Gorman, 'Christ as Composite', *Traditio*, 55 (2000).
30. See, *Compendium*, 213; *ST* III, q. 7, a. 1, *ad*. 3.
31. See for instance the repeated references to Damascene's *De Fide Orth*. in *ST* III, q. 4.

32 *ST* III, q. 53, a. 2, *respondeo*.
33 For a defence of this view, see Thomas Joseph White, 'The Voluntary Action of the Earthly Christ', *Thomist*, 69 (2005).
34 The co-assumpta are discussed in *ST* III, qq. 7–15, with qq. 14 and 15 focusing on the co-assumed defects in both and soul (respectively).
35 The treatise runs from *ST* III, q. 27 (the sanctification of the Lord's mother) through to q. 59 (post-ascension judiciary power). For an introduction to the importance of this treatise and its scope, see Paul Gondreau, 'The Life of Christ', in *Cambridge Companion to the Summa Theologiae,* eds Philip McCosker and Denys Turner (Cambridge: Cambridge University Press, 2016), pp. 240–54.
36 Especially the (as yet untranslated) Jean-Pierre Torrell, *Jésus Le Christ Chez Saint Thomas D'aquin*, (Paris: CERF, 2008); Jean-Pierre Torrell, *Le Christ En Ses Mystères* (Paris: Desclée, 1999).
37 See, for instance, the analogy used for sacramental character (a seal pressed into wax): *ST* III, q. 63.
38 An overview of Thomas's account of salvation in Christ, including its development through the course of his career, can be found in: Rik van Nieuwenhove, 'Soteriology', in *The Theology of Thomas Aquinas,* eds Joseph Wawrykow and Rik van Nieuwenhove (Notre Dame, IN: University of Notre Dame Press, 2005), pp. 277–302.
39 *ST* III, q. 46, especially a. 5 and a. 6.
40 Nicholas M. Healy, 'Redemption', in *Cambridge Companion to the Summa Theologiae,* eds Philip McCosker and Denys Turner (Cambridge: Cambridge University Press, 2016), pp. 255–68.
41 On the importance, sanctity and uniqueness of the passions of Christ's human soul, see the magisterial Paul Gondreau, *The Passions of Christ's Soul in the Theology of St Thomas Aquinas*, (Washington DC: Catholic University of America Press, 2018).
42 *ST* III, q. 52, a. 1.
43 *ST* III, q. 52, a. 3 and a. 4.
44 ST III, q. 52, a. 3. Thomas's actual use of the Lazarus story is surprisingly thin in the *Summa Theologiae*.
45 *ST* III, q. 56.
46 *ST* III, q. 51, a. 3.
47 *ST* III, q. 50, a. 4.
48 *ST* III, q. 50, a. 2, a. 3.
49 *ST* III, q. 28, a. 3.
50 *ST* III, q. 54, a. 4.

CHAPTER 8

1 John Steinbeck, *Sweet Thursday* (London: Penguin, 1954), p. 260.
2 Frederick J. Roensch, *Early Thomistic School* (Dublin: Priory Press, 1964); Romanus Cessario, *A Short History of Thomism* (Washington DC: Catholic University of America Press, 2005).
3 Romanus Cessario and Cajetan Cuddy, *Thomas and the Thomists: The Achievement of Thomas Aquinas and His Interpreters* (Philadelphia, PA: Fortress Press, 2017);

NOTES

Fergus Kerr, *After Aquinas: Versions of Thomism* (Oxford: Blackwell, 2002); Gerald A. McCool, *From Unity to Pluralism: The Internal Evolution of Thomism* (New York, NY: Fordham University Press, 1989).

4   Francis J. Beckwith, *Never Doubt Thomas: The Catholic Aquinas as Evangelical and Protestant* (Waco, TX: Baylor University Press, 2019).

5   See, for instance, Bruce L. McCormack and Thomas Joseph White, *Thomas Aquinas and Karl Barth: An Unofficial Catholic–Protestant Dialogue* (Grand Rapids: Eerdmans, 2013). See also David H. Kelsey, 'Aquinas and Barth on the Human Body', *Thomist*, 50 (1986); Louis Roy, 'A Note on Barth and Aquinas', *American Catholic Philosophical Quarterly*, 66 (1991).

6   Walter Farrell, *A Companion to the Summa* (New York: Sheed and Ward, 1938).

7   Brian Davies, *Thomas Aquinas's Summa Theologiae* (Oxford: Oxford University Press, 2014).

8   Brian Davies, *Thomas Aquinas's Summa Contra Gentiles: A Guide and Commentary* (Oxford: Oxford University Press, 2016).

9   Joseph Wawrykow and Rik Van Nieuwenhove, *The Theology of Thomas Aquinas* (South Bend, IN: University of Notre Dame, 2005).

10 Matthew Levering and Marcus Plested, *The Oxford Handbook of the Reception of Aquinas* (Oxford: Oxford University Press, 2021).

11 *ST* III, qq. 63–69.

12 Especially *ST* III, qq. 39–41.

13 *ST* I-II, q. 49, qq. 90–92.

14 *ST* I, qq. 118–19.

15 Alasdair MacIntyre, *After Virtue: A Study in Moral Theory*, 3rd edn (London: Bloomsbury, 2007), p. 263.

16 Rod Dreher, *The Benedict Option: A Strategy for Christians in a Post-Christian Nation*, (New York, NY: Sentinel, 2017).

Acknowledgements

Michael Polanyi argued that we always know more than we can tell. This never seems to be truer than when we attempt to acknowledge the debt of gratitude we owe to others.

Before doing so, I would like to make a (somewhat half-hearted) apology to Aquinas's most devoted students. In arguing that Aquinas matters now, I have omitted many things it would be important for another book to mention, especially if it aspired to give a comprehensive account of Thomas's thought. I have also occasionally made interpretative moves that will make committed Thomists blanch.

Above all this book has been a work of conversation with and through the thought of Thomas Aquinas, in which I have grappled with what I have come to see as the central feature of Thomas's philosophical and theological legacy. Writing this book has helped me come to terms with the extent to which I do or do not belong to the intellectual tradition of Aquinas, but it has equally made me more aware of other voices that impinge upon and inform my reading of Thomas: Etienne Gilson, Martin Heidegger, Cornelius Ernst, Jean-Pierre Torrell and even Karl Barth. Along the way, it turns out that I have – almost unwittingly – imbibed a good deal of Herbert McCabe, mediated to me by a trio of excellent teachers: Fergus Kerr, Richard Conrad and Simon Francis Gaine.

Thomas would probably have remained just another dead white man for me, had he not come to life in conversation with students, colleagues and teachers. Graham Ward, Silvianne and Barnabas Aspray, Tobias Tanton, Amber Bowen, Nicholas Crowe, Victoria Lorrimar, Timothy Radcliffe, Georgina Arando and Lexi Eikelboom deserve special thanks

ACKNOWLEDGEMENTS

for their support and encouragement. Elsie Illidge asked a poignant question at just the right moment.

I have now spent a decade or so discharging the obligation to teach Thomas's thought and owe a great deal to several groups of extraordinarily engaged students, not least a lively Tuesday evening doctrine class at Ripon College, Cuddesdon. Whether at the University of Oxford, in the Blackfriars Studium or at the Rosary Catholic Primary School on Haverstock Hill in London (where I was chaplain), students have repeatedly pushed me to connect Thomas's complex ideas with the equally complex reality of being human.

Amid so 'great a cloud of witnesses', none has been – or could be – more supportive than Rachel Cresswell. I dedicate this book to her as a token of gratitude for a decade of friendship.

Bibliography

Aertsen, Jan A., 'The Philosophical Importance of the Doctrine of the Transcendentals in Thomas Aquinas', *Revue Internationale de Philosophie*, 52 (1998).
———, 'Truth as Transcendental in Thomas Aquinas', *Topoi*, 11 (1992).
Anscombe, G. E. M., 'Modern Moral Philosophy', *Philosophy* 33, no. 124 (1958).
——— and P. T. Geach, *Three Philosophers: Aristotle, Aquinas, Frege* (Oxford: Blackwell, 1961).
Barad, Judith, *Consent: The Means to an Active Faith According to St Thomas Aquinas* (New York: Peter Lang, 1992).
Bauerschmidt, Frederick Christian, *Thomas Aquinas: Faith, Reason and Following Christ* (Oxford: Oxford University Press, 2013).
Beckwith, Francis J., *Never Doubt Thomas: The Catholic Aquinas as Evangelical and Protestant* (Waco, TX: Baylor University Press, 2019).
Berkman, John, 'Towards a Thomistic Theology of Animality', in *On Creaturely Theology*, eds David Clough and Celia Deane-Drummond (London: SCM Press, 2013).
Boesel, Chris, and Catherine Keller, *Apophatic Bodies: Negative Theology, Incarnation, and Relationality* (New York: Fordham University Press, 2009).
Boyd, Craig A., 'Participation Metaphysics in Aquinas's Theory of Natural Law.' [In English]. American Catholic Philosophical Quarterly 79, no. 3 (2005).
Bradley, Denis J. M., *Aquinas on the Twofold Human Good: Reason and Human Happiness in Aquinas's Moral Science* (Washington DC: Catholic University of America Press, 1997).
Candler, Peter M., *Theology, Rhetoric, Manuduction: Or Reading Scripture Together on the Path to God*, Radical Traditions (London: SCM Press, 2006).
Cessario, Romanus, *A Short History of Thomism* (Washington DC: Catholic University of America Press, 2005).
——— and Cajetan Cuddy, *Thomas and the Thomists: The Achievement of Thomas Aquinas and His Interpreters* (Philadelphia, PA: Fortress Press, 2017).
Chenu, Marie-Dominique, 'Le Plan de la Somme Théologique de Saint Thomas', *Revue Thomiste*, 47 (1939).
———, *Toward Understanding Saint Thomas*. trans. A.-M. Landry and D. Hughes (Chicago: Henry Regenry, 1964).

———, *Nature, Man and Society in the Twelfth Century* (Chicago: Chicago University Press, 1968).
Chesterton, G. K., *St. Thomas Aquinas* (London: Hodder and Stoughton, 1933).
Chrétien, Jean-Louis, *The Ark of Speech* (London: Routledge, 2003).
Clarke, W. Norris, 'Action as the Self-Revelation of Being', in *Explorations in Metaphysics* (South Bend, IN: University of Notre Dame Press, 1994).
———, *The One and the Many: A Contemporary Thomistic Metaphysics* (South Bend, IN: University of Notre Dame Press, 2001).
Coakley, Sarah, 'Person of Christ', in *The Cambridge Companion to the Summa Theologiae*, eds Philip McCosker and Denys Turner (Cambridge: Cambridge University Press, 2016).
Cory, Therese Scarpelli, 'The Distinctive Unity of the Human Being in Aquinas' in *The Oxford Handbook of the Reception of Aquinas*, eds Marcus Plested and Matthew Levering (Oxford: Oxford University Press, 2021).
Davies, Brian, *Thomas Aquinas's Summa Theologiae* (Oxford: Oxford University Press, 2014).
———, *Thomas Aquinas's Summa Contra Gentiles: A Guide and Commentary* (Oxford: Oxford University Press, 2016).
———, 'The Summa Theologiae on What God Is Not', in *Aquinas's Summa Theologiae: A Critical Guide*, ed. Jeffrey Hause (Cambridge: Cambridge University Press, 2018).
De la Torre, Miguel A., *Embracing Hopelessness* (Minneapolis: Fortress Press, 2017).
Dodds, Michael J., 'Unlocking Divine Causality: Aquinas, Contemporary Science and Divine Action', *Angelicum*, 86 (2009).
Dreher, Rod, *The Benedict Option: A Strategy for Christians in a Post-Christian Nation* (New York, NY: Sentinel, 2017).
Eco, Umberto, *The Aesthetics of Thomas Aquinas*, trans. Hugh Bredin (Cambridge MA: Harvard University Press, 1988).
Eikelboom, Lexi, *Rhythm: A Theological Category* (Oxford: Oxford University Press, 2018).
Emery, Gilles, *Trinity in Aquinas* (Ypsilanti: Sapientia Press, 2005).
———, *The Trinitarian Theology of St Thomas Aquinas* (Oxford: Oxford University Press, 2007).
———, 'Theologia and Dispensatio: The Centrality of the Divine Missions in St. Thomas's Trinitarian Theology', *Thomist*, 74 (2010).
Ernst, Cornelius, *Multiple Echo: Explorations in Theology*, eds Timothy Radcliffe and Fergus Kerr (London: Darton, Longman Todd, 1979).
Farrell, Walter, *A Companion to the Summa* (New York: Sheed and Ward, 1938).
Finnis, John, *Aquinas: Moral, Political and Legal Theory* (Oxford: Oxford University Press, 1998).
———, *Natural Law and Natural Rights* (Oxford: Oxford University Press, 2011).
Fitzpatrick, Antonia, *Thomas Aquinas on Bodily Identity* (Oxford: Oxford University Press, 2017).
Friedman, Russell L., *Medieval Trinitarian Thought from Aquinas to Ockham* (Cambridge: Cambridge University Press, 2010).
Gleason, Philip, 'Neoscholasticism as Preconcilliar Ideology', *Catholic Historian*, 7 (1988).

Gondreau, Paul, 'The Life of Christ', in *The Cambridge Companion to the Summa Theologiae*, eds Philip McCosker and Denys Turner (Cambridge: Cambridge University Press, 2016).

———, *The Passions of Christ's Soul in the Theology of St Thomas Aquinas* (Washington DC: Catholic University of America Press, 2018).

Gorman, Michael, 'Christ as Composite', *Traditio*, 55 (2000).

Griffiths, Paul J., *Christian Flesh* (Stanford, CA: Stanford University Press, 2018).

Hadot, Pierre, *Philosophy as a Way of Life: Spiritual Exercises from Socrates to Foucault* (Oxford: Wiley-Blackwell, 1995).

Healy, Nicholas M., 'Redemption', in *The Cambridge Companion to the Summa Theologiae*, eds Philip McCosker and Denys Turner (Cambridge: Cambridge University Press, 2016).

Heidegger, Martin, *Basic Concepts of Aristotelian Philosophy*, trans. Robert B. Metcalf and Mark B. Tanzer (Bloomington: Indiana University Press, 2009).

Hemmerle, Klaus, *Theses Towards a Trinitarian Ontology* trans. Stephen Churchyard (Brooklyn: Angelico Press, 2020).

Hemming, Laurence Paul, '*Analogia Non Entis Sed Entitatis*: The Ontological Consequences of the Doctrine of Analogy', *International Journal of Systematic Theology*, 6 (2004).

Henry, Michel, *Incarnation: A Philosophy of Flesh* (Evanston, IL: Northwestern University Press, 2015).

Hewitt, Simon, *Negative Theology and Philosophical Analysis* (London: Palgrave Macmillan, 2020).

Hittinger, Russell, *Critique of the New Natural Law Theory* (South Bend, IN: University of Notre Dame Press, 1988).

Houck, Daniel W., *Aquinas, Original Sin and the Challenge of Evolution* (Cambridge: Cambridge University Press, 2020).

Hunter, Justus, *If Adam Had Not Sinned: The Reason for the Incarnation from Anselm to Scotus* (Washington DC: Catholic University of America Press, 2020).

Jones, L. Gregory, 'The Theological Transformation of Aristotelian Friendship in the Thought of St. Thomas Aquinas', *New Scholasticism*, 61 (1987).

Kaczor, Christopher, and Thomas Sherman, *Thomas Aquinas on the Cardinal Virtues* (Washington DC: Catholic University of America Press, 2020).

Keating, Michael, 'The Strange Case of the Self-Dwarfing Man', *Logos* 10, no. 4 (2007).

Keenan, James F., 'Virtues', in *The Cambridge Companion to the Summa Theologiae*, eds Philip McCosker and Denys Turner (Cambridge: Cambridge University Press, 2016).

Keenan, Oliver James, 'Divine Antecedence and Pretemporal Election', *New Blackfriars*, 98 (2017).

Kelsey, David H., 'Aquinas and Barth on the Human Body', *Thomist*, 50 (1986).

Kent, Bonnie, 'Aquinas and Weakness of Will', *Philosophy and Phenomenological Research* 75, no. 1 (2007).

Kerr, Fergus, *Theology after Wittgenstein*, 2nd ed. (Oxford: Blackwell, 1997).

———, *After Aquinas: Versions of Thomism* (Oxford: Blackwells, 2002).

———, 'A Different World: Neoscholasticism and Its Discontents', *International Journal of Systematic Theology*, 8 (2006).

———, 'Ansombe, Ernst and Mccabe: Wittgenstein and Catholic Theology', *Josephinum* 15, no. 1 (2008).
Kerr, Gaven, *Aquinas's Way to God* (New York: Oxford University Press, USA, 2015).
Klubertanz, George Peter, *St Thomas Aquinas on Analogy* (Chicago: Loyola University Press, 1960).
Ku, John, *Baptist God the Father in the Theology of St Thomas Aquinas* (New York: Peter Lang, 2013).
Lamont, John, 'Aquinas on Subsistent Relation', *Recherches de théologie et philosophie médiévales*, 71 (2004).
Laporte, Jean-Marc, 'Beatitude in the Structure of Aquinas', '*Summa*: Is Ia 26 a Stray Question?', *Toronto Journal of Theology*, 18 (2002).
Lash, Nicholas, 'Are We Born and Do We Die?', *New Blackfriars* 90, no. 1,028 (2009).
Legge, Dominic, *The Trinitarian Christology of St Thomas Aquinas* (Oxford: Oxford University Press, 2017).
Levering, Matthew and Marcus Plested, *The Oxford Handbook of the Reception of Aquinas* (Oxford: Oxford University Press, 2021).
Lisska, Anthony J., *Aquinas's Theory of Natural Law: An Analytic Reconstruction* (Oxford: Wiley-Blackwell, 1998).
Lombardo, Nicholas E., *The Logic of Desire: Aquinas on Emotion* (Washington DC: Catholic University of America Press, 2011).
Long, Steven A., *Natura Pura: On the Recovery of Nature in the Doctrine of Grace* (New York: Fordham University Press, 2010).
Maritain, Jacques, *The Angelic Doctor: The Life and Thought of Saint Thomas Aquinas* (New York: Dial Press, 1931).
———, *Existence and the Existent* (Mahwah, NJ: Paulist Press, 2015).
MacIntyre, Alasdair, *Three Rival Versions of Moral Enquiry* (London: Duckworth, 1990).
———, *After Virtue: A Study in Moral Theory*, 3rd ed. (London: Bloomsbury, 2007).
McCabe, Herbert, *Law, Love and Language* (London, Sheed & Ward, 1968).
———, 'A Note on "Analogy"', in *Summa Theologiae*, Vol. 3, Knowing and Naming God: 1a. 12–13, eds Thomas Gilby and Herbert McCabe (1975).
———, 'Original Sin', in *God Still Matters* (London: Bloomsbury, 2002).
———, *On Aquinas* (London: Burns and Oates, 2008).
McInerny, Ralph, 'Natural Law and Human Rights', *American Journal of Jurisprudence* 36, no. 1, 1991.
———, *Aquinas and Analogy* (Washington DC: Catholic University of American Press, 1996).
———, *Aquinas on Human Action: A Theory of Practice* (Washington DC: Catholic University of America Press, 2012).
McCool, Gerald A., *From Unity to Pluralism: The Internal Evolution of Thomism* (New York: Fordham University Press, 1992).
McCormack, Bruce L. and Thomas Joseph White, *Thomas Aquinas and Karl Barth: An Unofficial Catholic–Protestant Dialogue* (Grand Rapids: Eerdmans, 2013).
McDermott, Timothy, *How to Read Aquinas* (London: Granta Books, 2007).
Mondin, Battista, *The Principle of Analogy in Protestant and Catholic Theology* (The Hague: Nijhof, 1963).

Montagnes, Bernard, '*La Doctrine de l'analogie de l'être d'après Saint Thomas D'Aquin*' (Thèse Louvain, 1963).

Mortensen, John R., *Understanding St Thomas on Analogy* (Rome: Gregorian University, 2010).

Muers, Rachel, *Keeping God's Silence: Towards a Theological Ethics of Communication* (Oxford: Blackwell, 2004).

Mulhall, Stephen, *The Great Riddle: Wittgenstein and Nonsense, Theology and Philosophy* (Oxford: Oxford University Press, 2015).

Murray, Paul, *Aquinas at Prayer: Bible, Mysticism and Poetry* (London: Bloomsbury, 2013).

Novikoff, Alex J., *The Medieval Culture of Disputation: Pedagogy, Practice and Performance* (Philadelphia: University of Pennsylvania Press, 2013).

Ogle, Nicholas, 'Trinitarian Charity: Aquinas and Lombard on Charity and the Holy Spirit', *Scottish Journal of Theology*, 74 (2021).

Paasch, J. T., 'The Trinity', in *Aquinas's Summa Theologiae: A Critical Guide*, ed. Jeffrey Hause (Cambridge: Cambridge University Press, 2018).

Pasnau, Robert, 'Aquinas's Thoughts on Linguistic Nature', *Monist* 80, no. 4 (1997).

Perl, Eric David, *Thinking Being: Introduction to Metaphysics in the Classical Tradition* (Leiden: Brill, 2014).

Pieper, Josef, *The Silence of St Thomas* (London: Faber & Faber, 1957).

———, *The Four Cardinal Virtues* (South Bend, IN: University of Notre Dame Press, 1966).

———, *Living the Truth*, trans. Lothar Krauth (San Francisco: Ignatius Press, 1989).

Pilsner, Joseph, *The Specification of Human Actions in St Thomas Aquinas* (Oxford: Oxford University Press, 2006).

Polanyi, Michael, *The Tacit Dimension* (London: Routledge, 1967).

Principe, Walter H., 'Affectivity and the Heart in Thomas Aquinas' Spirituality', in *Spiritualities of the Heart*, ed. Annice Callahan (New York: Paulist Press, 1990).

Przywara, Erich, Analogia Entis: *Metaphysik* (München: Kösel, 1932).

Rikhof, Herwi, 'The Trinity', in *The Theology of Thomas Aquinas*, eds Rik Van Nieuwenhove and Joseph Wawrykow (South Bend: University of Notre Dame Press, 2005).

Robertson, Kellie, 'Medieval Nature and the Environment', in *The Cambridge Companion to Christianity and the Environment* (Cambridge: Cambridge University Press, 2022).

Roensch, Frederick J., *Early Thomistic School* (Dublin: Priory Press, 1964).

Rogers, Eugene F., 'Trinity', in *The Cambridge Companion to the Summa Theologiae*, eds Philip McCosker and Denys Turner (Cambridge: Cambridge University Press, 2016).

Rogers, Paul M., *Aquinas on Prophecy: Wisdom and Charism in the* Summa Theologiae (Washington DC: Catholic University of America Press, 2023).

Roy, Louis, 'A Note on Barth and Aquinas', *American Catholic Philosophical Quarterly*, 66 (1991).

Ryan, Fáinche, *Formation in Holiness: Thomas Aquinas on* Sacra Doctrina (Utrecht: Thomas Instituut/Peeters Leuven, 2007).

Schrader, Dylan A., *Thomistic Christocentrism: Recovering the Carmelites of Salamanca on the Logic of the Incarnation* (Washington DC: Catholic University of America Press, 2021).

BIBLIOGRAPHY

Schwartz, Daniel, *Aquinas on Friendship* (Oxford: Oxford University Press, 2020).
Scruton, Roger, *Fools, Frauds and Firebrands* (London: Bloomsbury, 2015).
Sherwin, Michael S., *By Knowledge and By Love: Charity and Knowledge in the Moral Theology of St Thomas Aquinas* (Washington DC: Catholic University of America Press, 2005).
Sigurdson, Ola, *Heavenly Bodies: Incarnation, the Gaze and Embodiment in Christian Theology* (Grand Rapids: Eerdmans, 2016).
Sonderegger, Katherine, *Systematic Theology 2: The Doctrine of the Holy Trinity, Processions and Persons* (Minneapolis: Fortress Press, 2020).
Steinbeck, John, *Sweet Thursday*, (London: Penguin Modern Classics, 1954).
Stump, Eleonore, *Aquinas* (London: Routledge, 2003).
Taylor, Charles, *The Language Animal: The Full Shape of the Human Linguistic Capacity* (Cambridge, MA: Harvard University Press, 2016).
te Velde, Rudi A., *Aquinas on God* (London: Ashgate, 2006).
Torrell, Jean-Pierre, *St Thomas Aquinas: The Person and His Work*, trans. Robert Royal (Washington DC: Catholic University of America Press, 1996).
———, *Le Christ En Ses Mysteres* (Paris: Desclée, 1999).
———, *Saint Thomas Aquinas: Spiritual Master*, trans. Robert Royal (Washington DC: CUA Press, 2003).
———, *Aquinas's* Summa: *Background, Structure, Reception*, trans. Benedict M. Guevin (Washington DC: Catholic University of America Press, 2005).
———, *Jésus Le Christ Chez Saint Thomas D'aquin* (Paris: CERF, 2008).
Tugwell, Simon, *Thomas: Selected Writings* (Mahwah, NJ: Paulist Press, 1988).
Turner, Denys, 'One with God as to the Unknown', in *God, Mystery and Mystification* (South Bend, IN: Notre Dame University Press, 2019).
Ulrich, Ferdinand, *Homo Abyssus*, trans. D. C. Schindler (Washington DC: Humanum Press, 2018).
van Nieuwenhove, Rik, 'Soteriology', in *The Theology of Thomas Aquinas*, eds Wawrykow, Joseph and Rik van Nieuwenhove (Notre Dame, IN: University of Notre Dame Press, 2005).
Ventimiglia, Giovanni, *Aquinas after Frege* (London: Palgrave Macmillan, 2020).
Verbeke, Gerard, 'Man as Frontier According to Aquinas', in *Aquinas and Problems of His Time*, eds Gerard Verbeke and Daniel Verhelst (Leuven: University Press, 1976).
Wawrykow, Joseph, 'Hypostatic Union', in *The Theology of Thomas Aquinas*, ed. by Rik Van Nieuwenhove and Joseph Wawrykow (Notre Dame, IN: University of Notre Dame Press, 2005).
Wawrykow, Joseph and Rik Van Nieuwenhove, *The Theology of Thomas Aquinas* (South Bend, IN: University of Notre Dame, 2005).
Weisheipl, James A., *Friar Thomas D'aquino: His Life, Thought and Works* (Oxford: Blackwell, 1974).
White, Thomas Joseph, 'The Voluntary Action of the Earthly Christ', *Thomist*, 69 (2005).
———, *Wisdom in the Face of Modernity: A Study in Thomistic Natural Theology* (Naples, FL: Sapientia Press, 2009).
———, 'Beauty, Transcendence, and the Inclusive Hierarchy of Creation', *Nova et Vetera*, 16 (2018).

———, '*Ressourcement* Thomism', in *The New Cambridge Companion to Christian Doctrine*, ed. Michael Allen (Cambridge: Cambridge University Press, 2022).

———, 'Essence and Existence, God's Simplicity and Trinity', in *The New Cambridge Companion to Aquinas*, eds Eleonore Stump and Thomas Joseph White (Cambridge: Cambridge University Press, 2022).

White, Victor 'The Unknown God', in *God the Unknown* (London: Harvill Press, 1956).

———, *Holy Teaching: The Idea of Theology According to St Thomas Aquinas* (London: Blackfriars Publications, 1958).

———, 'Prelude to the Five Ways', in *Aquinas's* Summa Theologiae: *Critical Essays*, ed. Brian Davies (Oxford: Rowman & Littlefield, 2006).

Wilhelmsen, Frederick D., *The Paradoxical Structure of Existence* (London: Routledge, 2017).

Zeitz, James V., 'Przywara and Von Balthasar on Analogy', *Thomist*, 52 (1988)

Index

After Virtue (Macintyre) 202
alienation, sense of 2, 198
analogy, doctrine of 74–80
anger 117–20
Anscombe, Elizabeth 130
approaches to reading Aquinas 26–7
Aquinas (Stump) 23
Aquinas, St Thomas
   approaches to reading 26–7, 200–2
   attunement to otherness 16–17
   conflict experience 15
   continued relevance of 1–2
   as conversationalist 13–14
   current interest in 199–200
   death of 13, 14, 20
   feeling of change 15–17
   as friar preacher 14–15
   in hedgehog or fox categories 22–5
   impact on European culture 4–5
   life of 13, 14
   marginality awareness 15–16
   movement in thought 29–31
   plausibility of 6–9
   religiosity of 19
   remoteness of 27–9
   as theologian 5, 21–2
   university life 16, 17–19
   writings as 'straw' 20–1
Aristotle 17, 63, 136, 144, 171, 173
authority 170–1

Barth, Karl 162, 199
being and becoming 36–7
belonging
   biology of 128
   and communication 129–31
   in culture 128–9
   and fortitude 155–7
   and freedom 131–4
   friendship in 143–5
   and happiness 134–5
   justice in 145–55
   moral lives 126–8
   and prudence 137–43
   and temperance 157–9
   theological 129
   and virtue 134–7, 138
   vulnerability of 155–9
Berlin, Isaiah 22
biology of belonging 128
bliss 82–3
body-soul composite 100–2
Bonaventure, St 104

Cathars 15
change
   feeling of 15–17
   in reality 47–50
charity 165–7, 177–9
Chenu, Marie-Dominique 17, 23, 31
Chesterton, G. K. 23

Christ
- centrality of   161–3
- death and resurrection   191–6
- and development of Christology   185–7
- human experience of   188–91

co-creation   97–9
communication   3–4
- and belonging   129–31
- and conversational stimulation   13–14
- and reality   33–5

conflict, experience of   15
continuity in reality   47–50
conversational stimulation   13–14
creation   23–5
Crusades   15
culture of belonging   128–9

death of Christ   191–3
Descartes, René   35, 99, 101
discursive thought   124–5
Disputed Questions on Truth (Aquinas)   50
divine persons   83–9, 90–6
divine simplicity   70–2
Dreher, Rod   202
Scotus, John Duns   184

Emery, Gilles   85
emotions   113–20
Ernst, Cornelius   22
esse   38–41
eucharist   196–7

faith   165–70
Fitzpatrick, Antonia   23
Five Ways   58–63, 66, 174–5
form in reality   41–3, 121–2
fortitude   155–7
Foucault, Michel   5
Frederick II, Emperor   15
freedom   131–4
friendship
- and belonging   143–5
- with God   177–80

Freud, Sigmund   10

Gilby, Thomas   201
God
- analogies for   74–80
- and bliss   82–3
- divine persons in   83–9, 90–6
- divine simplicity of   70–2
- essence of   63–5, 70–1
- as Father   92–3
- and the Five Ways   58–63
- and friendship   177–80
- and grace   163–5
- gratuity of   180–2
- horizon of   56–7
- and negation   69–72
- and other possible worlds   183–5
- and productive human mind   85–8
- reality of   70–1, 72–4
- relationality of   88–92
- and speech   74–80
- and the trinity   81–2, 83–5, 92–6, 179–80
- unknowability of   61–3

grace   163–5
Granada   15
gratuity of God   180–2

Hadot, Pierre   79
happiness   134–5
hedgehog or fox categories   22–5
Heidegger, Martin   13, 95
Hemmerle, Klaus   95
Heraclitus   36
hope   165–7, 175–7
horizons
- of God   56–7
- of reality   57–9

humans
- ability to 'step back'   120–2
- and anger   117–20
- bodily relations of   99–100
- as body-soul composite   100–2
- as co-creators with God   97–9
- difference from other living things   97–8, 109–10
- and discursive thought   124–5
- and emotions   113–20

INDEX

intellect of 122–4
interior senses 110–12
and love 118–19
and memory 112–13
in reality 102–3
and senses 106–12
and truth 120–2
unity of 104–6
Husserl, Edmund 95

ignorance 65–6
intellect of humans 122–4
interior senses 110–12

John of Damascus 187
justice 145–55
and belonging 150–3
description of 145–6
and fortitude 155–7
limitations of 154–5
and morality 153–4
and rights 146–50

Kant, Immanuel 35, 99

language 3–4
Lazarus 194
living/non-living things 45–7
Lombardo, Nicholas 23
love 118–19

Macintyre, Alasdair 202
Manichaeism 181
marginality, awareness of 15–16
McCabe, Herbert 23
McCosker, Philip 164
meaningfulness in reality 43–5
memory 112–13
modalism 86
'Modern Moral Philosophy'
(Anscombe) 130
Monte Cassino Abbey 15–16
moral lives 126–8
movement
in Aquinas' thought 29–31
in reality 45–7

Naples, University of 15, 16
negation 63, 64, 65, 67, 68, 69–72
Nicomachean Ethics (Aristotle) 136

On Aquinas (McCabe) 23
Order of Friar Preachers 14
original sin 182–3
other possible worlds 183–5
otherness, attunement to 16–17
Oxford Handbook of the Reception of Aquinas 201

Parmenides 36
Paul, St 10
Pieper, Joseph 23–4
plausibility of Aquinas 6–9
plenitude 69
Pontifical University of St Thomas Aquinas 199
Posterior Analytics (Aristotle) 171, 173
productive human mind 85–8
providence 140–3
prudence 137–43
Przywara, Erich 95
purposiveness in reality 43–5

quidditative knowledge 63–5

reality
being and becoming in 36–7
change and continuity in 47–50
and communication 33–5
and *esse* 38–41
form in 41–3, 121–2
of God 70–1, 72–4
horizon of 57–9
humans in 102–3
living/non-living things 45–7
meaningfulness in 43–5
in natural extremities 32–3
purposiveness in 43–5
and speech 33–5, 49–50
substance in 48–50
transcendental properties 50–2
truth in 52–5
as a verb 35–6

reason   7–8
relationality   88–92
religiosity of Aquinas   19
remoteness of Aquinas   27–9
resurrection of Christ   191–6
Rogers, Paul   23

self-movement   45–7
senses   106–12
Sigmund (cat)   37, 38–9, 41
Sonderregger, Katherine   162
speech
   and God   74–80
   and reality   33–5, 49–50
'stepping back'   120–2
Stump, Eleonore   23
subordinationism   86
substance in reality   48–50
Summa Contra Gentiles (Aquinas)   27, 201
Summa Theologiae (Aquinas)
   and alienation   198
   approaches to reading   27, 201
   centrality of Christ   162
   difficulty of   9
   and the eucharist   196
   and events in life of Christ   160
   and the Five Ways   58
   movement in   29–30, 31
   and negation   68
   style and structure of   6
   translations of   201

temperance   157–9
theology
   of Aquinas   5, 21–2
   and belonging   129
   and philosophy   8–9
   science of   171–5
Thomistic Institute   199
Torrell, Jean-Pierre   14
Toward an Understanding of Saint Thomas (Chenu)   23
transcendental properties   50–2
trinity, doctrine of   81–2, 83–5, 92–6, 179–80
trust   170–5
truth
   human capacity for   120–2
   in reality   52–5
Tugwell, Simon   14

Ulrich, Ferdinand   95
unity of human beings   104–6
university life   16, 17–19

violence   182–3
virtue   134–7, 138, 165–7
vulnerability   155–9

War of the Keys   15
Weisheipl, James   14
Wittgenstein, Ludwig   31
writings as 'straw'   20–1